DENSE+GREEN

Foreword by
Chan Heng Chee
*Lee Kuan Yew Centre for
Innovative Cities
Singapore University of
Technology and Design*

Contributions by
Kees Christiaanse
Herbert Dreiseitl
Foster + Partners
T. R. Hamzah & Yeang
MVRDV
Naree Phinyawatana
WOHA
Jean W. H. Yong

**Birkhäuser
Basel**

Foreword by
Chan Heng Chee
*Lee Kuan Yew Centre for
Innovative Cities
Singapore University of
Technology and Design*

Contributions by
Kees Christiaanse
Herbert Dreiseitl
Foster + Partners
T. R. Hamzah & Yeang
MVRDV
Naree Phinyawatana
WOHA
Jean W. H. Yong

**Birkhäuser
Basel**

Layout, cover design and typography
Yoshiki Waterhouse, Waterhouse Cifuentes Design
with Steve Engert

Cover photograph
Roland Halbe

Assistance and preparation of texts and case study materials
(research, photographs, drawings)
Peter Christensen
Alexander Cornelius
Khew Yu Nong
Aloysius Lian
Thomas Wortmann

Copyediting, proofreading
Michael Wachholz, Michael Eisenbrey

Editor for the publisher
Andreas Müller

Production
Amelie Solbrig

Paper
Hello Fat Matt 1.1

Printing
Grafisches Centrum Cuno GmbH & Co. KG
Printed in UltraHDPrint

We would like to thank the Lee Kuan Yew Centre for Innovative
Cities at the Singapore University of Technology and Design for
the generous support of this publication.

Library of Congress Cataloging-in-Publication data
A CIP catalog record for this book has been applied for at the
Library of Congress.

Bibliographic information published by the German
National Library

The German National Library lists this publication in the Deutsche
Nationalbibliografie; detailed bibliographic data are available on
the Internet at http://dnb.dnb.de.

This publication is also available as an e-book
(ISBN PDF 978-3-03821-014-6; ISBN EPUB 978-3-03821-674-2).

© 2016 Birkhäuser Verlag GmbH, Basel
P.O. Box 44, 4009 Basel, Switzerland
Part of Walter de Gruyter GmbH, Berlin/Boston

Printed on acid-free paper produced from chlorine-free pulp. TCF ∞

Printed in Germany

ISBN 978-3-03821-579-0

9 8 7 6 5 4 3 2 1

Table of Contents

Dense + Green Case Studies

Foreword

The growth of cities is all about people. The accelerating trend of people moving to cities to seek employment, raise a family, find a better life and future is unstoppable. UN statistics predict that in 2030, 60% of the world's population or 4.9 billion people will be urban, and by 2025 there will be 35 megacities in the world compared to 22 in 2011.

One of the leading challenges for architects and urban planners today is how to deal with density—density that comes from the natural increase of population and density that comes from migration, both internal and external. We have seen cities in developed regions that must address the task of creating a congenial environment, designing for the diverse demands of a larger population that wants the best of city life and aspires to the best of living close to nature. In developing regions, cities have to design, plan, and build to house a population that is urbanizing at exceptional speed, which means dealing with overwhelming numbers and yet provide a liveable environment.

The sustainability conversation, ongoing for some time, has achieved a new urgency lately because the awareness of global warming has spread and the effects of climate change are already felt in many ways, in the extremes of weather and the unexpected floodings and snowstorms that wreck cities, especially coastal cities. But we must think of sustainability in a new way. Important though green technology is, we have to be concerned with liveability and of how people can adapt to their environment. How does the integration of nature in architecture, adding sky terraces, vertical parks, and green facades in high-density buildings, enhance liveability?

We understand that proximity to and living with natural green has its healing and rejuvenating effects, and as we move forward in a technology-driven age, it is all-important to bring back nature into our lives. This seems to be particularly so in the case of Gen Y, those aged between 15–34 years and even Gen X, those aged 35–50 years. And we can predict with confidence that Gen Z, those aged 5–14 years now, will also embrace the same ideals. Nature is the essential touchstone that converts a teeming, bustling, and harassing part of reality into a calm, soothing, and liveable oasis. Furthermore nature, like technology, can be used to help screen off heat, increase cooling, and promote energy efficiency. It depends on how we use nature and green technology together.

So what means sustainable and liveable for high-density cities or regions, and how to achieve it? Singapore, a city-state and nation-state at the same time, is but a little red dot on the map of the world, yet Singapore has achieved a reputation as an innovative city and country. It is a country that is space-challenged and has coped with the substantial increase in population in a planned and purposeful way: it opted for high-density high-rise living. Singapore is also known as a green city. Right at the beginning of urbanization in the 1970s, the Singapore Prime Minister, Lee Kuan Yew, was intuitively aware of the symbiotic relationship between density and green as a proposition for a sustainable and liveable city. He challenged urban designers and builders to implement this principle.

This book is an exercise in figuring out the many imaginative ways in which ecological design has been executed all over the world. The author and the contributors, who are architects, urban designers, and urban planners, proffer typologies of dense and green buildings, dense and green building technology, as well as green design in the landscape of the city and what dense and green urbanism means. What they do is very much in the spirit and mission of what the Lee Kuan Yew Centre for Innovative Cities at the Singapore University of Technology and Design aspires to do, which is why we are proud to associate ourselves with this book.

Chan Heng Chee
Ambassador-at-Large and Chairman
Lee Kuan Yew Centre for Innovative Cities
Singapore University of Technology and Design

DENSE+GREEN AGENDAS

The Dense and Green Paradigm

Thomas Schröpfer

A Paradigm of Paradigms

The rapid urbanization of our global society is, by now, an incontrovertible reality. From Lagos to Lahore, Seoul to São Paulo economic, political, and social dynamics are driving people into cities in breathtaking numbers. In 1800, Beijing was the only city with a population of one million or more. By 1900, 16 cities had reached this figure. By 2000, it was 378 cities. By 2025, there will be about 600 cities of one million or more worldwide.[1] The accompanying continual and radical recasting of the form of our urban environments is often considered as a process of unadulterated metastasis which, depending on a host of variables, tends to result in a sprawl that maintains the preceding human density or even increases not only the net area of human population centers, but also their density. Density, as many leading architects of the 20th Century have demonstrated, can be designed and designed well. It can be the ultimate test of intelligent design and, at its best, make our lives more practical, more manageable, and more urbane.

In the midst of the current ecological turn, one cannot omit from that list of desirable benefits the one of being in greater sync with our natural environment. To be sure, dense living has the potential to bring a certain amount of marked ecological benefits, chief among them the consolidation of resources, which—be they fossil fuels or food—are more likely to be economically utilized. Yet like urbanization, the process of becoming ecological in a dense world is not a process that necessarily happens without design volition. Design, on the other hand, would appear to be more integral to becoming more ecological than it is to becoming more dense. In other words, being dense and being "green" are not synonymous to the extent that they sometimes have been thought to be. This book advocates for an integrative understanding of the two and a more holistic formulation of a 21st-Century architecture and urban design paradigm.

The effort to define such a paradigm and to set forth templates and examples for it, while new in itself, emerges organically from earlier paradigms—paradigms that began to coalesce in the wake of the environmentalist and reurbanization movements of the 1960s. A particularly critical moment was the publication of Reyner Banham's *Architecture of the Well-Tempered Environment* in 1969. While many seeking to contextualize ecological thinking in architecture have duly looked to his 1971 publication *Los Angeles: The Architecture of Four Ecologies,* Banham's articulation of the so-called "well-tempered" environment was not as divorced from urban issues as has hitherto been thought and it is perhaps even more instructive as a metathesis. The *Well-Tempered Environment* makes the compelling case that the harmonization of major population centers with architecture is a question of mass. Banham explains how physical massiveness in architecture emerged from antiquity as the Western architectural tradition's foremost preoccupation. Massiveness comprised not only the advantages of "perdurable" shelter but also the symbolic power of technological achievement vis-à-vis monumentality.[2] Yet in the modern era, the actual reverence for massiveness came into crisis with the new realities of the industrial (and post-industrial) "machine age": "… such constructions bring with them environmental advantages that had become so customary in three millennia of European civilization, that they were falsely supposed to be inherent in all structural techniques, and there were baffled complaints when they were found to be absent from light-weight methods promoted out of the futuristic enthusiasm for the 'Machine Age.'"[3]

Banham's observation makes clear the dramatic paradigm shift wrought on our relationship with nature by the rise of the machine and explains it as primarily a question of the level of density, more precisely of material density. Rammed earth, massive stone, and bulky wood construction techniques would give way to the balloon frame, cast iron, and lightweight steel with the beginning of the modern era. Along with this shift from relatively heavy to relatively light materials came a higher mediation with mechanized systems integrative to the lightweight architectural mainframe. Buildings became apparatuses of minimized physical appearance for "perfect" environments in general and cities in particular, where they were most commonly staged—a "subnature," as David Gissen has described it.[4] This transformation furnished unprecedented human comfort that went along with an alienation from the natural world that, until recently, was thought of as lamentable only by the postmodern and poetic sensibilities.

However, in recent decades it has become clear that more was lost in this process than just a romantic vista and the smell of flowers (or of brick, or even concrete). We have ceded the possibility of the city being a part of *nature* in favor of *naturalizing* it into our technological, and consequently architectural, repertoire. This specific ecological turn is not to suggest a "return to nature" but instead a more sustained attempt to transpose the benefits of mass and massiveness from the scale of material to the scale of architecture.[5] We can achieve ecological balance in today's cities comparable to the way we once had at the scale of the building.

To do so, it is necessary to retool our understanding of human density to become a question of the massivity of scale, not of large size, and in turn see our cities as places where being dense *and* green holds the promise of paradigms that have been difficult to achieve through the trials and errors of the 20th Century.

One can find antecedents for this shift in thinking in many historical examples, from the Hanging Gardens of Babylon via the tight knitting of medieval European cities to Le Corbusier's subtle but critical placement of the "landscape" atop, rather than next to, the Villa Savoye in 1931. Yet the issues at stake are ultimately specific to our time, negotiating the technological and population conditions in which we have found ourselves in recent decades.

Genesis of an Idea

The new dense and green paradigm is one that has coalesced around a multiplicity of recent architectural, urbanistic, and conceptual developments. In tracing the paradigm's roots through the postwar period to the present, one is struck by just how diverse the sources of its conceptual, formal, and technological genesis have been.

In its origins, the new dense and green paradigm can in large part be seen as an outgrowth of an important, yet somewhat understudied approach of architecture and urban planning strategies that came to be known under the popular term of "Vancouverism." Vancouverism owes its name to the Canadian city's particular geographic context. Wedged between the Pacific Ocean to the west and a strip of crucial agricultural land and further the Canadian Rockies to the east, the city was given codes and guidelines that were developed by the municipal authorities during the rapid growth in the 1950s to delimit urban sprawl, which was on display in the USA directly to the south, and instead direct it toward a steady densification of the existing core, without necessarily promoting an excessive skyline.[6]

In terms of types, the result was the steady consolidation of a specific building, which pliantly adapted the new codes while also addressing the basic needs of the city. It consisted of a medium-rise multi-use structure of about 10 to 15 stories, in combination with a relatively modest footprint so as to preserve the existing street and traffic. Commercial spaces typically occupied the pedestrian level, while residential spaces were accommodated on the upper levels. The actual typology became the canvas for a number of regional architects who saw its pragmatic qualities as a springboard for conceptual developments, many of which hinted toward ecological principles. This was particularly evident in the work of Arthur Erickson, whose Project 56 sought to intensify Vancouver's West End neighborhood, a scheme anathema to those elsewhere in the Western world. Although not realized, Erickson's principles were in large part adapted and turned the West End into the highest-density residential neighborhood on the West Coast by the 1960s.[7]

Over subsequent decades, Vancouver's repeated ranking as one of the world's most liveable cities has proven that density and quality of life were not mutually exclusive, as many had argued, but could rather be mutually beneficial. To a great degree this confirmed Jane Jacobs' theory, as stated in her seminal book *The Death and Life of Great American Cities*,[8] that there was such a thing as "good" and "bad" density, and it was telling that Vancouver's Director of Planning for the City paid tribute to Jacobs when asked about his city's immensely successful model for dense architecture, noting: "I know what she [Jacobs] means about people misunderstanding density—that's why we emphasize density done well rather than density as a mathematical exercise. [But] people 'round the world praise Vancouver's liveability, and she had a big hand in it."[9]

To a large degree, Vancouverism has been explored in Europe. Many European cities have, for the last couple of decades, made efforts to realize better human ecologies with the built environment—often more so than Vancouver and most certainly more so than North America in general, where unchecked growth and boundless space have particular historical foundations. In this context, Timothy Beatley's study *Green Urbanism: Learning from European Cities* was a seminal effort to transmute the relative ecological and life quality of many European cities into a set of metrics and methods that could have resonance well beyond Europe.[10] Many European cities have become exemplary for their combination of denseness and greenness. With metrics varying from study to study, the notable measures of the ecological success of European cities are their intelligent land use practices—comprising compact growth districts with ample green space as well as well-designed housing and living environments that resist the idealized images of freestanding homes purported by many other non-European countries—innovative and extensive public transportation systems that create attractive and cheaper alternatives to the automobile usage, good governance, and a "closed-loop" eco-cycle that marks the city's capacity for minimizing its reliance on resources that originate from beyond its immediate area. The image of the bike-mounted European businessman commuting

to work has proven its potency beyond cliché, as numerous local governments in the USA, for example, nowadays initiate and install extensive bike-sharing programs in their own cities.

In this context, it is important to note that a great deal of the relevant changes made in Europe were pre-empted by legislation and development policy. For example, in 1989, the Dutch government ratified a comprehensive plan to draft, integrate, and implement a massive switch of policies that sought to improve environmental quality, stressing long-term plans that bore no effect on the generation drafting it but rather on the next one and the one after.[11] The program, called the National Environmental Policy Plan (NEPP), was very bold and set standards for the entire European Union.

Today, there is indeed a great deal to learn from Europe, but to do so requires an understanding of what exactly it means that the rest of the world has come to emulate cities like Amsterdam and Copenhagen. After all, even a resident of the ecologically-conscious city of Stockholm produces five times more carbon emissions per year than a resident of Dhaka, Bangladesh.[12] The crux here is the concept of "liveability" which has emerged as one of the major, nonetheless abstract crucibles contributing to our fuller understanding of the dense and green paradigm. Indeed, a comprehensive evaluation of the term demonstrates how the use of the words "liveability" and "liveable" has accelerated considerably in the post-World War II era and that this concept has become a common goal, even though the paths to that goal have varied. Harold Ickes, the US Secretary of the Interior, described the notion of liveability as early as 1935 as the balance between life's three basic requirements on the built environment: health, comfort, and safety. He pried his definition out of one that was less concerned with the outward appearance of cities (or architecture) than in Europe, but rather with the spatial qualities of their interiors.[13] Meanwhile, in Europe, architects and urban planners did contend with the concept's metrics and meaning in the aftermath of the war, when cities across the continent that had evolved organically for centuries had to be rebuilt from scratch in a comprehensive manner. European architects sought ways to implement and amend Le Corbusier's Athens Charter of 1943 into a reconstruction culture where liveability was largely imagined as a balm for the trauma of the postwar landscape.[14]

Today, the concept of liveability, although still ambiguous in theory, has a life as an unambiguous appraisal factor used, for example, to measure salaries when companies determine what is needed to recruit workers to a city. This task has been led by

The Economist, which has established a ranking system with five basic categories (stability, healthcare, culture and environment, education, and infrastructure) and five "grades" (acceptable, tolerable, uncomfortable, undesirable, intolerable).[15] Within those categories, specific appraisal factors have a direct relationship to the work of architects and urban planners, e.g. the quality of the road network and public transportation and the availability of good-quality housing. Obviously, as the American-European differences suggest, the very definition of what is "good" and what is "quality" has different meanings for different people and demonstrates the largely subjective nature of the term, even today. Yet in coalescing around ecological principles, international design practices since the 1950s have functioned as one of the greatest standardizing forces for defining a more universal liveability through architecture and urban design.

At the specifically architectural scale, a key precedent is Kevin Roche and John Dinkeloo's Ford Foundation Building in New York City, USA, completed in 1968. The 12-story building in the heart of Midtown Manhattan represents an evocative translation of International Style norms, exploring, in particular, unconventional spatial arrangements involving greenery and interiorized public spaces as well as novel subsystems of environmental controls. The volume comprises an L-shaped office block surrounded by an enormous, publicly accessible winter garden, highly unusual in the middle of the dense metropolis, to form a nearly perfect cubic volume. The building envelope contains weathering steel that abuts the main structural frame, while the extensive use of glass underscores Roche's desire to foster transparency as a "moral" character to the building, *à propos* of its philanthropic and humanitarian function. Ada Louise Huxtable stressed the civic qualities of the green-ness of the Ford Foundation Building in 1967, noting: "Ford will never give most New Yorkers anything except this civic gesture of beauty and excellence, and that is a grant of some importance in a world where spirit and soul are deadened by the speculative cheapness of the environment."[16]

The Metabolism movement in Japan is another important precedent. Aphoristically driving an architectural style through a manifesto, the movement's leaders—Kenzo Tange, Kisho Kurokawa, Kiyonori Kikutake, Arata Isozaki, and Fumihiko Maki—pioneered a coterminous interest in organic congruence and reason, density, and the importance of the city. As Udo Kultermann has described it, the Metabolist premise is one where "the human community is a living perpetuum, a continuous biological process, which does not allow for the application of rigid, schematic principles."[17] The Metabolist

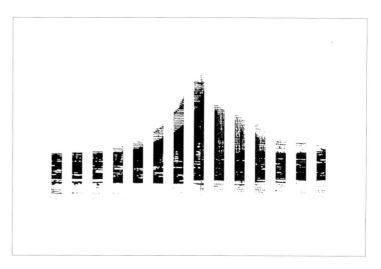

assault on rigid and schematic principles flies in the face of the tenets that made Vancouverism a resounding success. Yet its approach to architecture and urban design is not necessarily diametrically opposed to the qualitative concerns of phenomena such as Vancouverism or buildings like the Ford Foundation. In transmuting organic life to design principles and considering architecture's formal articulation and life cycle as an analogue to the organic world, the Metabolists—through projects like the Nakagin Capsule Tower of 1972 by Kisho Kurokawa or the Clusters in the Air project of 1962—shaped a movement that was interested in total systems. Often comforts were spared in the process and in projects like the Nakagin Capsule Tower; in particular, the belief in density reached a threshold that some critics deemed oppressive and inhumane, much as they did with the allied Brutalist movement. Yet this assessment misses

the main thrust of the carefully crafted argument, which is that organic-inspired design is non-ideological and in following nature fundamentally avers the conventions for human habitation. Metabolism remains a counter-narrative, one which has had important consequences for the formation of the new dense and green paradigm.

Together with the Metabolist experiments came the evolution of the megastructure, which further melded techno-centric ideology with utopian ideas. A definition of the megastructure by Fumihiko Maki alludes to its affinity with Metabolist principles: "The Megastructure is a large frame in which all the functions of a city or part of a city are housed… In a sense it is a man-made feature of the landscape. It is like the great hill on which Italian towns were built."[18] What is envisioned here are man-made

structures that to some extent can mimic natural parts of the landscape, like the hills of Italian towns, for the construction of dense and habitable zones, explaining to a large degree the ecological underpinnings of an architectural movement that often looked anything but ecological.

The megastructure had its greatest theoretical ally, unsurprisingly, in Reyner Banham, who advocated for its widespread adoption in urban environments in his 1973 essay "A Clip-On Architecture."[19] At least in the beginning, Banham saw megastructures as an architectural solution to the issues of urban sprawl and diffusion and the tendency that those processes had to make architectural forms more banal and less innovative. The concept was brought to life by a number of avant-garde designs, realized and unrealized, by architects including

Superstudio, Archigram, Rem Koolhaas, Geoffrey Copcutt, Moshe Safdie, Zvi Hecker, Ettore Sottsass, Buckminster Fuller, as well as the core Metabolist group.

Peter Cook, a member of the Archigram collective, designed the Sponge City project in 1974: an exemplar of the burgeoning landscape-as-apparatus idea mentioned by Maki, which epitomizes the marriage of density and the "well-tempered" landscape in an iconic form whose prescience today cannot be overstated. The project used the sponge as a formal analogy for an urban substance up to seven stories high, which would support extensive communal living while nestled in an extensive "earthscape" of plants as well as vegetal and animal life.[20] The "spongy" qualities of the project are perhaps most evident in the project's plan, which incorporates biomimetic ideas of skin,

Peter Cook, Sponge Building, 1975, elevation.

orifices, "gunge" openings, and elastic zones that coalesce around an inner core structure with vertical circulation and a clip-able framework to connect "soft" (i.e. flexible and/or demountable) and "hard" (fixed) elements, most commonly domiciles conceived as "nests."[21] The landscape consists of two large mounds that overlap and even integrate classicizing columns and fenestration, to bring a touch of historicism and gravity to the structure despite its *tabula-rasa*, utopian thrust.

Zvi Hecker's Ramot Polin housing complex in Jerusalem, Israel, which began construction in 1972, came as close as any project to realizing a design in the spirit of Sponge City. The project consists of 726 housing units tightly packed in a honeycomb structure, providing housing for refugees of the Six Day War.[22] Many of the settlers had initially been housed in *ma'abarot* (refugee settlements), which were slowly phased out by Hecker's design that, nonetheless, took some of its inspiration from the improvisational nature of the *ma'abarot*. Ramot Polin comprises five separate "fingers" of star-shaped buildings encircling courtyards and pedestrian walkways. The first stage, completed in 1975, employed prefabricated building technology for its economic efficiency. Yet that did not preclude formal innovation—hundreds of dodecahedrons abut one another, with each planar facade element cast from a single pentagonal slab of precast concrete. The elements, lifted in place by a crane, recall the metabolic process of adding and subtracting pieces. Yet the project relinquishes the framework of the megastructure by simply imagining the dense units as building blocks that literally rest one atop the other. Terraces were facilitated by each unit's usage of the rooftop of the unit below and functioned as critical elements for the tenants, serving the residents during the holy holiday Sukkot as living, eating, and even sleeping spaces in accordance with the customs established by Jewish law. Meanwhile, the shared courtyards harkened back to the regional typology of the courtyard house. Rather than stressing the capacity for the individual units to plug in and out, as the Metabolists did, Hecker emphasized permanence and solidity à *propos* of the context of the residents, who were seeking permanent domiciles and green space after displacement.

The storied confrontation between the long-running CIAM (*Congrès International d'Architecture Moderne*) and the breakaway group of architects known as Team 10, who sought to challenge the Congress's doctrinaire principles of urban planning, had perhaps its most visionary leaders in Peter and Alison Smithson. They derived principles for the New Brutalism movement in the various sessions of the Congress held between

1953 and 1981. The Smithsons foregrounded the importance of density and environmental synchronicity in many of their projects, none more ambitious than their development plan for Kuwait City, which they began on commission from the Kuwaiti government in 1968. The Smithsons leveraged the massive scale of the Kuwait project to test their evolving concept of the "mat fabric" that literally wove notions of density and porosity (often conceived as opportune moments for green space) into a unified strategy for urban and architectural design.

The Smithsons derived the term "mat" from the motif of the traditional small carpet from Central Asia (Le Corbusier had used the same term to describe his design for the Venice Hospital in 1964).[23] The notion of "mat fabric," with its crevices and holes, horizontal and vertical articulations, functioned as an operative design tool in Kuwait.[24] Within the continuous, largely undifferentiated fabric of the dense scheme, situated on an elevated level lifted off the ground by piers, one can observe an emphasis on the courtyard, the promenade, and the *wadi* (a small artificial stream of water common to the Arab world and used for natural cooling). The "crevice" of the "mat" is utilized as a visual device, providing guiding sight lines to the minarets as a way-finding system and also space for planters with trees and other indigenous vegetation.

Despite the obvious aversion to the CIAM planning principles as a one-size-fits-all solution, the balanced design applies mostly normative practices of Western urban master planning, with the exception of two massive *maidans*, or open spaces for large-scale civic functions. The more important of the two, dubbed the "Orangerie Maidan," is a space inspired by the Orangeries of Versailles and Potsdam.[25] Planters with citrus trees could provide "spaces for fragrant nighttime walks, or, when removed, spaces suitable for light exhibitions, or spectator stands for Kuwaiti civic and religious festivals."[26] Here we see the large-scale public space acting as an antidote to a tightly packed urban fabric, in a coupling that, while born of references to traditional regional architecture, has had a marked contemporary resurgence.

The dense and green conjunction did not originate from architectural discourses only. Political, cultural, and environmental upheavals have also played an important role in accelerating and fomenting the paradigm. One crucial event was the oil crisis of 1973. Because of the sudden embargo placed on the export of oil by numerous Arab oil-producing countries, oil prices around the world skyrocketed and prompted a number of entrepreneurial architects, designers, and non-professionals to recast both

urban and non-urban settings in the mold of a brave new world, free from the excessive reliance on fossil fuels for the operation of cars and buildings. The 2007 exhibition "1973: Sorry, Out of Gas; Architecture's Response to the 1973 Oil Crisis" at the Canadian Centre for Architecture underscored the ways in which such changes created vastly new ways of thinking about architecture's relationship with energy, ways that centered on three distinct ecological operations: the harnessing of wind power, the harnessing of solar power, and the use of the earth as an advantageous climatic environment.[27] Among the important actors of this primarily North American movement were Michael Reynolds, David Wright, Malcolm Wells, and Andy Davis.

While the majority of the architects and urban designers of this movement proved that passive systems could be introduced with aplomb to urban settings, eschewing the reliance on the local power grid and often even generating money by creating more energy than was consumed, it was Wells who offered some of the most lasting and synthetic principles for the dense and green model. His books *Underground Designs* of 1977 and *Recovering America: A More Gentle Way to Build* of 1999 are manifestoes on how better human-ecological coordination is largely a question of minimizing the amount of raw material we use to construct our built environment– a statement that offers both direct and indirect ways of praising dense, even impacted constructions. Wells' own home in Massachusetts served as the model for a reproducible and self-constructed Tiny Underground House. At only 35 sqm, the Tiny Underground House had an energy footprint of almost zero and was remarkably silent, dry, and, according to Wells, "easy on the land." Wells provided those interested in recreating his design with DIY plans, elevations, and a construction section.

Strategies like those of Malcolm Wells have an affinity to the more general environmental sub-movement of eco-centrism, essentially a grassroots effort to reclaim the earth as a place of natural symbiosis through the rejection of energy-consuming civic infrastructures.[28] In reality, eco-centrism finds itself much more as part of a framework of radical idealism, stressing the social and political elements over the environmental ones.[29] To be sure, the architectural manifestoes set forth by Wells and so many of his generation are concerned with ecology on the operative level, but at their core they propose a social contract to fellow humans—a contract that underscores interpersonal reciprocity, be the scenario set in nature or in a dense urban agglomeration. There is a lot to learn here, because this core orientation rejects the temptation to characterize these projects as mere "hippy" experiments on the one hand, and as programs

Malcolm Wells, Design for an Underground House, 1989, renderings.

unconcerned with conditions of urban density on the other. To see the dense and green paradigm as one construed from a fundamental desire for global balance, irrespective of formal appearance or location, was an important step in connecting these historical developments with our present circumstances.

The New Dense and Green Paradigm

A host of buildings completed mostly since the turn of the millennium offer important insights into the ways in which the diverse channels discussed above have rallied around an almost subconscious movement, which we are only just beginning to recognize as such. While the formal, ideological, and professional diversity of the paradigm was maintained, its basic ideas solidified and became recognizable.

The development of the new dense and green paradigm is in large part indebted to the pioneering work of two architects, Ken Yeang and Norman Foster, who are as instructive in their commonalities as they are in their marked differences. Yeang committed his academic research as well as his design practice to the issue of the ecological building in the city as early as in the 1970s, before such a topic had a major audience in architectural discourse.[30] Yeang's unique practice evolved as a perpetual push and pull of text and building, which effectively acted as experiments on one another. Bucking the common refrain that buildings in dense urban fabrics are inherently more ecological, Yeang has used less commonly cited trade data—mainly those that consider the energy consumption of skyscrapers in and of themselves—to shed light on the ways in which the architecture of dense urban fabrics, and skyscrapers in particular, are not necessarily predisposed to a greater level of ecological congruence.

Yeang, accelerating the tenets of Vancouverism for the needs of the contemporary city, embodies the role of the architect as mediator by negotiating these trade realities with an elemental belief in urban environments. In contrast to a return to nature, his buildings are manifestoes of the nature of return in the city. Yeang is deeply passionate about the importance of urban density and has communicated his ideas through a consistent body of articles, publications, and built projects. Whereas the books *Designing with Nature: The Ecological Basis for Architectural Design* (1995) and *The Skyscraper, Bioclimatically Considered: A Design Primer* (1997) give architectural practice some of its most compelling syntheses on the topic, it is his built projects that drive the point home.

One of the earliest manifestations of Yeang's professional position is the Menara Umno skyscraper in Penang, Malaysia, completed in 1998.[31] The 21-story, 1,920 sqm building can be completely naturally ventilated. It provides a work environment where no desk is more than 6.5 m away from an operable window.[32] The project embellishes its capacity for ventilation through specially designed "wing-walls" that funnel wind to an array of designated balcony zones, where air is locked in as a resource that can be drawn upon later through a secondary system of operable windows and doors. This system distinguishes the building from other skyscrapers that employ porosity as a source of ventilation and human comfort, but not of internal climatic calibration. Other passive features of Yeang's project include daylit lobbies and staircases as well as sophisticated sun-shading devices.[33] While the project lacks the bedecking greenery of many of his other projects, it lucidly articulates its spatial objectives of both passive environmental strategies and density.

Norman Foster and his firm Foster + Partners, founded in 1967 and undergoing several name changes since then, have been steadily demonstrating an unrivalled capacity for a synthesis of ecological sensitivity, intelligent urban solutions, and forthright architectural form. Foster's sensitivity to dense and green matters has been part of a cumulative process, originating from what he himself has described as the self-evident ethical necessity for architecture to respond to environmental conditions, rendering this approach an integral element of his office's culture, one not tied to any dogma or ideology. In his own words, Foster illuminates how this approach is fundamental to his practice's work: "Our buildings have always been driven by a belief that the quality of our surroundings directly influences the quality of our lives, whether in the workplace, at home or in the public spaces that make up our cities. This emphasis on the social dimension is an acknowledgement that architecture is generated by people's needs, both spiritual and material. Allied to this is a willingness to challenge accepted responses or solutions. Looking back I can see that our practice has been inspired by the polarities of *analysis* and *action*. This means trying to ask the right questions, allied with an insatiable curiosity about how things work—whether they are organizations or mechanical systems."[34]

The analysis Foster + Partners undertakes in the office and the action it engages in its buildings are perhaps not as polarized as Foster suggests. In fact, it may be their precise codependency and synchronicity that makes Foster's work compelling in regard to the dense and green paradigm. So often his Swiss Re Tower

Foster + Partners/Systematica s. r. l., Masdar City, Abu Dhabi, UAE, 1997, aerial view, rendering.

in London, UK, is cited as a watershed example for its fusion of intelligent, ecological systems and elegant architectural form. But the building also functions as a living, three-dimensional diagram of its own genesis, a genesis derived from the parity and coeval nature of analysis and action. The 40 story "gherkin" form is in all actuality more a product of its responsive qualities to its site than a product of image. Although the building has the same amount of volume as a rectangular building on the site of the same height would have, the widening of the building at its center and the tapering on the top and bottom give the undeniable optical impression that the building is not bulky and thus not contributing to the bulkiness or congestion of downtown London. The profile also creates reduced reflections and an increase in the amount of daylight at ground level. Addressing the "green" element quite literally, a series of swirling sky gardens support the building's ventilation system and assist in the oxygenation of the interior air quality. The rotation in the spatial arrangement of the sky gardens, evident on the outside from the difference in its fenestration, makes plain the dense and green ideas in diagrammatic form.

The Hearst Tower in New York City, USA, is another office building whose form functions as a living diagram of its own tension between analysis and action. The instantly recognizable diagrid structure afforded the opportunity to use 20% less steel by carrying loads diagonally as opposed to vertically.[35] 85% of that steel is recycled and HVAC systems have been maximized to reduce the building's energy consumption by 25% in comparison to a comparable building.[36]

The Swiss Re Tower, completed in 2003, and the Hearst Tower, completed in 2006, are both often lauded as symbols of Foster's ingenuity. Yet these are only part of a continuum in Foster's unique brand of dense and green design that can be traced back to the Commerzbank in Frankfurt, Germany, the European Union's tallest building at the time, whose planning began in the 1970s through support of the Frankfurt Green Party and which was realized after a long gestation in 1997.[37] In addition to employing a number of highly advanced energy reduction technologies, the design incorporates sky gardens that create communal garden atria at nine different levels across the 56-story building. The continuum of dense and green design extends to the present, with projects such as Masdar in the United Arab Emirates, a city built in the desert that aims to be entirely self-sustaining and zero-energy.

Another important moment in the evolution of the dense and green paradigm is the Netherlands Pavilion at the Expo 2000 in Hanover, Germany. The pavilion has largely been considered the Expo's most successful and likely the most adept interlocutor of the overall themes of the exposition: "man, nature and technology."[38] The fair's programming stressed the capacity for design to mediate a balance between those three entities through exploring the best practices for global human coexistence. MVRDV's interpretation of the task in the context of the Netherlands Pavilion consisted of a densely stacked, airy building comprising six distinct levels and exhibition features that signify distinct ecosystems of the Dutch landscape. A main ground level, conceived as a grotto, hoists the structure aloft through three root-like pillars and is in turn topped by layers addressing the themes of agriculture, oysters, forest, rain, and water. Each level or "plate" is conceived not only as its own exhibition, but also as an architectonically independent entity, connected through a staircase placed on the facade's exterior serving as the primary vertical circulation.

The tightly stacked plates and the didactic and immersive environments that they contain pay tribute to Dutch successes in negotiating one of the world's most densely populated nations with a progressive design culture. Each level creatively demonstrates or proposes architectural solutions to the problems of the day. While the structure's character is primarily that of a demonstrative showpiece, it also has a number of synthetic and original architectonic qualities. For one, the pavilion bears out the supposition that varying ecological strategies for buildings can be juxtaposed, as opposed to integrated, and that this can be a point of aesthetic interest, not discord. Moreover, the apparent trick of the densification and overlay of the programs further spurs the possibilities of thinking of a "green" architecture as one that could just as easily be oriented vertically as it could be horizontally.

Many recent works by Jean Nouvel are emblematic of how the dense and green paradigm has been brought to term by architects whose careers did not actually originate with ideas of ecological design. Nouvel's own shifts have been gradual and to some extent demonstrate the uneasy marriage of "autonomous" formal concerns and the contingent conditions of both ecological and density-driven design. Nouvel's 2008 design for a residential tower in Los Angeles' Century City, nicknamed the "Green Blade," is a case in point. Sitting on a 2.4-acre site and rising 45 stories, Nouvel's design appears at first glance to be a rather typical high-rise luxury condominium development. Upon closer inspection of the design, however, a number of

MVRDV, Netherlands Pavilion, Expo 2000, Hanover, Germany, 2000, section.

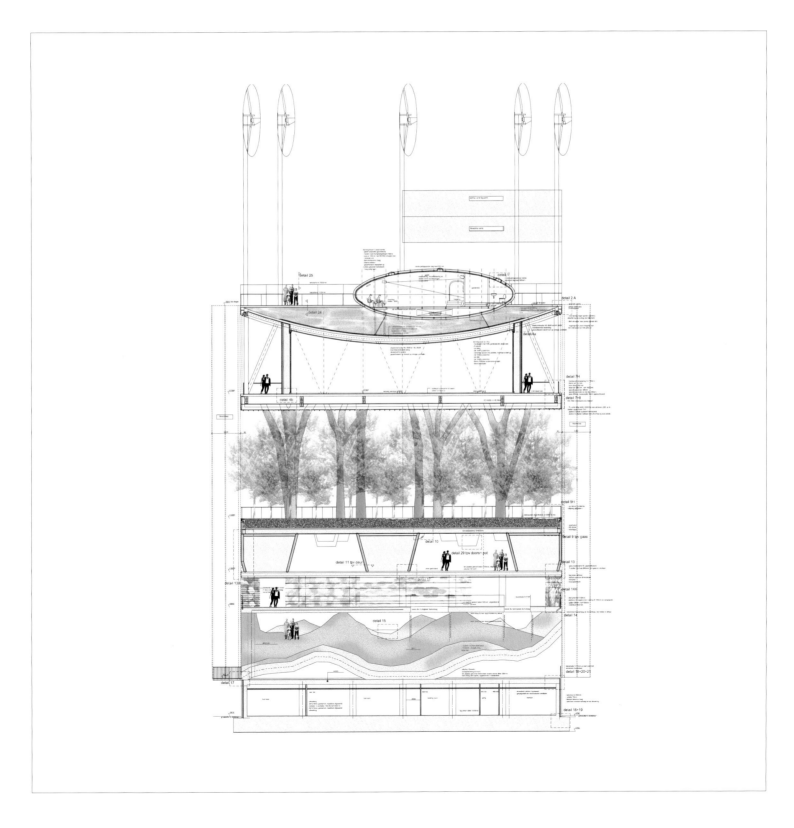

Ateliers Jean Nouvel, 10000 Santa Monica Boulevard (Green Blade), Los Angeles,
California, USA, 2008, exterior, renderings.
Ateliers Jean Nouvel, Seguin Island, Paris, France, 2009, garden spaces, rendering.

subtle and innovative adaptations make themselves evident, in particular the building's very thin profile and its extremely reductive treatment of the facade, which is rendered as not much more than scaffolding with affixed sheet glass. The building's profile is intended to create a floor-through plan, which eliminates the need for artificial lighting entirely during daytime, while the facade construction is intended to furnish the application of an extensive program of planters that cover the building with a display of plant life indigenous to southern California.

These two major moves are indicative of the *post-facto* surgery required to adapt what can be described as modernist glass boxes into "green" organisms. This approach, essentially the opposite of a holistic, bottom-up concept, and the fact that the project is a luxury condominium self-consciously jockeying for LEED status makes a project such as this an easy target for criticism. Yet at the same time, it can be seen to indicate how formal approaches, even ones that originate from different design ideas, can breathe new life into the polarized standards of "the ecological" and "the modernist."

Another project by Nouvel, a master plan redesign of Paris' Seguin Island still unfolding, illustrates a more bottom-up design scheme. This is largely amplified by the fact that the island in the Seine is not a *tabula rasa* but the site of a former Renault car factory. While Nouvel's design does call for the razing of the derelict buildings, the island's spatial configuration—including its throughways and general volumetric hierarchy—is left intact. The main greening element—the extensive planting of indigenous grasses, plants, and trees on a total of 7 ha—privileges the role of landscape architecture. The island's river banks are designed to provide a generous promenade as a major public amenity, rendered as an almost primordial landscape[39] and matched by an indoor garden space and commercial promenade 450 m in length and designed in conjunction with landscape architect Michel Desvigne, whose operable roof adjusts to the given environmental conditions. High-planted terraces pre-empt an array of buildings whose architectural qualities are, at least in these earlier stages of design, of secondary importance to the cohesive greening program of both the public and private realms.

In Milan, Italy, Stefano Boeri, Gianandrea Barreca, and Giovanni La Varra's Bosco Verticale is a veritable celebration of architecture as organism. The architects have collaborated closely with botanists and horticulturalists in their design of 119-m-tall residential towers in the rehabilitated industrial district of Porta Nuova. The design focuses on the science of the plants installed

on each successive level's perimeter to determine what can best mitigate the smog and increase the air quality of the area. Epitomizing the furry green building, the architects are fully aware and not afraid of the cliché, proving that the literal greening of the building envelope is more than a visual stunt: a true test for one of Europe's most polluted urban areas.

Another innovative approach to the dense and green paradigm that is driven by a typological agenda is BIG and JDS Architects' Mountain Dwellings in Ørestad, Denmark, completed in 2008. The building, charged with the unusual task of facilitating two thirds of its volume for local parking needs, comprises a bed of co-planar apartment units condensed on a single, tightly packed matrix and is subsequently tilted by about 45°. This single bold move creates a series of units, terraced in ten layers, each with its own private rooftop garden and the adjacent unit with exposure on three of four sides. The plantings of the roof gardens change with the seasons and are kept nourished by a massive integrated watering system. Apartments are separated from their gardens through a simple sliding glass door. Levels are connected through slanted elevators and stairwells.

This tilting and densification of the suburban ideal of a freestanding residence with a backyard has functional reasons. The volume left beneath the wedge-shaped void fulfills the requisite needs for parking, whose programmatic presence, rather than being camouflaged, is revealed plainly with massive supergraphics on three of its four facades. The rasterized graphic motifs allude to mountain landscapes and make plain the building's topographic analogy, its tacit geocentric and eco-mimetic qualities. In addition to appropriating a suburban typology into a decidedly urban one and effectively greening it in the most elemental way, the architects adhere to and exceed the progressive low-energy standards that are so important to the practice and construction of architecture in the Nordic countries. The result is a unique combination of social pleasure—even luxury—with a responsible, typologically innovative design.

The playfulness and blunt visual qualities of the Mountain Dwellings are not incidental. In fact, they are part of the key design ideas of Bjarke Ingels, BIG's director, who has promoted the notion of "hedonistic sustainability," an architectural strategy that seeks to enhance quality of life from—not in spite of—sustainable building practices.

Whereas densification and sustainability are intended to evoke pleasure in the inhabitants of the Mountain Dwellings, in Cloud 9's

Media ICT office building in Barcelona, Spain, completed in 2011, these features are intended to evoke downright awe. This striking building in a central Barcelona district articulates its diurnal and seasonal ecological life cycle entirely through its facade. The structure consists of a latticed box forming a nearly perfect platonic cube sitting on an area of 3,572 sqm.[40] Upper levels provide office space while the ground level contains a workshop, a "cibernarium" (an institute dedicated to internet-based technologies and programs), and an auditorium intended for general public usage. The most striking element of the facade is its inflatable ETFE cushions, which are infused with a nitrogen-based fog during the summer months to shield the building from the harsh Spanish sun. In the winter the plastic cushions are released to gain solar energy. The facades are also equipped with sensors that collect environmental information on variables such as humidity and barometric pressure in order to automatically adjust additional apertures. The photovoltaic roof provides the building with up to 55% of its energy needs and the building in total reduces its CO_2 emissions through its sensitive systems by an appraised 95%, giving it an absolutely minimal environmental footprint.[41] Visually, the project inverts the quotidian integrative strategies of active building systems and treats them—quite literally—as the ornamental elements of the facade, making a clear statement on the one hand and harkening back to other historical movements—namely the so-called British "high-tech" movement—that privileged mechanical and facade systems as one and the same.

While Cloud 9's sophisticated facade system in Barcelona emphasizes the importance of the architectural membrane, Ryue Nishizawa's Vertical Garden House in Tokyo, Japan, of 2011 does the precise opposite. The four-story private residence, tucked into an impossibly narrow site in the heart of the city, is stripped of all glazing apart from one component at ground level, presumably for security purposes, rejecting what the architect has described as a "true facade."[42] Instead, a simple palette of full-height windows, curtains, benches, and planters function as dividers within the interior space as well as between the building envelope and the exterior. What is left are white floor plates that accentuate the building's compositional appearance as a shelf with discrete objects resting on it, lyrically conveying a sense of a still-life painting come to life in three dimensions. The plates are punctuated by a sinewy spiral staircase, registering as its only discernible architectural object. Even so, it is largely camouflaged by the impromptu placement of plants in a wide variety of species. The plants further enhance the shelf-like appearance of the house and its qualities as a mere canvas for the lives and

OMA/Büro Ole Scheeren/RSP Architects Planners & Engineers, The Interlace, Singapore,
2015, aerial view.
WOHA, School of the Arts, Singapore, 2009.

belongings of its inhabitants. The project represents the dense and green paradigm at its most elemental, where density is derived from the urban site condition and green is derived from the relinquishing of complex enclosure systems and the poetic, almost sublime reification of the quotidian houseplant. Vertical Garden House has the ascetic, crystalline qualities for which Ryue Nishizawa and the affiliate firm SANAA have become renowned in architecture.

At the other end of the scale range of innovative dense and green housing is OMA Büro Ole Scheeren's Interlace Singapore project, an expansive, 170,000 sqm, 1,000-unit residential development in a city known for its experimentation with density and green design. The project consists of 31 apartment blocks of identical length, each six stories in height. These block-like horizontal components are stacked in a hexagonal arrangement (which incidentally recalls Zvi Hecker's Ramot Polin housing project, discussed above). In between the blocks are spacious courtyards. The overlaying of the units creates a network of nodal moments of connection, forming a continuous vertical corridor between the units that facilitates access for both shared and private elevated garden spaces. The project, sited in an already verdant neighborhood, completes a long-evolving green belt of municipal parks, recreation, and residential spaces. In a best-practice approach to environmental concerns, the project employs strategic systems based on the careful study of the sun, wind, and microclimate conditions of Singapore in general and the site in particular, as well as advanced passive energy strategies.[43]

Much like Jean Nouvel, Rem Koolhaas and OMA's arrival on the ecological scene is one of a productive revisionism to the firm's approach to environmental concerns over its nearly four decades of existence. The revision has an important innovative typological dimension to it when compared to the firm's projects in Asia in the past two decades of comparable or larger scales, such as the CCTV project in Beijing or the Togok (XL) Towers project in Seoul. Rather than articulating density through the traditional heroics of the skyscraper, there is an essential, almost ironic dismantling of the skyscraper typology, forming a building that alludes to a skyscraper dissected into equal sections and laid flat in an organic honeycomb arrangement. This rejects a symbolic presence on the city's impressive skyline without sacrificing its formal boldness. In fact, the unusual massing of the project creates the very opportunities that facilitate its green features, communal nature, and makes good on its promise to be a creative addition to Singapore's many other experiments with the dense and green typologies.

A recent issue of *A+U Magazine* entitled "Singapore, Capital City for Vertical Green" demonstrates at the urban scale what OMA Büro Ole Scheeren are accomplishing at the architectural scale. In his response to the question "What is the state of urban development in Singapore?" the Danish architect and urban designer Jan Gehl duly notes the Corbusian legacy that many of Singapore's architects and planners still follow. "In terms of planning ideology, the modernist principles coined in the Athens Charter of city planning from 1933 have definitely provided the leading principles for Singapore's development. Corbusier and the other authors of the modernist planning and architecture principles would be proud today if they could drive around and see their dreams fulfilled. They envisaged the modern city as a machine for living and working—efficient, healthy, green and pretty. This indeed has been accomplished and as I personally see it, coming from afar, herein also lie some of the problems, or perhaps some of the indicators, rather, for where to go next."[44]

Indeed, a number of fortuitous and strategic conditions have facilitated this quasi-utopian agenda and made Singapore a leader in dense and green typologies. Projects like WOHA's School of the Arts, completed in 2010, and PARKROYAL on Pickering, completed in 2013, have led the way on the design side with visionary leadership. However, if there is to be a "Singaporism" for the 21st Century, one must also understand how, if at all, the semi-utopian nature of the Singapore model is actionable in settings with less capital, more poverty, and different historical circumstances.

Asia in general and Singapore in particular have great potential for the further exploration of dense and green as well as liveability principles. The breathtaking scale of many of the new developments here captures the attention of politicians and developers and the imagination of citizens. For example, Shenzhen Logistic City by JDS Architects, a project in Shenzhen, China, that was unveiled in 2010, is a proposed 1111-m-tall tower (making it the tallest building in the world) that is to house a vertical community. Cascading loggias of verdant green space and embedded wind turbines are to reduce its energy consumption to next to nothing.

While many are familiar with the blank-slate setting of Masdar, the Sydney Central Park project in Australia represents a more viable option in that it is situated within an existing infrastructure and pre-existing urban conditions that truly test the veracity of dense and green ideas. The project's site is a 6 ha area steps away from Sydney's Central Station and central business district. The site's footprint, which abuts a number of major

thoroughfares, comprises a campus of buildings designed by an array of architects, including Jean Nouvel and Foster + Partners as well as Jeppe Aagaard Andersen, Tonkin Zulaikha Greer, Johnson Pilton Walker, and Turf Design.[45] The project is subject to an exacting range of solar, wind, water, and acoustic parameters, among others, that will make it Australia's bellwether of green design.[46]

On the infrastructure side, a recent wave of so-called "vertical farms" support the density of the green city while minimizing both the literal and ecological footprint of the traditional farm. For example, the Harvest Green Project by Romses Architects in Vancouver, British Columbia, Canada, features farms for vegetables, herbs, fruits, fish, chickens, and a boutique goat and sheep dairy facility housed in discrete compartments saddled from a core tower. The tower is designed to be powered by photovoltaic glazing, small- and large-scale wind turbines, and methane generated from compost of organic materials originating from the farm. A rainwater cistern atop provides a water source for the vertical irrigation of the crops and roof gardens. Expanding beyond the farm and garden programs, the tower's design also houses a plant and seed lab, an organic foods store, a supermarket and restaurant that serves food harvested on site, a transit station, and underground parking. The project is a step forward for the design of vertical farms, which, in addition to not having had taken off with the same success as dense and green residential and commercial typologies, have also maintained staid aesthetic schemes (which are nonetheless big on innovation of the agriculture sector).

As the agriculture agenda demonstrates, we are just now breaking free of the idea that dense and green is a topic limited to certain typologies—the typologies of apartment and office buildings. A city, if we are to understand it as an organism, as green thinking tends to emphasize, is more than work and life. It is play, it is eating, it is shopping, and it is all the spaces that we inhabit in between these programs. What agency might an average resident possess to activate dense and green environments at the tactical and micro-scale, and might this change the way we talk about the issue, which is so often seen exclusively through the prism of apartment and office building typologies?

This holistic view calls up what has become an important, if still not clearly defined, term—resilience, which generally refers to the ability of a community to exist within its immediate vicinity—that is, to draw its food, its building materials, its water, and so

WOHA, PARKROYAL on Pickering, Singapore, 2013, sky terraces.

on from this area—without being dependent on the vicissitudes of geopolitical events and overly relying on distant economies. Resilience is key to Masdar, for example, and it has a great deal of promise as well as potential problems. On the one hand, it goes without saying that a lowering of international reliance on fossil fuels, a reduction of emissions, and sustainable farming, building, and development practices will benefit all. Yet in cultural terms, resilience also has the potential pitfall of becoming synonymous with insularity and anti-cosmopolitanism. A global flow of goods, particularly non-natural resources, remains crucial to cross-cultural understanding and tolerance. The resilience of natural resources cannot and should not become associated with the shutting down of global, cosmopolitan culture.

Conclusion

William McDonough has posited that the proverbial "greening" of architecture is a project beyond quantitative calculations, and rather emphasizes its expressive aspects and potential for synergy. Green buildings, he states, "seek to replace dominion over nature with a more fulfilling relationship with the natural world. If this century is to be known for peace, prosperity, beauty, and the restoration of our world, the integration of nature into our built environment needs to become one of the foundations of our design agendas. Architecture, with its profound ability to create new relationships to place, is uniquely positioned to lead such a development."[47] Architecture is already leading that relationship and the dialogue has been steadily building for some time now: the dialogue between city and nature, between the dense and the green.

1. World Urbanization Prospects. The 2007 Revision, vol. 1, "Comprehensive Tables." United Nations publication (source: http://www.un.org/esa/population/publications/wup2007/2007WUP_Highlights_web.pdf).
2. Banham, Reyner. The Architecture of the Well-Tempered Environment. Chicago: University of Chicago Press, 1969. p. 22.
3. Ibid.
4. See Gissen, David. Subnature: Architecture's Other Environments. New York: Princeton Architectural Press, 2009.
5. A symposium on the topic of the proverbial "return to nature" and its relationship to the design fields was held at the Harvard University Graduate School of Design from 2009–2010, the forthcoming records of which recount an important array of reflections on the topic for contemporary architecture from historians, practicioners, and critics.
6. See, for example: Boddy, Trevor. "Vancouverism vs. Lower Manhattanism: Shaping the High Density City," presented at the Institute for Urban Design, New York, 20 September 2005, and reprinted on the website ArchNewsNow, http://www.archnewsnow.com.
7. Liscombe, R. W. The New Spirit: Modern Architecture in Vancouver, 1938–1963. Montreal: Canadian Center for Architecture, 1997. p. 152.
8. Jacobs, Jane. The Death and Life of Great American Cities. New York: Random House, 1961.
9. Wikens, Stephen. "Jane Jacobs : Honoured in the Breach," in Globe and Mail, 6 May 2011.
10. See Beatley, Timothy. Green Urbanism: Learning from European Cities. Washington, D.C.: Island Press, 2000.
11. See an official account of the legislation in: Organisation for Economic Cooperation and Development. Governance for Sustainable Development. Paris: OECD, 2002. p. 231.
12. Hoornweg, D., L. Sugar, and C. L. Trejos Gomez. "Cities and greenhouse gas emissions: moving forward," in Environment and Urbanization, vol. 23 (2) (2011). doi:10.1177/0956247810392270.
13. Ickes, Harold L. "The Place of Housing in National Rehabilitation," in The Journal of Land & Public Utility Economics, vol. 11, no. 2 (May 1935). p. 109–116.
14. Basic introductions to CIAM, which picked up this task, as well as its offshot Team X include: Mumford, Eric. The CIAM Discourse on Urbanism, 1928–1960. Cambridge, Mass.: The MIT Press, 2000; and Risselada, Max and Dirk van den Heuvel (eds.). TEAM 10. In Search of a Utopia of the Present, 1953–1981. Rotterdam: nai publishers, 2005.
15. The Intelligence Unit of The Economist explain their rating system for the world livibility index on their website: https://www.eiu.com/public/topical_report.aspx?campaignid=Liveability2012
16. Huxtable, Ada Louise. "The Ford Foundation," in The New York Times, 26 November 1967.
17. As cited by Johnson, Donald Leslie and Donald Langmead. Makers of 20th Century Modern Architecture, A Bio-Critical Sourcebook. London and Chicago: Fitzroy Dearborn, 1997. p. 211.
18. Maki, Fumihiko. Investigations in Collective Form. (A special publication, no. 2) The School of Architecture, Washington University, St. Louis, 1964. p. 8.
19. Banham, Reyner. "A clip-on architecture," in Architectural Design, 35 (November 1965). pp. 534–535.
20. Spens, Michael. "From Mound to Sponge: How Peter Cook Explores Landscape Buildings," in Architectural Design, vol. 77, no. 22 (2005). p. 14.
21. Ibid.
22. Bergdoll, Barry and Peter Christensen (eds.). Home Delivery: Fabricating the Modern Dwelling. New York: The Museum of Modern Art, 2008. p. 158.
23. For a discussion of Le Corbusier's use of the mat and the mat-building revival, see Sarkis, Hashim, Pablo Allard, and Timothy Hyde. Case: Le Corbusier's Venice Hospital and the Mat Building Revival. London: Prestel, 2002.
24. Kohte, Susanne. "Tropical Architecture: The Beginnings of Sustainable Architecture," in Archithese, 6 (June 2009). pp. 67–69.
25. Ibid.
26. Ibid.
27. See Borasi, Giovanna (ed.). Sorry! Out of Gas!: Architecture's Response to the 1973 Oil Crisis. Montreal: Canadian Center for Architecture, 2007.
28. See, for example: Eckersley, Robyn. Environmentalism and Political Theory: Towards an Ecocentric Approach. Albany: State University of New York Press, 1992.
29. See, for example: Westphal, Merold. "Hegel's Radical Idealism: Family and State as Ethical Communities," in Pelczynski, Z. A. (ed.). State & Civil Society: Studies in Hegel's Political Philosophy. Cambridge: Cambridge University Press, 1984. p. 77–92.
30. Ken Yeang's key early essays include: "Bases for Ecosystem Design," in Architectural Design, July 1972; "The Energetics of the Built Environment," in Architectural Design, July 1974; "Bionics: The Use of Biological Analogies in Design," in Architectural Association Quarterly, no. 4 (1974).
31. Source: http://www.trhamzahyeang.com/project/skyscrapers/umno01.html
32. Ibid.
33. Ibid.
34. This is excerpted from a 2003 statement written by Foster and posted on the firm's website as an essay entitled "Architecture and Sustainability" (http://www.fosterandpartners.com/data/practice-data/essays/essay13.pdf).
35. Source: http://www.fosterandpartners.com/projects/hearst-tower/
36. Ibid.
37. Scott, Andrew. Dimensions of Sustainability. New York: E & FN Spon, 1998. p. 173.
38. Flamme-Jaspers, Martina. Expo 2000 Hannover: Architecture. Ostfildern: Hatje Cantz, 2000.
39. Source: http://www.arcspace.com/features/ateliers-jean-nouvel/seguin-island/
40. Ruiz-Geli, Enric. Media-ICT Building: Cloud 9. Barcelona: Actar, 2011. p. 58.
41. Ibid.
42. Zancan, Roberto. "Tokyo's Vertical Thresholds #2: Ryue Nishizawa," in Domus, 16 December 2011.
43. Information culled from the OMA website (http://www.oma.eu/projects/2009/the-interlace).
44. Gehl, Jan. "What's Next Singapore?," in A+U, 05 (2012). p. 28.
45. Information culled from the development's website (http://www.frasersbroadway.com.au/broadway/).
46. Ibid.
47. Gissen, David (ed.). Big & Green: Toward Sustainable Architecture in the 21st Century. New York: Princeton Architectural Press, 2002. back cover.

Dense and Green Technologies

Naree Phinyawatana

Linear use of natural resources.
"Virtuous cycle" of natural resources.

Urbanization involves a great change in human behavior, lifestyle, and more importantly, urban ecosystems. Increase in urbanization induces increase in natural resources consumption, specifically energy consumption for lighting, heating, and cooling. Because sustainability is the result of a carefully integrated collaborative process, pushing the boundaries of sustainable design through innovation requires an initial holistic concept of guidance that supports strategies for long-term planning, designing, and ease of operation by rigorous technical analysis and recommendation. During the initial-stage reviewing, defining opportunities and challenges are crucial aspects for a project to meet its fullest innovation potential.

A traditional design can be illustrated as a linear use of natural resources, in the sense that a resource is used once and disposed of afterwards. By contrast, a "virtuous cycle" represents a setting to ensure that all resources are used to their fullest potential before being disposed of from a project, a neighborhood, or a city. This requires a new way of thinking to push the design and operation boundaries beyond fundamental pragmatism. A deep understanding of the basis of sustainability strategies is indispensable, which includes taking full advantage of site orientation, building massing, daylighting, natural ventilation, passive cooling, system efficiency, integrated controls for measurement and verification on performance, and even incorporating landscape and green elements into the design.

Facade Matters

Good buildings begin with good envelopes. The most important step toward designing a better dense and green environment lies in establishing a proper building massing along with facade optimization during an early phase of a project in order to balance all external factors, which in turn will reduce the overall internal energy demand by at least 5–10%. Major external factors that influence internal conditions include outdoor air temperature, air movement, relative humidity, and solar radiation. Building facades serve as the first line of defense to reduce the required internal loads to operate a building.

There are several analyses that can be studied in this early stage of the design in order to determine the effectiveness of the massing design. Overshadowing analysis can be used to determine direct daylight availability at a given point when looking up toward the sky, especially when daylight access from ground is a critical factor in the overall development design.

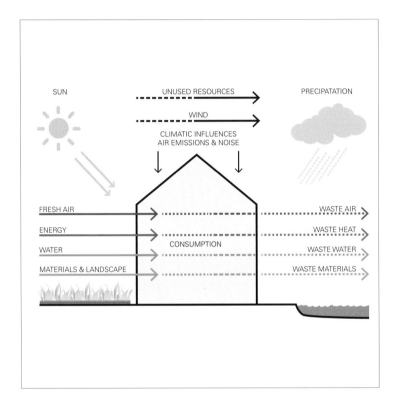

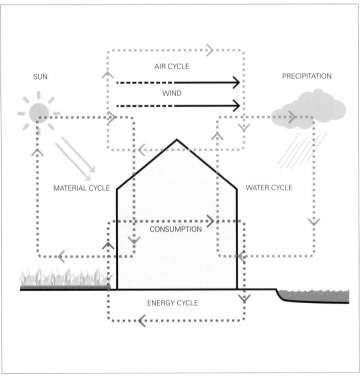

Overshadowing study.

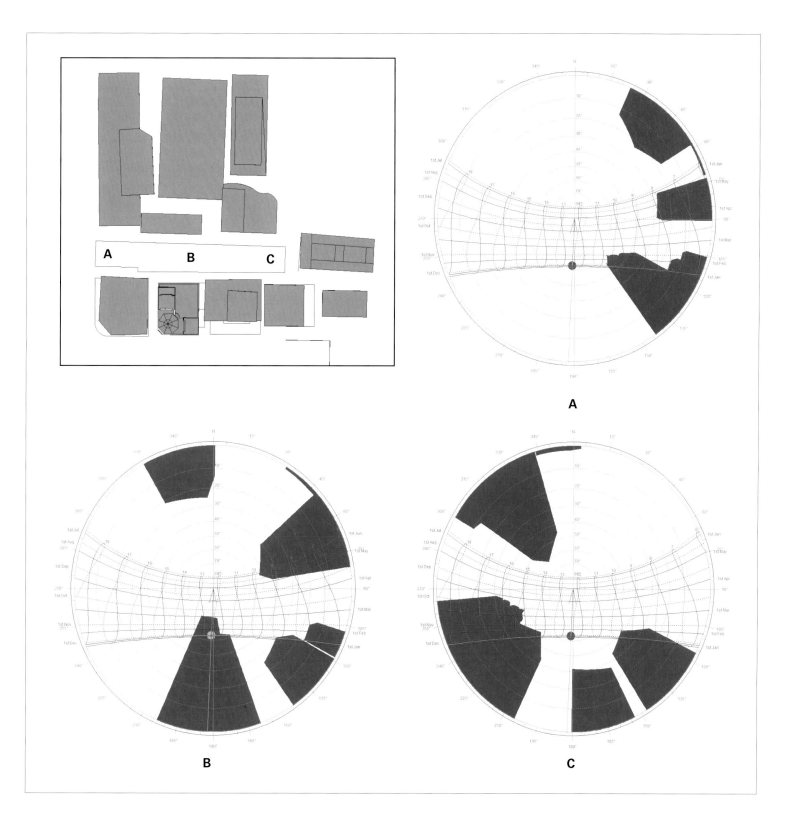

A

B

C

Indoor conditions and outdoor climatic parameters.
Annual solar radiation study.

Seasonal components of solar radiation.
Building envelope: single layer vs. double layer.

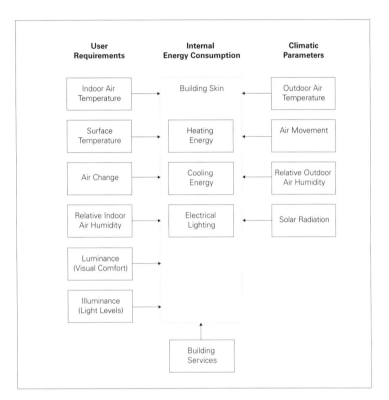

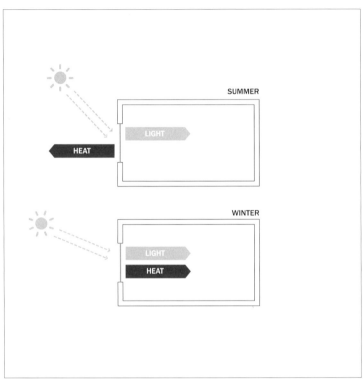

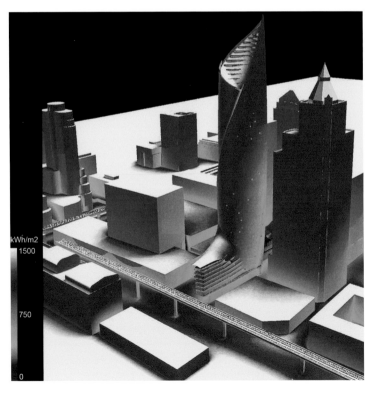

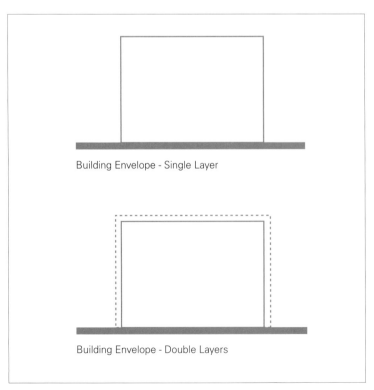

Building Envelope - Single Layer

Building Envelope - Double Layers

Another common study is annual cumulative solar radiation, which assesses the overall solar radiation received on all exposed facades and landscape surfaces over the course of a year. Both analyses are useful in determining a proper massing design and identify the building envelopes or landscape zones that would require less daylight access or that are overexposed to solar radiation loads. Additionally, both studies are helpful in specifying appropriate locations for green roofs or sky gardens to ensure ample exposure to daylight throughout the year. This initial study is imperative for sky gardens because daylight is crucial for plants to survive. As different plant species require different daylight levels and total daylight exposure per day, it is important to discuss early in the process those to be used and the location of sky gardens, vertical greenery, and green roof areas. Building envelope systems can be divided into two major types: single-layer and double-layer systems. A single layer has all facade elements combined within a single facade system, while a double-layer system typically consists of an internal facade system in combination with an external system, such as a shading system, as a separate outer layer. The double-layer system is a preferred option for building with complex geometries because the internal layer can be constructed using a standard facade system. Both system types aim to reduce the external solar radiation loads while maintaining a useful daylight level for building occupants.

The glazing ratio, or window-to-wall ratio, represents the percentage of the overall glazing area relative to the opaque wall areas. In general, buildings tend to have a glazing ratio of approximately 40% to 50%, depending on the facade exposure to the external environment. A full curtain wall system may have a glazing ratio of up to 70%. With a higher glazing ratio, more daylight will be admitted into the space, which can affect the cooling or heating demand inside a building. Spandrel, a term borrowed from a different context where it describes the area between two arches, is an architectural material used to cover up the lower or upper portion of a glazing unit to reduce the overall direct facade exposure to the external environment. Spandrel can help to reduce the glazing ratio of full curtain wall buildings to at least 50%. Therefore, it is a balancing act to select the proper glazing system to perform together with a good external shading according to the orientation and solar exposure of the individual facade.

The selection of an appropriate shading system and the glazing performance are imperative in order to balance solar loads and daylight availability. Understanding the spectrum of solar radiation

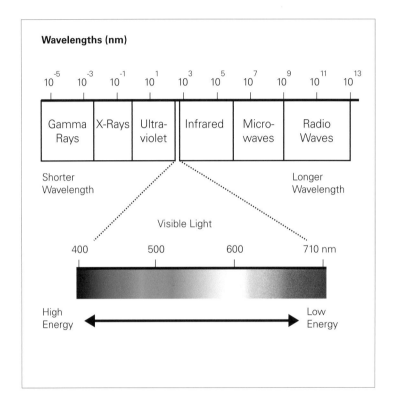

and daylight is critical in designing a high-performance facade. Solar radiation has three main spectrum ranges: ultraviolet light, visible light, and infrared light. While the most common spectrum is the spectrum visible to human eyes, the invisible spectrums affect the overall building performance and occupants' comfort level. Infrared light, which is transmitted into a building as heat, can be divided into shortwave incoming infrared and longwave emitting infrared. High-performance glazing is able to reduce ultraviolet and infrared light while admitting visible daylight into buildings.

Visual Transmittance (Tvis) is the most common glazing property that should be carefully reviewed. Tvis ranges from 0 to 1, with a higher value of Tvis meaning that more daylight will be admitted into a space. A typical recommended Tvis ranges from 0.5 to 0.7 for high-performance glazing. Shading Coefficient (SC) and Solar Heat Gain Coefficient (SHGC) are two other technical terms for describing the effectiveness of shading or glazing systems. Both range from 0 to 1, where 1 represents a full direct sun exposure and 0 equals no daylight passing through a window. For a high-performance glazing system, SHGC of 0.3 to 0.4 is a common range to be specified. Light to Solar Gain (LSG) is another coefficient that indicates the ratio between the Solar

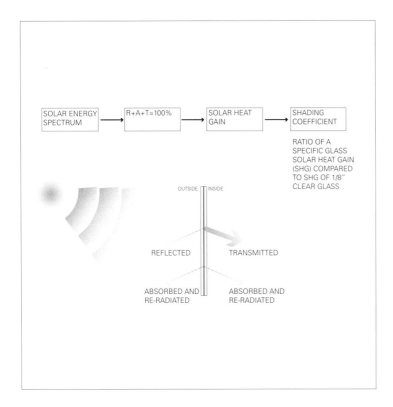

```
┌─────────────┐     ┌──────────┐     ┌──────────┐     ┌──────────┐
│SOLAR ENERGY │ ──> │R+A+T=100%│ ──> │SOLAR HEAT│ ──> │SHADING   │
│SPECTRUM     │     │          │     │GAIN      │     │COEFFICIENT│
└─────────────┘     └──────────┘     └──────────┘     └──────────┘
```

RATIO OF A
SPECIFIC GLASS
SOLAR HEAT GAIN
(SHG) COMPARED
TO SHG OF 1/8"
CLEAR GLASS

OUTSIDE | INSIDE

REFLECTED   TRANSMITTED

ABSORBED AND   ABSORBED AND
RE-RADIATED   RE-RADIATED

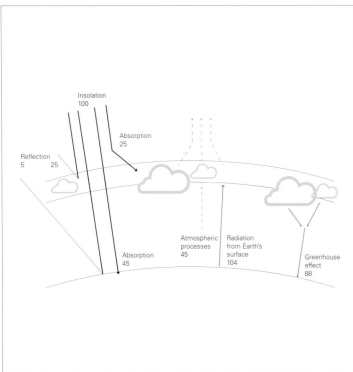

Insolation
100

Absorption
25

Reflection
5   25

Atmospheric   Radiation
processes   from Earth's
45   surface   Greenhouse
              104   effect
Absorption   88
45

Heat Gain Coefficient and Visual Transmittance. A higher LSG means that high-quality daylight will be transmitted into a space with low solar heat gain. A good LSG range is 1.6 to 1.8. The U-Value, which measures the heat loss in a building element, should be at approximately 1.45 W/m^2°K or 0.25 Btu/hr.ft^2°F for a high-performance glazing system.

Low-emitting glass (low-e glass) has been developed to minimize ultraviolet and infrared light that passes through glass without compromising the amount of visible light transmitted to daylit spaces. When solar radiation has been absorbed or transmitted through the glass, it is cooled by the moving air or re-radiated by the glass surface. The ability of a material, in this case glass, to radiate energy is known as emissivity. Generally, a higher reflective surface has a lower emissivity, while a dull and rough surface has a high emissivity. Radiant energy is one of the important heat transfer modes that occur at a window. Reducing the emissivity of a glazing system will assist in the overall improvement of the energy performance of a building. The lower the emissivity, the less heat gets transmitted into a building. For example, clear uncoated glass has an emissivity value of 0.8, while low-e glass has an emissivity value of 0.02. Low-e glass has an extremely thin low-e coating that reflects the longwave infrared energy. low-e glass will mitigate heat or cold air escaping through windows. The common solar-control low-e coating is a soft coating through a Magnetron Sputter Vacuum Deposition (MSVD) coater, in an off-line process to apply coating on precut float glass. This type of coating, which requires that it be sealed in laminated glazing or an insulated glazing unit, offers a superior level of solar control. MSVD coating or soft coating is ideal for mild and hot climates with dominant use of air-conditioning, such as tropical dense urban areas.

For interior sky gardens, it is imperative to coordinate all design measures with the required daylight levels as well as the minimum daylight hours for specified plants. Although in an urban context a building's roof space may be a small surface area compared with the overall building envelope exposure, green roofs for podiums or at building tops will provide pleasing views, serve as relaxing amenities, and assist in mitigating urban heat island effects. Additionally, green roofs can contribute to the reduction of overall stormwater runoff from buildings, while green walls or vertical gardens can serve as an external shading system to reduce solar heat gains. Optimizing the massing and specifying a high-performance building envelope system are the first two important steps in minimizing the internal condition requirements for urban buildings.

Integrated System Design

The primary challenge in dense and green buildings is how to minimize the demand for natural resources and how to limit natural resource consumption. This section will focus on how integrated advanced building systems can contribute to further reduce energy consumption, while providing a comfortable interior environment for occupants. High urban density in itself represents a good first step toward sustainability, because the required infrastructure will be utilized with the highest efficiency in high-density areas. A simple analogy is to compare a city's infrastructure system to a tree's roots. A tree with far-reaching roots would require more energy and effort to seek nutrients and fresh water for its branches and leaves. Similarly, a widely spread city infrastructure system would be less efficient and suffer more energy loss depending on the length of the transmission process. Distant energy and fresh-water sources would require more energy for transferring electricity and water into cities. Integrating innovative building system design and using renewables, where applicable, are critical steps to reducing the ever-growing energy demand.

Net Zero represents a recent concept to push building performance to its highest efficiency limits. This concept fits the dense and green approach well: the lower the energy consumption at the building level, the lower the demand at the urban infrastructure scale. According to the US National Renewable Energy Laboratory (US NREL),[1] there are four major types of Net Zero Energy Buildings that look at different aspects of reducing impacts from energy use through carbon emissions:

Net Zero Site Energy
produces as much as it uses

Net Zero Source Energy
produces as much as it uses at sources

Net Zero Energy Costs
aims for an annual energy bill of $0

Net Zero Energy Emissions
aims for a carbon-neutral result

Specifying a highly efficient building system design is complex for high-rise buildings. Developing a space-conditioning strategy appropriate to the climate and the building use can ensure high indoor air quality and occupant comfort, reduce energy use, and should also aim for low maintenance requirements.

Ventilation systems increase the oxygen levels as well as the overall comfort levels for occupants by introducing fresh air into buildings. Fresh air can be introduced passively via natural ventilation through windows and actively through fans or centralized air-handling units. In order to reduce the energy use for cooling or heating air from outside, the recent technologies of Heat Recovery Ventilation (HRV) and Energy Recovery Ventilation (ERV) have been widely specified in conjunction with ventilation systems.

HRV, commonly also known as heat or air exchanger, exchanges the inbound and outbound air flow within buildings. HRV may appear as a counter-intuitive measure in hot and tropical climates because of the terminological focus on heat. However, HRV works well in hot climates by providing dry-cool outgoing air to exchange with hot-humid incoming air. Depending on the internal program of the building and the specified building systems, HRV can provide up to approximately 5 to 10% of energy savings. The closely related ERV also transfers both sensible and latent heat to the incoming air. Devices that perform the actual exchange of heat within HRV and ERV are the recuperator, thermal wheel, heat pipe, plate heat exchanger, and plate fin heat exchanger. Efficiency rates for HRV and ERV range from 50 to 80%. Full conditioning may not be necessary in cases where the exhaust air from the occupied space may be used for the benefit of sky gardens or atria.

There are two main types of systems for conditioning fresh air to a set point for the use for specific building programs: the air system and the hydronic system. The air system is suitable for high-occupancy areas where a high ventilation rate is required, while the hydronic system will serve low-occupancy areas where ventilation rate requirements are low. Hydronic systems will always have a higher efficiency level because energy can be transferred more efficiently through water than through air. Therefore, high-performance buildings will typically prefer a water-cooled over an air-cooled chiller system because of the higher Coefficient of Performance (COP) of the former. Distribution methods for delivering the conditioned air include Variable Air Volume (VAV) fan coils, chilled beams, displacement ventilation, and radiant heating and cooling, for use depending on the program type, occupancy rate, as well as conditioning and ventilation requirements. The VAV fan coil system is common for offices, while displacement ventilation is suitable for atrium spaces.

Environmental section.

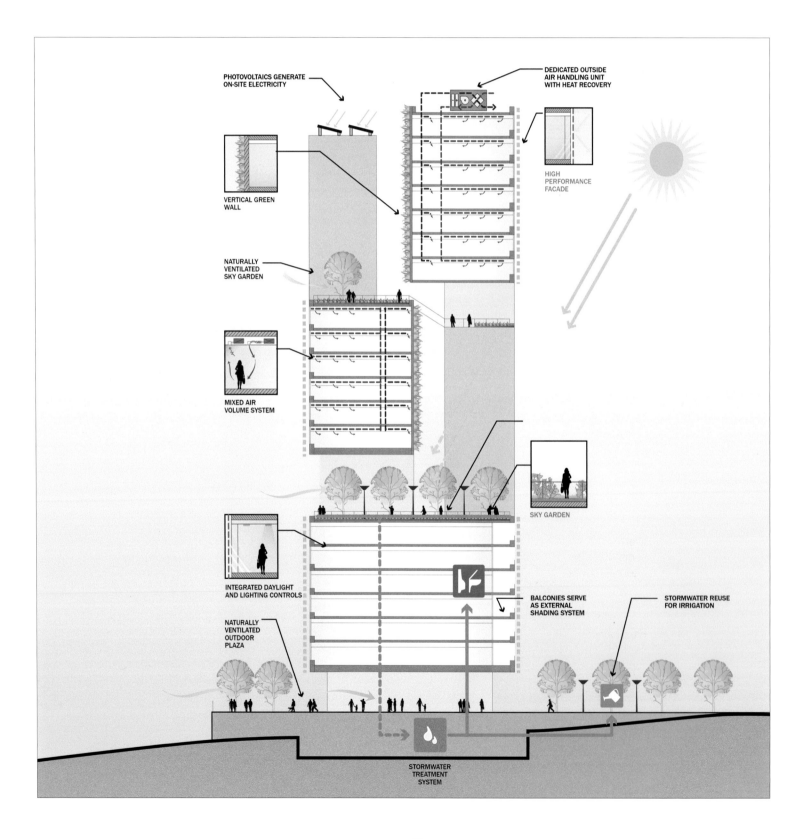

PHOTOVOLTAICS GENERATE
ON-SITE ELECTRICITY

DEDICATED OUTSIDE
AIR HANDLING UNIT
WITH HEAT RECOVERY

VERTICAL GREEN
WALL

HIGH
PERFORMANCE
FACADE

NATURALLY
VENTILATED
SKY GARDEN

MIXED AIR
VOLUME SYSTEM

SKY GARDEN

INTEGRATED DAYLIGHT
AND LIGHTING CONTROLS

BALCONIES SERVE
AS EXTERNAL
SHADING SYSTEM

STORMWATER REUSE
FOR IRRIGATION

NATURALLY
VENTILATED
OUTDOOR
PLAZA

STORMWATER
TREATMENT
SYSTEM

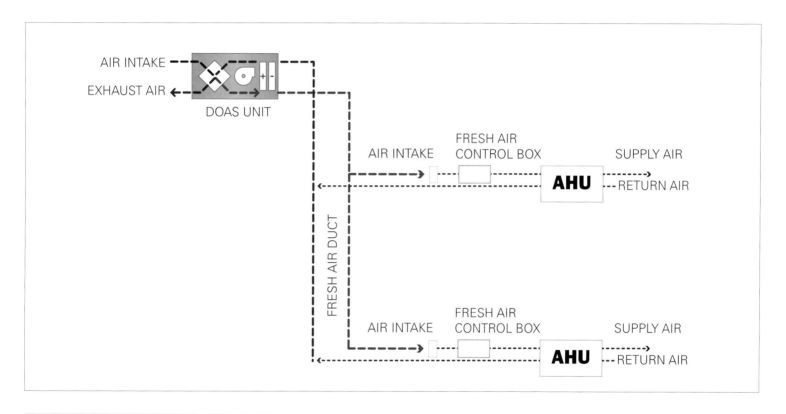

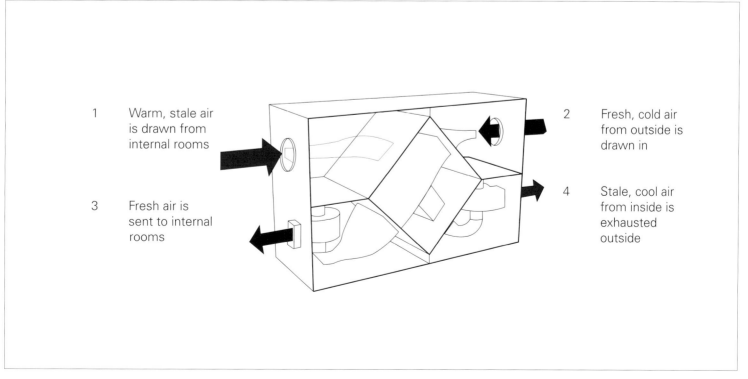

1   Warm, stale air is drawn from internal rooms

2   Fresh, cold air from outside is drawn in

3   Fresh air is sent to internal rooms

4   Stale, cool air from inside is exhausted outside

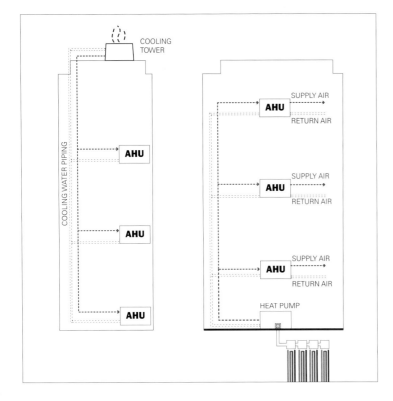

Heat sink methods are another option in the context of conditioning systems. They can perform by means of air, water, and a ground heat exchanger. The heat exchange of air systems occurs at the condensing unit, while hydronic systems require cooling towers, which exchange heat at the rooftop by blowing water droplets, or ground source heat pump systems, which exchange heat with underground water.

Conditioning system selection	Refrigeration (tons)
Split-Type Air-Conditioning System	> 50
Variable Refrigerant Flow Conditioning System	> 100
Air-Cooled Package Conditioning System	> 100
Water-Cooled Package Conditioning System	> 250
Air-Cooled Water Chiller Conditioning System	> 250
Water-Cooled Water Chiller Conditioning System	< 250

Lighting is another large internal demand, sometimes combined with external loads of exterior open space, podium, or rooftop. Optimizing the building envelope's design to control daylight levels can help to decrease interior lighting demand, thereby reducing the overall energy loads by at least 5 to 10%. High-efficiency lighting systems, such as Light Emitting Diodes (LEDs), with integrated lighting controls can cut the lighting load by half compared to traditional luminaires. Advanced lighting controls include occupancy sensors and daylight sensors. Occupancy and vacancy sensors are suitable in low-occupancy areas. Daylight sensors work effectively in large open-plan spaces.

Energy centers or central plants for large mixed-use developments combine the main electrical substation, a chiller plant, and possibly a boiler plant. Energy centers and central plants are classified as supply side, while the ventilation and conditioning distribution systems are classified as demand side. In order to reach optimal efficiency, the supply side should be designed to properly accommodate the loads of the demand side. Minimizing external and internal loads on the demand side will entail reductions on the supply side. The energy center or the central plant should be located near the center of load or demand: the further away the energy center, the less efficient it becomes. Intermediate mechanical transfer floors are typically integrated in high-rise buildings at intervals of 80 to 100 m.

Another critical building component is the water management system. Fresh potable water is a limited resource and should be treated and reused before disposing to sewers or stormwater drains. A typical building could save up to 40% of water by specifying efficient water fixtures. Blackwater from restrooms will require a more intensive water treatment system than greywater from bathroom or kitchen sinks and showers. The treated water may be reused for flushing or irrigation. By specifying native or adaptive vegetation for general landscapes, sky gardens, and green roofs, a project can reduce the overall potable water demand by half and supplement the other half with greywater, blackwater, or stormwater reuse to achieve net zero in potable water demand for irrigation.

Concerning the use of on-site and off-site renewables, roof areas of urban high-rises have high asset values because they are very limited and often occupied by building system equipment. Allocating photovoltaics (PV) to generate electricity or solar hot water systems should be carefully considered, including the payback period. There is currently an emerging trend of see-through building-integrated photovoltaics (BIPVs) on vertical facade areas. In addition to the definition of Net Zero Energy Buildings, US NREL has established four Net Zero categories for on-site and off-site renewables:

On-site

NZEB: A
Use renewable energy sources available only within building footprint

NZEB: B
Use renewable energy sources as described in NZEB: A, plus use renewable energy sources available at the building site

Off-site

NZEB: C
Use renewable energy sources as described in NZEB: A & B, plus use renewable energy sources available off-site such as biomass, wood pellets, ethanol or biodiesel to generate energy on-site. Energy sources can also be collected from non-petroleum base waste streams on-site such as used vegetable oil.

NZEB: D
Use renewable energy sources as described in NZEB: A, B & C, plus purchased certificate off-site renewable energy-sources, from the Green-E or other equivalent renewable energy certification.

As PV will typically produce DC current, it is advisable to tie the energy production to a battery system for reuse. The power production of a PV system in an urban area may be limited and the use of PV becomes more meaningful if it is focused on specific areas like facade lighting, landscape lighting, or sky garden lighting, which can potentially be powered by a rooftop PV system. For sky gardens and landscaped zones, integrated LED/PV lighting systems are an efficient emerging technology, more commonly available for commercial use.

Designing for Dense and Green Communities

The efforts to rethink our effect on the environment, which have become known as "sustainability," are a key component of the dense and green approach. Conventional environmental efficiency is about doing more with less, using fewer resources, reducing pollution and waste, and minimizing damage to human health and the environment. Optimizing the massing and facade design, providing highly efficient systems, incorporating renewables to reduce the natural resource demands, and introducing greenery in buildings are imperative strategies to be included in dense and green buildings. Integrated green areas such as sky gardens, atria, and green roofs are emerging strategies that increasingly become common features of high-rise buildings in urban areas. The implementation of sustainable strategies can have very positive effects on buildings as well as create and support dense and green communities. The ultimate goal is to understand and establish ways in which man can have a beneficial impact on the environment.

1. Source: http://www.nrel.gov/sustainable_nrel/rsf.html

Blue-Green Infrastructures for Buildings and Liveable Cities

Herbert Dreiseitl

A Turning Point

Blue and Green in nature are never static but in a state of constant flux. The dynamic of water and greenery is the environment's resilient language, its potential to create living systems and enhance evolution. Blue and Green in nature are the living landscape.

The ever-changing character and process of landscape have always been a challenge for the human desire for comfort and freedom. Our imaginations and desires to be more independent created architecture as we know it today. In today's urban fabrics, buildings of any function are mostly conceived as shelters. They define and separate an inner space from the outer environment. Here are the defined and controlled conditions of such urban rooms and there is the uncontrolled "wilderness" with its unforeseen and unpredictable surprises of instability like temperature extremes, wind and rain, and limited natural light. Even though we may not be fully aware of all the benefits for our civilizations that this strict separation of the inside and the outside brings along, we often call architecture the "third skin," in a metaphor suggesting that we experience it as the most exterior layer beyond our natural skin as the first and our clothes as the second layer.

Buildings have been getting more and more efficient in this separation of inner space from the exterior environment. For the first time in history, and due to our very high standards of insulation, air control, integrated intelligent control systems, light regulation, etc., we can live in buildings in the urban fabric for weeks and months almost without any contact with the natural environment. Cities, like perfect machines and the supporting infrastructures, seem to make the natural environment a byproduct and dependency on nature a relic of the past.

Today, and probably even more so in the future, we can clearly see that this is not true. We are not independent but are instead embedded in and supported by our environment, in the many ways of which we are well aware. In light of this awareness of environmental damage and problems, it seems that today we are at a turning point. Missing vital aspects of interaction of the interior of buildings with the exterior environment is creating more and more challenges not only in physical terms but also in terms of the mental and cultural dimensions of society.

Buildings tell stories and create awareness. Basically any building receives water, air, comfort, energy, and virtual information from its outside. Consumers in buildings rely on natural resources that are coming from the outside, in the broadest sense. This also includes our daily food supply. We rely on minerals, nutrients, on good soil for agriculture, products from forests, oceans and so on, resources that often come from far away and that are transported into the urban fabric to feed each building and its inhabitants. Disposing of the remaining substance, including wastewater and sewage, is a challenge for which we have not yet found solutions that are not harmful for the environment.

Natural resources are the basis of our standard of living and the liveability of our cities. Even in the most sophisticated communities, especially children often have only a little knowledge about how food is produced, how e.g. tomatoes grow and where cheese comes from; they may see water and earth as something unaesthetic and dangerous that is better to watch on television than to touch with their own hands. Having encountered in my own practice and involvement with people many unreasonable fears and strange ideas about the environment, I think that such reactions show to what degree we have become alienated from the natural context in which we live. A lack of trust and confidence in values is often the reason for doubtful behavior, vandalism, and self-destruction, and constitutes a high risk for society.

How can new architecture bridge the division between outside and inside? How can we integrate green elements into buildings by creating win-win situations that produce better air, acoustics, biodiversity, and eventually liveability? How can we overcome the traditional separations in the building professions?

Blue-Green Infrastructures is a concept in response to such questions. While it is becoming more and more important, it is not yet properly understood in its functions and values for the infrastructures of the city and its inhabitants: as a backbone for liveability and a dynamic repository for balancing and stabilizing life processes. To measure, count, and quantify the value of blue and green components in the urban context is a much more complex task than to do the same for the hard forms of engineered infrastructure, buildings, and real estate developments. As a first step, it is important to understand and design fluids like water and to learn how to imagine the processes of change related to green factors in design.

From Horizontal to Vertical

Why is it that parks and other green spaces are so often uninteresting and uninspiring, reduced to the role of placeholders for future developments or gaps in between buildings, fragmented and disconnected, so much unlike the seamless spaces of transition that would be needed for plants and animals to create a rich and diverse bio-habitat? Why are waterways, rivers, and streams often so unattractive and poorly treated in our cities today? For decades cities have been turning their backs on green corridors and especially on water bodies. The ensuing dilemma appears as flooding, erosion, and pollution. One major reason is that we have occupied much if not all of the spaces that previously belonged to the waterways, leaving only limited room for water after heavy storms and downpours. The rapid growth of urban sprawl in many parts of the world will continue to cover the earth's surface with asphalt and concrete, creating direct runoff effects that channel large amounts of water at the same time to the same place instead of slowing it down and holding it back to avoid such concentrations.

This state of affairs also has a significant effect on microclimates. The lack of Blue-Green Infrastructures limits filtration and fails to hold back the microscopic wind-blown particles. The resulting increase in dust particles contributes to unhealthy living conditions. In city centers with fewer green spaces and water bodies, the concentration of dust particles is significantly higher; streets and buildings with greenery and trees have lower dust particle concentrations than those without. According to the WHO, 7.1 million people died as a result of air pollution in 2012.

As is well known from hot deserts, an absence of water incurs temperature extremes, with very high temperatures during daytime and a drop as low as below the freezing point at night. Similar microclimatic effects are observed in cities, where city center temperatures can easily deviate from those of the surrounding countryside by up to 10° C. Water and vegetation are the buffers that help to regulate temperature extremes.

Buildings and urban structures that are not flexible enough will not be able to cope with the dynamic forces of change, neither in the unpredictable rhythms of the environment nor in terms of socio-economic and political transformations. A comparison between structures in the natural environment and structures in the urban setting of most cities today reveals a significant difference: natural structures work with flexible spaces and resilient principles over time, using them as a potential for dynamic reactions and maintaining the balance in any event from a soft change to an unexpected disaster—including extreme climate conditions. It is all about processes over time,

processes that have resources like integrated spaces, such as wetlands, available to function as buffers.

In our cities, we are confronted with even short-term changes between different needs at different times at one and the same place. Urban spaces can completely change in function throughout the day. For example, in India, a space that is used as a market in the morning can be used as a food court at noon, a bazaar in the afternoon, and an event space for a wedding in the evening. The urban planner Rahul Mehrotra calls this phenomenon "the kinetic city."

In this context, one can say that running out of space is one of the biggest challenges we are confronted with in most cities today. Growing populations that result in a growing demand for housing are in conflict with the different needs for infrastructures. In this ongoing conflict of priorities and ownership, all too often Blue-Green Infrastructures are the losers, for a large number of reasons. Therefore, it would be insufficient to limit Blue-Green Infrastructures to the remaining spots on the ground floors, so to speak, of cities. To keep cities healthy and to react to climate change with mitigation and resiliency, we have to explore other opportunities. One is to occupy the building itself.

Connecting Inside and Outside

For centuries, buildings have mostly been constructed with bricks, concrete, steel, and glass, and there has been no space for plants and water. Water, indeed, was seen as one of the biggest enemies; grass and moss were regarded as signs of deterioration. In this context we encounter historical examples of green roofs and breathing walls with willow bushes and trees.

In cities like Singapore, we now see a new trend in that innovative buildings contribute to urban Blue-Green Infrastructures. Buildings like the PARKROYAL on Pickering, the Tree House, or the Khoo Teck Puat Hospital are examples of a new generation of vertical green in the city. This includes the topic of water for irrigation, evaporation, and filtration and has many side effects for Blue-Green Infrastructures in the urban environment.

Milestones, Experiments, and Change

Looking back to the development of Blue-Green Infrastructures, there are some pilot projects that have changed architecture and introduced a new mindset.

Joachim Eble Architektur/Atelier Dreiseitl/Transsolar, Prisma, Nuremberg, Germany, 1991,
interior public areas.

The Prisma in Nuremberg, Germany, built in 1991, was a pioneer project with integrated vertical and horizontal green terraces, featuring a rainwater harvesting system that also functions as an air-conditioning, air filtration, and stormwater infiltration system. It is a mixed-use facility with 61 residential units, 32 offices, nine stores, a coffee house, and a kindergarten, developed for Karlsruher Life Insurance Company A.G. in a cooperation between Eble Architects in Tübingen, Atelier Dreiseitl in Überlingen, and Transsolar in Stuttgart. The urban ecology approach and technology employed at the time is still up-to-date today. Rooftop water is collected, cleansed, and sent through the building in two separate cycles. The first cycle irrigates the plants in the 15-m-high greenhouse, supporting an interesting waterscape of creeks and ponds. The other cycle pumps water between colorful, tall glass walls. Fresh air from the outside is filtered and conditioned by seven waterfalls with a height of 5 m each as part of an innovative rainwater management system. It features a process in which air enters the interior through open crevices and exits purified and cooled together with the waterfall into the greenhouse. The jet effect is not only an innovative technical solution but also an artfully designed environmental feature that encourages awareness of natural resources.

The combination of external rainwater harvesting and internal water usage results in a pleasant interior climate, as demonstrated by the air quality both in winter and summer and by the vitality of the plants. The sound of the waterfall creates a special and relaxing atmosphere in the greenhouse. In the infiltration system below the underground garage, remaining rainwater seeps into the ground under the building and refills the groundwater aquifer.

Visitors to Frankfurt can enjoy a grand view over the city from the Commerzbank Tower, completed in 1997 and for a long time Germany's tallest office building, designed by architects Foster + Partners and engineers Arup and Krebs & Kiefer. Designed as both a symbolic and functional green building, the Commerzbank Tower, although provided with active climate control systems, uses natural ventilation to reduce energy consumption, which has made the building one of the world's first ecological skyscrapers. The most prominent innovation are three interior sky gardens that are situated in the east, south, and west of the tower, contributing additional green layers and offering ideal climatic conditions for the various plants they house. Sycamores, cypresses, and a redwood tree reach up to the 16-m-high glass ventilation flaps. Another feature are winter gardens on many different levels, which in the relatively

harsh climate of Frankfurt that is characterized by cold and dark winter days, provide spaces for the inhabitants to get fresh air and to socialize. The gardens also allow for vast amounts of natural light in the interior and provide pleasant views. Operable facade elements permit natural ventilation throughout the entire structure. Since 2008, the roof on the 57th floor has been home to a pair of rare and endangered peregrine falcons, tenderly cared for by the facility managers.

As one of the tallest buildings in Europe, the Commerzbank Tower brought ecological architecture out of its alternative niche and into the focus of some of the most ambitious architectural designs of the time. By opening up the previously mostly closed facades of tall buildings, the project proved that natural air and light can be brought into skyscrapers by way of stacked green spaces.

The Nikolaus Cusanus House in Stuttgart, Germany, a nursing and retirement home for 135 residents, responds to the desire to live close to nature in a central urban location. The generous 800 sqm entrance hall provides plants, natural light, and water in a grand green space. No concrete or other hardscape seals the floor of this space. It is all natural earth, with air ventilation funnels embedded in it. A creek, fed by rainwater collected in cisterns, travels through the entrance hall. Water channels, or rills, are partly formed by local rocks found during construction, with meanders chiseled in or several rocks layered on top of each other. The tropical plants and natural stones make the courtyard a pleasant space on hot summer as well as on cold winter days. A small waterfall provides a calming sound, while a constant splashing and gurgling of water allows for private conversations. The adjacent platform-like floors reach out to the courtyard, making it, in an emphatic sense, the central space of the building.

In Berlin, Germany, in the heart of the city formerly divided into an eastern and western part, the teams of Renzo Piano, Christoph Kohlbecker, and Herbert Dreiseitl designed a sustainable city quarter in which water is used as a symbol of healing and to bring the two parts together again. The redevelopment of Potsdamer Platz with its urban water bodies employs sustainable stormwater management strategies in interactive water features and urban open space design. The large urban pond and watercourse use biologically cleansed stormwater collected from the surrounding buildings. The combination of green roofs, cisterns, cleansing biotopes, and watercourses used for natural drainage was the first urban waterscape at such a scale (1.2 ha). At the central Marlene-Dietrich-Platz, water forms

*Renzo Piano Building Workshop/Kohlbecker Architekten & Ingenieure/Atelier Dreiseitl,
Potsdamer Platz, Berlin, Germany, 2000. Dialogues between concrete and water.
A large naturalized pond acts as cleansing biotope and retention basin.*

Atelier Dreiseitl, Strategic Flood Master Plan, Copenhagen, Denmark, 2013. Rendering of Gasværksvej street during normal rain. Rendering of Sankt Jørgens Sø with new park, of which the lower parts act as a retention basin during heavy rain events.

floating images that are shaped by flowing steps and cascades. Harvested rainwater is used to flush toilets and to irrigate the adjacent green spaces. Another innovative feature is a water cleansing system on the basis of natural filter substrates that function without any additional chemicals.

These innovative Blue-Green Infrastructures in the heart of a European capital created enormous interest and became a model for other parts of the world including the booming city developments in China. An example is the City of Tianjin, located half an hour by high-speed train southeast of Beijing and among China's top five cities. Situated close to the sea and endowed with a high groundwater table, Tianjin needs to prevent seawater from encroaching on inland areas. The design of a new cultural district, including a new opera house and a city hall, used the Berlin experience as a model for integrated Blue-Green Infrastructures. The urban pond system of 90 ha (222 acres) functions as a stormwater feature, a balancing water body that can process a once-in-a-decade storm event and buffer a once-in-a-century downpour. Avenues of trees and other plants shield the spectacular waterfront from cold Mongolian winds. The urban pond reduces temperature extremes, while its picturesque beauty sets the scene for Tianjin's outstanding cultural architecture.

A lesson learned from these examples is that sustainable solutions function best when they are networked on the scale of a large watershed, in an expansive urban context connected to a full range of other infrastructural systems, and when they are socio-culturally integrated. Many cities have lost almost all of their ecological structures and green corridors, including open waterways, productive landscapes, and park networks. By contrast, the most successful contemporary cities have managed to maintain and further develop their Blue-Green Infrastructures to their benefit. Among these is Copenhagen, Denmark. The Green Finger Plan of 1947, a strategy that was easy to understand and that in fact was implemented, has kept urban corridors free of construction. Today, Copenhagen is among the greenest cities, with the highest liveability and lifestyle rankings in the world.

Engineering and Beyond

Much research and development has gone into engineering in terms of mathematical models for hydraulics, flood risk analysis and settlement protection, energy efficiency, and other topics. Yet we still know very little about how an urban society can live

Atelier Dreiseitl, Strategic Flood Master Plan, Copenhagen, Denmark, 2013.
Sectional renderings of Sonderboulevard during fine weather and during a cloudburst
event, where the landscaped area in the middle acts as retention basin.

in harmony with its natural environment. The Blue-Green resources are there, but what kind of water systems are adequate and will work effectively in the long term? What kind of infrastructure fits the scale of individual buildings with their specific functions and users?

In whatever scale we conceive of architecture, the Blue-Green Infrastructures are a driver of, and play a fundamental role in, connecting buildings to urban regions with their specific environments. Without proper management of water systems and green structures on a larger scale, there is no basis for the long-term sustainability of the implementation of small-scale solutions on the level of individual buildings. Having worked on urban landscape and water issues in many different regions and climate zones for more than three decades, it is my view that principles and guidelines can help but, as Blue-Green structures are alive and subjected as living systems to resilient change, solutions have to be individually adapted.

Obviously, climate zones with high levels of humidity, much rain, and warm temperatures have an advantage and work well for lush greenery. There is a higher risk that traditional engineering with water and greenery fails in projects and cities of arid regions. It would be unrealistic to expect the same intensive green in Abu Dhabi as in the Garden City of Singapore. Instead of planting non-local vegetation that requires enormous water and nutrient inputs, it would be preferable to use local plants with specific sensitivities and adapted characteristics. This would require an appreciation of the different aesthetics of desert plants with their subtle forms and colors. In the planning process for the new Zayed National Museum in Abu Dhabi, a project I pursued in collaboration with Foster + Partners, we succeeded in convincing our clients that local plants with minimal water consumption would fit best in terms of sustainability and enhance both the biophilic design and the unique local aesthetics.

A new language and awareness regarding Blue-Green issues is expected of engineering today. We can no longer divide projects into separate tracks of work and have to go beyond traditional working modes that are often characterized by disciplinary boundaries.

Blue-Green Technologies

Vertical structures using plants are becoming an important trend as a symbol for green architecture. In the last decade, many architects and engineers have discovered how to integrate plants to give buildings an environmentally friendly facade and character. Spectacular projects of artists and architects like Friedensreich Hundertwasser in Vienna, Austria, the Vertical Gardens by Patrick Blanc, early buildings by Ken Yeang, or examples like Arcadia by Chua Ka Seng & Partners and the PARKROYAL on Pickering by WOHA in Singapore have set new standards and encouraged others to follow suit.

The concept of buildings as being enclosed and encapsulated objects that are separated from the natural environment is being increasingly challenged. There is no doubt that this is a very positive development in architecture. But there are also critical sides of this trend that need to be addressed. Often a project looks good in the first few years but may have serious problems in terms of its functionality and maintenance later and sometimes fails completely in the long term. Plant structures are living systems and very complex in their specific environmental needs, growth patterns, rhythms, and lifecycles. Already the creation of a successful horizontal landscape structure at ground level in the midst of building blocks and urban structures can be a challenge. Softscapes are in a process of permanent transformation. We have to think differently to grasp the natural conditions of plants and allow for their processes of change including growth, aging, and renewal. The challenge is even more complex when implementing green elements on more exposed vertical surfaces and in stacked positions.

As early as in the 1960s, the green roof movement in Germany, Switzerland, and Austria considerably increased our knowledge of these issues and set new standards. The current vertical green structures go beyond green roofs in their complexity. Today we know more about plant performance, substrates, and structures, but we still have to learn much more about sustainable integration, especially in terms of the water cycle.

Beyond differences in climate, every location differs in temperature, direct and indirect sun exposure, humidity and rain exposure, wind conditions, the orientation of buildings and facades, and surface materials. Together these factors create a microclimate that plants need to adapt to in order to remain healthy. Every cardinal direction, for example, has its own strong influence on diminishing or supporting plant growth. The same goes for the position on the building in terms of height. Some plants such as clamberers need structural support, others prefer to grow directly on vertical geotextiles rooted in planters, or like to hang over. Sometimes it is helpful to have different species live in symbiosis in order to prevent invasive species from taking over.

Of prime importance is the preparation and selection of the substrate as well as the irrigation and drainage system. In contrast to natural ground soil, the substrate is per se limited in space. It has to support the plants in terms of appropriate humidity, nutrients condition, salt and pH value, all of which are critical for root development and symbiosis with microorganisms and fungi. All these factors keep the plants strong and healthy. Often, salt concentration increases over time and can become a problem. Therefore, water drainage is not only needed to avoid an excess of water but also to regulate the salt content in the substrate.

Nutrients are important as well, although many plants can survive with very little and in many cases natural rain is sufficient to water the plants. On the extended green roof systems of Berlin's Potsdamer Platz, we tested various substrates and finally decided not to use additional fertilizers. Fertilization may be useful in the beginning and for intensive greenery but is liable to create significant problems in water systems, as most nutrients cannot be completely absorbed by the root systems and end up in the water bodies. Nutrient-rich water will create algae growth and problematic eutrophic situations.

Automatic maintenance as well as periodic manual care are essential to keep the system vital and in good condition. Both horizontal and vertical green structures on buildings need particularly high levels of technical functionality in terms of design for maintenance.

Greenery needs water. Here is the dilemma we are facing today and will face even more in the future. If green structures demand substantial water supply from public systems under conditions of drought, plants might look green but we will create more water scarcity in times when we need every drop of water in our cities. The Blue factor needs to be combined with the Green infrastructures of the contemporary city.

The best Blue-Green urban infrastructure is a combination of decentralized and centralized systems. The reason is that water is often unevenly distributed by nature. While in natural landscapes this can be compensated for by water being retained in open lakes, swamps, rivers, streams, and in groundwater, the capacity of water storage in cities is limited, as water is drained as quickly as possible out of the city. The challenge lies not only in the

technology but also in its implementation within the surrounding urban fabric.

Density as a Challenge and an Opportunity for Liveability

Blue-Green Infrastructures are most often located in the public realm and therefore at the forefront of public awareness. In vibrant cities, we can all see and experience how space is getting tighter and that there is a growing competition between functions, programs, and jobs. Better ways of sharing and multi-functional structures need to be developed. Increasing density is forcing us to come up with a better understanding and ways to better quantify the values that give even higher priority to Blue-Green systems. As many studies have shown, doing nothing is more expensive in the long run and will generate many problems for future generations. The issue is not only how to avoid floods but how to create healthier environments that provide better air quality, food security, and biodiversity. In this way, increasing density will help us focus on a more holistic and integrated approach to Blue-Green Infrastructures, with the aim of sharing spaces with different functions. This in turn necessitates that we overcome disciplinary boundaries and better integrate all design and planning processes.

Biological Functionalities of Green

Jean W. H. Yong

"Development that meets the needs of the present generation without compromising the ability of future generations to meet their own needs." Definition of "Sustainable Development," *Brundtland Report* (1987) [1]

Plants are the backbone of all life on earth and an essential resource for human well-being. While there are strong connections between plants and our daily food for sustenance, ironically, we have not developed good linkages between plants and our built environment. In the past, attitudes toward plants and their biological functions in the landscape and built environment were generally restricted to "romantic gardenesque" applications. Because of the aesthetic qualities of plants, many people understandably still hold this attitude. Moving beyond aesthetics, the biological functionality of greenery plays a critical role in creating useful applications and defining sustainable approaches within the realm of any built environment. Through integrating greenery inthe built environment, previously unfavorable areas can be designed, engineered, and built to create more liveable spaces.

Plants are central to a functioning global ecosystem: they are providers of natural resources, environmental moderators, natural pollution filters, and carbon sinks. Through the light-driven process of photosynthesis, they oxygenate the atmosphere, remove carbon dioxide, and maintain humidity and, to a lesser extent, ambient temperature, in both natural and urban settings. Through the process of transpiration, plants help to restore evapotranspiration, which is diminished by urbanization through the loss of vegetation and the creation of impervious areas. Plants also provide aesthetic and microclimatic benefits (shading and passive cooling) through controlled evaporation via the leaf pores or stomata.

Vegetation, essentially a collection of plants, forms a greenbelt that plays a critical role in the management of urban stormwater by helping to filter out pollutants, maintaining the permeability of the "filter" layers, as well as contributing to nutrient removal through direct uptake and by housing the microbial communities that facilitate the process (phytoremediation). In urbanized areas, greenbelts are used as screens to reduce atmospheric pollutants and as natural curtains against noise. Looking beyond cities with a broader perspective, greening, especially with trees, is in both developed and developing countries a primary strategy for mitigating the effects of man-made greenhouse gas emissions through carbon sequestration by plants.

Greenery Reduces Soil Erosion and Regulates Water Flow

The continual development of the land brings certain undesirable effects. One of these is soil erosion, the wearing away of the topsoil layers. Damage from impact and runoff of water can take the form of small troughs, leading to larger gullies, and ending with more massive slips. Plants can be placed on steps and exposed slopes to prevent the formation of troughs and gullies. Leaves and branches lessen the impact of raindrops and slow water runoff, while shallow, fibrous root systems hold soil in place. The organic matter added to soil by plants acts as a sponge to soak up and retain water. In addition, plants improve the aesthetic appearance of the slope in comparison to constructed erosion-mitigation civil engineering materials. Plants with shallow, fibrous root systems are the most effective immediate controllers of erosion. The larger evergreen plants are generally considered more effective controllers of erosion for the long term. A strategic combination of several plant types offers the best mitigation approach to resolve any soil erosion issues.

Greenery Improves Water Quality

As cities develop, more and more land is laid with impervious surfaces that do not allow water to infiltrate. These include vehicular roads, civic squares, parking lots, walkways, and shopping malls. Impermeable land alters the hydrologic cycle and affects the water quality in water catchment areas and adjacent water bodies. Rainwater running on top of these impervious surfaces (e.g. road surfaces, concrete channels, etc.) carries potentially harmful pollutants (metals, high nutrients, microbes, etc.). There are many plant-based systems, for example vegetated swales, bioretention systems, cleansing biotopes, constructed wetlands, or sedimentation basins, that are currently in use worldwide to reduce the levels of pollutants entering adjacent water catchments.

Greenery Improves Air Quality

Plants can purify the air by removing carbon dioxide, limit quantities of sulphur/nitrous oxides, and replace them with oxygen. The fresh air produced by plants along expressways and major roads mixes with and dilutes the heavily particulated air. Plants can also cleanse the atmosphere by removing dust, ashes, and particulates from the air: the particles settle on the leaves and branches, and are eventually washed by the rain to the ground. Studies have shown that roads planted with trees contain one quarter of the number of dust particles of roads without trees in the same area of the city. [2]

Plants and the tropical built environment (Singapore).
Plants and the subtropical built environment (Australia).

Plants and the temperate built environment (USA).
Plants and the temperate built environment (Japan).

Measuring photosynthesis and transpiration simultaneously in a leaf (Australia).
Visualization of transpiration cooling in a leaf using a sensitive thermal imaging camera (Australia).

Air quality in homes and offices has become a major health issue. Volatile organic compounds (VOCs) found in indoor air emanate from adhesives, furnishings, clothing, and solvents, and have been shown to cause illnesses in people. The VOCs tested included benzene, xylene, hexane, heptane, octane, decane, trichloroethylene (TCE), and methylene chlorides. By simply introducing common ornamental plants to indoor spaces, the quality of indoor air can be significantly improved through the removal of harmful VOCs.

Greenery Can Be Used to Reduce Noise

Effective sound/noise control is governed by several factors. The interaction of these factors is deemed complex and unpredictable at present. Although more research is needed, the current knowledge is supportive of a role for plants in mitigating the higher, more irritating frequencies of unwanted sound.[3] For example, effective sound control depends on direction, frequency, and intensity of noise; topology, wind direction, temperature and humidity of the site; plant species, spacing, and planting density. Plants with thick, fleshy leaves and thin petioles were shown to be most effective in reducing noise pollution. In principle, a combination of trees, shrubs, and ground covers is sufficient to provide a useful sound barrier. The most effective sound barrier can be created by using a combination of plants with embankments and berms. For example, a 2-m-high wall covered with suitable climbers, combined with a 1.8-m-high hedge, offers a practical and effective solution for many small-scale noise mitigation projects.

Greenery as Alleviator of Stress in Humans

The continual push to improve the standard of living in cosmopolitan cities increases the stress levels among individuals in urban areas. As modern society becomes more and more reliant on technological innovations, plants and greenery are often overlooked. Practitioners can incorporate soft elements in the hardscape and rigid architectural lines in the built environment. Defining spaces with greenery in urban architecture can provide opportunities for long-term stress management. Roadside landscapes, water-sensitive urban designs, and the presence of trees along walkways can contribute to a calmer atmosphere for commuters.

The Center for Urban Horticulture of the College of Forests Resources, University of Washington,[4] concluded that people receive positive social benefit from greenery where the so-called

The surfaces of a multi-story car park (left) and a housing estate (right) can serve as urban water catchments; the collected rainwater is purified using a water-cleansing biotope system (Singapore).
Water-sensitive urban design in highly urbanized areas can vastly improve the liveability of the city (Hokkaido, Japan).

Certain resilient plants can be used to mitigate air pollution (Singapore).
The larger specimens of certain air pollution-resilient plants can be trimmed to form shelters (Shenzhen, China).

Small plants such as bryophytes can be used to improve indoor air quality (Singapore).
Large plants can be used to improve indoor air quality (Hangzhou, China).
Plants can be used to improve indoor public space air quality (Singapore).

"immunization effect" shapes their response and smoothens the transition to stressful environments in a calmer manner. Research from the University of Wisconsin found that living near green spaces can lower stress, anxiety, and depression.[5] At Edinburgh, a brain wave analysis study revealed interesting results about the positive influence of greenery on human brain function.[6] In the research, the participants started a walk of a mile and a half through an area with a high frequency of pedestrians and buildings, later moving on to greener space and ending up in a very busy area with heavy traffic. Interestingly, the walk through the green spaces lowered brain fatigue. In a similar study, green spaces have also been linked to improved performance and concentration in children with attention deficit issues.[7] These recent studies provided scientific evidence that greenery plays a beneficial role not only in defining spaces, but it also plays

an important role in pollution control, human therapeutic stress regulation, and in fostering social and community interactions in urban settings. Therefore, incorporating greenery into architectural design converges into a multi-disciplinary approach in creating sustainable spaces and improving the liveability for humans within the built environment.

Maximizing the Benefits of Green in Buildings

Plants can perform two key roles in the context of architecture. They can complement and reinforce the existing architectural features of the house, building, or structure, and they can also contribute to create outdoor space. Greenery can help to define a spatial development through the definition of space by introducing a sense of scale and by creating focal points for users

indoors and outdoors. Trees, shrubs, and ground covers can be used to emphasize architectural lines and dimensions of the built environment.

Plant forms and branching patterns can further soften and balance harsh or awkward buildings, materials, and structures. It is also possible to use plants to frame desirable views of building structures. Views from the inside of buildings can be framed, for example, by large shrubs or medium-sized trees with attractive foliage and branching patterns that provide a sense of scale and a visually attractive foreground. A good example to illustrate changing aspects in regions with distinct seasonality is the Sheraton Hotel at Niagara Falls, Ontario, Canada. This hotel features an impressive amalgamation of new and historic structures, situated on a historic site overlooking the Falls. It has undergone several rounds of re-building and improvements over the last 100 years. In addition to changes through seasonality, one may select special non-green variants of a species and induce changes in foliage, branching, or even flowering by controlling water availability or adding plant growth regulators. In the tropics, it is especially important to size and space the selected plants so that they do not overgrow and block other structures or openings.

Integrated Design (ID) is a comprehensive approach to sustainable planning and building that merges architectural design with greenery and other salient environmental considerations. Seen from another perspective, ID is essentially a framework for increasing the quality of the built environment through maximizing existing natural systems to create productive and healthy work and residential environments. One ID strategy that adopts and considers the local natural elements and climatic conditions is passive design. Passive design considers microclimatic parameters during the design process. As external environmental factors influence site microclimates, it is vital to consider the various options of harnessing greenery to modulate these environmental factors in order to augment occupant comfort.

One of the main environmental conditions is the amount of solar irradiation or natural daylight present on site. Another factor is the availability of space; if there are constraints for putting greenery horizontally, green ceilings and walls are alternatives for placing greenery vertically.

The intensity of solar irradiation also determines the magnitude of temperature and humidity on site. Greenery in outdoor spaces around buildings acts as a natural air-conditioner through

There are many options in the tropical regions for plant selection, including freshwater aquatic and saltwater plants (mangroves) that soften the appearance of built environments (Singapore).
Building with multiple levels for greenery (Bali, Indonesia).

Natural daylight can enter through the building roof (Niagara Falls, Canada).
Evaluation of different plant species for green roofs and vertical greenery (Chicago, Illinois, USA).
Vertical greenery system (Thailand).

the process of evaporative cooling via plant transpiration. Plants can serve as insulators as well as air purifiers from busy and therefore dusty roads. In seasonal countries, plants can be used as natural insulators during the winter months and coolers during summer months. In countries with hot climates such as desert areas and tropical regions, plants are utilized to reduce the heat received by buildings and to allow ample air movement. Regarding temperate/seasonal regions, studies conducted at four different sites at the Cambridge city center[8] suggested that thermal comfort outdoors and indoors is strongly influenced by quantitative microclimate parameters and eventually leads to psychological adaptations to counter thermal discomfort.

Greenery is beneficial to mankind through its biological functionalities. Any natural elements can be integrated to define a three-dimensional space with beauty and positive attributes within the built environment. Apart from the appropriate selection of plants incorporated as design elements during the planning and design stage, architects, landscape architects, and urban planners need to recognize the short-term and long-term aesthetics plants provide for the built environment. Beyond aesthetics, greenery enhances architectural design by harmonizing it with natural microclimate factors to create a balanced, sustainable, and more liveable built environment. Pragmatically, an effective and desirable green entity successfully incorporated within a well-designed built environment will also enhance the property value of the place. As a component of the urban planning and/or architectural design process, greenery provides positive social, economic, and environmental benefits.

Many cities are introducing water-sensitive urban design to improve the liveability of the built environment (Hokkaido, Japan).

1. World Commission on Environment and Development (WCED). *Our common future.* Oxford: Oxford University Press, 1987. p. 43.
2. Sarajevs, V. *Health benefits of street trees.* The Research Agency of the Forestry Commission, UK, 2011.
3. Cervelli, J. A. *Landscape design with plants: creating outdoor rooms.* University of Kentucky, College of Agriculture, Cooperative Extension Service publication, 2005.
4. Wolf, K. L. *The calming effect of green: roadside landscape and driver stress.* Factsheet no. 8, Center for Urban Horticulture, University of Washington, Seattle, 2000.
5. Beyer, K. M. , A. Kaltenbach, A. Szabo, S. Bogar, F. J. Nieto, and K. M. Malecki. "Exposure to neighborhood green space and mental health: evidence from the survey of the health of Wisconsin," in *International Journal of Environmental Research and Public Health* 11 (2014). pp. 3453-3472.
6. Aspinall, P., P.Mavros, R. Coyne R, and J. Roe. "The urban brain: analysing outdoor physical activity with mobile EEG,"in *British Journal of Sports Medicine* 49 (2015). pp. 272-276.
7. Kuo,F. E., A. Faber Taylor. "A potential natural treatment for attention-deficit/ hyperactivity disorder: evidence from a national study," in *American Journal of Public Health* 94 (2014). pp. 1580-1586.
8. Nikolopoulou, M., K. Steemers K. "Thermal comfort and psychological adaptation as a guide for designing urban spaces," in *Energy and Buildings* 35 (2003). pp. 95-101.

Green Urbanism
Models of a Dense and Green Urban Context

Kees Christiaanse

What is green urbanism? Can we call a zero-emission building devoid of plants a green building? Can we call a traditional oil-heated building covered with plants a green building? I propose to frame the term "green urbanism" with a number of associations that point toward a preliminary definition.

Obviously, the term "green" refers to the role of nature in urbanism, either managed by man or proliferating by itself, and to green politics, which combine a social-democratic and an ecological attitude focusing on a decentralized, resource-friendly, low-energy, and low-carbon society.

The term nature both refers to green in the city, and to natural phenomena related to growth, process, transformation, or open-ended developments.

In Eliel Saarinen's designs for the city as an "archipelago," a green framework surrounding the city's districts enables the urban population to enjoy the presence of nature in short distances from their homes.

Siegfried Kracauer writes in his 1931 article "Straßen in Berlin und anderswo" (Streets in Berlin and Somewhere Else)," … above all, the urban appearance of Berlin has the characteristics of a landscape: as informally shaped as nature, and looks like a landscape in that it sustains itself unconsciously."[1]

Fumihiko Maki writes in his *Investigations in Collective Form* [2] of 1964: "We must now see our urban society as a dynamic field of interrelated forces. It is a set of mutually independent variables in a rapidly expanding infinite series. Any order introduced within the pattern of forces contributes to a state of dynamic equilibrium—an equilibrium which will change in character as time passes." Maki's idea of "group form," which one may see as stemming from the political ideas of the late CIAM and of Team X, in a certain way represents what we would now call "bottom-up urbanism."

The term "ecology," next to its meaning as a description of the dynamics of natural ecosystems, was used by Rayner Banham in his book *Los Angeles: The Architecture of Four Ecologies* [3] and by Mike Davis in his book *The Ecology of Fear* [4] to describe complexes of relations between lifestyles, social behavior, and their crystallization in the physical environment.

With the above in mind, I would like to frame "green urbanism" with the following keywords: Green Archipelago, An Inclusive Micro-Urban Concept, Urbanized Landscape, and The Ecology of Green.

"Green Archipelago"

The archipelago as a metaphor to describe a city is rather old. The Romans already called their residential blocks *insulae*, suggesting the surrounding public space to be something fluid. Some cities, like Venice, literally form an archipelago where transport is effected by boat. One of the first architects who proposed the archipelago as a concept for urban design was Eliel Saarinen. His master plans for the cities of Tallinn of 1913 and Helsinki of 1918 propose a decentralization of the city into clearly distinct quarters, surrounded by a sea of landscape, woodlands, and water. The street pattern consisted of axial roads that simultaneously formed the main streets of the quarters. Saarinen may have been inspired to this image of a green archipelago by the rough coastline and peninsula-like geography of his Finnish hometown. The main driver for his concept seems to have been a social vision inspired by the Arts and Crafts movement of William Morris and John Ruskin as well as by Ebenezer Howard's idea of the Garden City. However, the districts in Saarinen's projects are really urban and dense, in addition to being green, and can be read most appropriately as an early serious attempt to put Metropolis and Arcadia in a reciprocally productive relationship.

We can also read Patrick Abercrombie's *Social and Functional Analysis of London* of 1944 [5] as a hierarchical archipelago, in which districts are relatively autonomous while being part of a larger organism. This apprehensive representation of London was informed by the fact that this city was divided into many districts by railroads, valleys, and waterways, and more specifically by the decentralized administration of the city's boroughs, which acted almost like independent municipalities.

In 1977, when I studied at TU Delft, Rem Koolhaas came to our studio with a typewritten manuscript full of corrections by hand, entitled "Berlin: A Green Archipelago." This text became the storyline of an article with the title "Cities within the City," published in *Lotus* magazine, under the leadership of Oswald Mathias Ungers, to whom Koolhaas was an assistant at Cornell University.[6] Here, the fragmented and collaged character of Berlin, resulting from the war and the expected decline in population, is accepted as a positive factor to let parts of the city shrink in a controlled way, whereby other parts are protected and consolidated. This intervention results in a federation of distinct urban islands. Ungers saw the importance of Berlin in

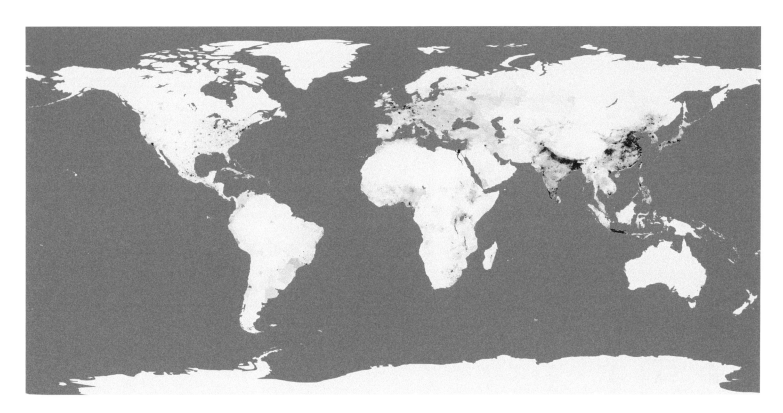

the "critical antithesis of contradictory elements in favour of a divergent multiplicity."[7] The residual spaces between the islands form a network of green zones, in which traffic infrastructure, large public buildings, allotments, sports facilities, and recreational amenities can be easily accommodated. In case the Cold War would end and the Berlin Wall be taken down, the Wall zone could be integrated into the green network.

The idea of Berlin as a metropolis impregnated with green was not new. Elements of this idea can be found in the work of Schinkel, Taut, the competition for Greater Berlin of 1910, and most strikingly in Albert Speer's *Generalbebauungsplan* for Berlin of 1938. In 1957, before the Berlin Wall was built, Hans Scharoun won the second prize in a competition for the redesign of Berlin as the capital of a future reunited Germany. In his design for the city center, large surfaces of derelict city areas were cleared for a spacious green center, where valuable old buildings like the Reichstag were given a new, green context. A network of freeways was elegantly embedded along existing infrastructural lines like waterways, railroad corridors, and parks. While the concept of the freeway had been developed simultaneously in Europe and America, the first freeway ever was constructed in Berlin in 1921, and in the 1930s the Nazis propelled the

construction of a system of *Reichsautobahnen* (state freeways). Over time, the layout of freeways was developed as a careful balance between traffic efficiency, landscape design to create scenic routes for the pleasure of driving, and ecological motives. Today, freeway verges are among the areas with the highest biodiversity.

In America, the parkway, originally conceived in New York City by the Olmsted Brothers to create scenic green routes between destinations within and outside the city, evolved into the landscaped freeway of the type well known from Los Angeles and New York City. In the 1960s, the parkway underwent a revival and retrofit in Singapore, becoming a symbol for Asia's freeway system.

An Inclusive Micro-Urban Concept

In 1963, Singapore's Prime Minister Lee Kuan Yew proclaimed a campaign to make Singapore a "City in a Garden," in a deliberate wink to Howard's "Garden City." The 1963 Master Plan for Singapore consisted of a Ring City, comprised of the city center and several new towns that were connected by a freeway system, roughly based on the idea of "bundled de-concentration"

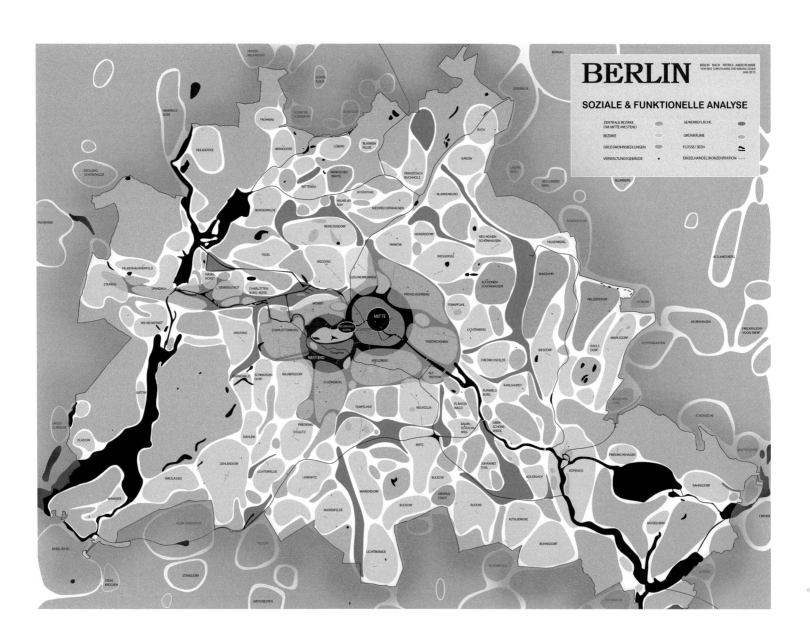

Kees Christiaanse and Miriam Züger, Social and Functional Analysis of Berlin, after Patrick Abercrombie, 2013.

Albert Speer, Generalbebauungsplan Berlin, 1938, landscape wedge diagram by Willy Schelkes.
Hans Scharoun, Competition for Berlin as German Capital, 1957.

developed for Randstad in the Netherlands. The freeways were designed as spacious parkways with lush greenery on the verges and the median strip. A specific rain tree, imported from Africa, with a huge, umbrella-like foliage covered the freeway like a canopy, providing shade. These green corridors were connected with the parks, hill ridges, and natural reservations they ran along, but also with airports, housing estates, and university campuses, with which they were to form an integrated green framework for the built surfaces of the island state.

For a long time, the concept of "City in a Garden" remained limited to the green freeways and green public spaces as additions to the city's built areas. More recently, it has evolved into a complex, inclusive culture by integrating vegetation inside, on top of, and alongside buildings. There is great potential in vertical and horizontal green surfaces within the framework of an inclusive water-management and climate concept on a micro-urban level. At the interface of urban and architectural design, there is a growing awareness that cities need large water-absorbing public spaces that hold and filter water before it is re-used, and that well-designed collective space has a positive social impact. Green, in this sense, has an immense capacity to endow buildings with a feeling of permeability and to soften the transition between public and private space.

The idea of liveability was propagated in the early 20th Century by the Modern Movement, symbolized by Le Corbusier's *Ville Radieuse*, where lush buildings with generous apartments stood on *pilotis* amidst the greenery and where functional zoning was the harbinger of a healthy and beneficial living environment. Many of the numerous post-war Modernist city extensions have turned into socially problematic ghettos for the urban poor. Contrary to this trend, Modernism has survived rather well in different forms in the tropics. This is especially true in Singapore, where the idea of "City in a Garden" was translated into a sophisticated social housing program by the Housing Development Board (HDB) in the form of large green estates, where residential buildings on *pilotis* hover over a variety of sports, play, educational, food, and leisure amenities. Unlike in Western estates in colder climate zones, the open-access deck and semi-covered ground-floor space in a pedestrian green setting provide comfortable, shaded collective spaces, where the generations of the extended Asian family can linger. Tending extends beyond the semi-public spaces and includes the maintenance of the buildings proper by the HDB, while the apartments are privately owned. This system goes along with a strong social control, actually a mild form of "gatedness,"

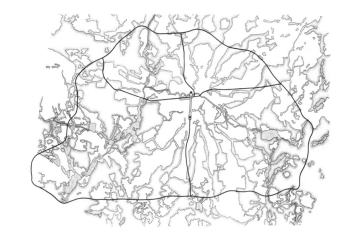

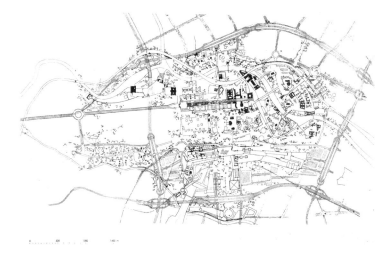

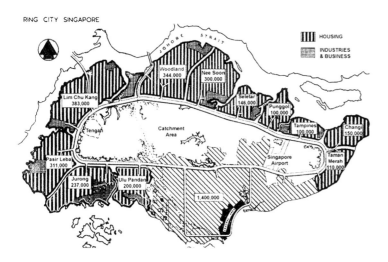

by the residents on the collective space, avoiding the neglect that generally characterizes Western social housing estates.

This social housing concept also informed the typological development of the Singaporean condominium, which has become the paradigm for middle- and upper-class living throughout Southeast Asia and China. A hybrid between a resort and an apartment complex, the typical condominium consists of one or more apartment towers surrounded by a fenced garden, containing a swimming pool, tennis courts, party rooms, and other collective facilities. Recently, under the pressure of increased demand for and scarcity of land, condominiums have started scraping the sky, accompanied by enhanced collective spaces like sky gardens, roof terraces, and green voids, partly compensating for the diminishing plot sizes at grade level.

The Pinnacle@Duxton complex in the center of Singapore, for instance, consists of five high-rises connected by sky bridges with a 400-m-long jogging track cutting through the towers and covered by a "shelf" with a public roof park. Together with the Marina Bay Sands Hotel, the complex has become an icon of a gradually evolving "shelf typology" of buildings connected at the top level and with collective amenities on the roof.

In many Asian cities, parts of the city form a continuous landscape of condominium complexes, producing districts that look all green, although their density is enormous. Their residual urban tissue of *kampung* and the permeability of the gate do not necessarily lead to a lack of urban vibrancy, a fact that may be very significant for the debate on urbanity in the contemporary Southeast-Asian city. Despite the overall Modernist layout of mono-functional clusters and *cul-de-sac* access systems, the resulting "green archipelago" became a successful blueprint for urban planning in Southeast Asia, among others for the city of Shenzhen in the Pearl River Delta.

The early master plans for Shenzhen rested heavily on the urbanistic concept implemented in Singapore. Deng Xiao Ping's visit to the city state in 1978 was one of the factors that triggered the installation of the first Special Economic Zone (SEZ) in Shenzhen. The original villages, dispersed across Shenzhen's vast countryside with interconnecting roads, served as an underlay for a framework of green freeways *à la* Singapore, creating a giant green mesh complemented with what was left of the shaved hill ridges used for landfill (also à la Singapore). The former agricultural land in between the freeway grid was filled with factories, business parks, housing, and other developments in a

continuous transformation that took place with incredible speed and continues today. After years of economic growth and the consequent erosion of the landscape and human resources, the Chinese government and Shenzhen's municipality recently acknowledged the need for a green policy. A public transport system has been installed, with a constantly extended network constructed in tunnels beneath the green freeways, whose generous dimensions allow for a smooth integration.

The redevelopment of Shenzhen's western coastline is a gigantic New Town project and at the same time an enormous urban renewal project intended to correct the consequences of recent development decisions. My office, KCAP Architects & Planners, participated in the competition for this coastal strip with a length of more than 40 km. Due to the "hard and fast" development, much of the historic landscape has vanished and at certain points the original coastline has receded by up to 5 km. Our design, which was awarded second prize, is an attempt to reconcile the planning "efforts" from the recent past and the development potential with a re-naturation and restoration approach.

The Baoan city district, stretching along the large Pearl River Delta, used to be a delta in itself, as more than 45 creeks and

rivers streamed through the area in former times. The coastline redevelopment project embraces this forgotten supply of fresh water. Via "repair by development," the forgotten rivers and creeks are elaborated into an area-wide freshwater network that complements the saltwater coastline with an extensive network of fresh and brackish water and a variety of green spaces. This water network is to form the basis for the transformation of the area into a rich and differentiated coastal city with three centers (New Airport City, XiWan, and QianHai).

In many cities worldwide, heavy transport infrastructure is being put under ground or removed and replaced by green corridors with public spaces and amenities. In Seoul, for example, an elevated freeway was removed to revitalize the original Cheonggyecheon Stream, resulting in the recovery of one of the city's most important public spaces. In New York City, an obsolete elevated railroad was turned into the High Line Park, thanks to the collective effort of stakeholders in the surrounding districts. In Boston, elevated freeways that strangled the peninsula were turned into park zones. And in Singapore, the old railroad track to Malaysia, to be replaced by a high-speed railroad, will be turned into a linear park. These examples are indicative of the fact that the archipelago idea has become a model for a

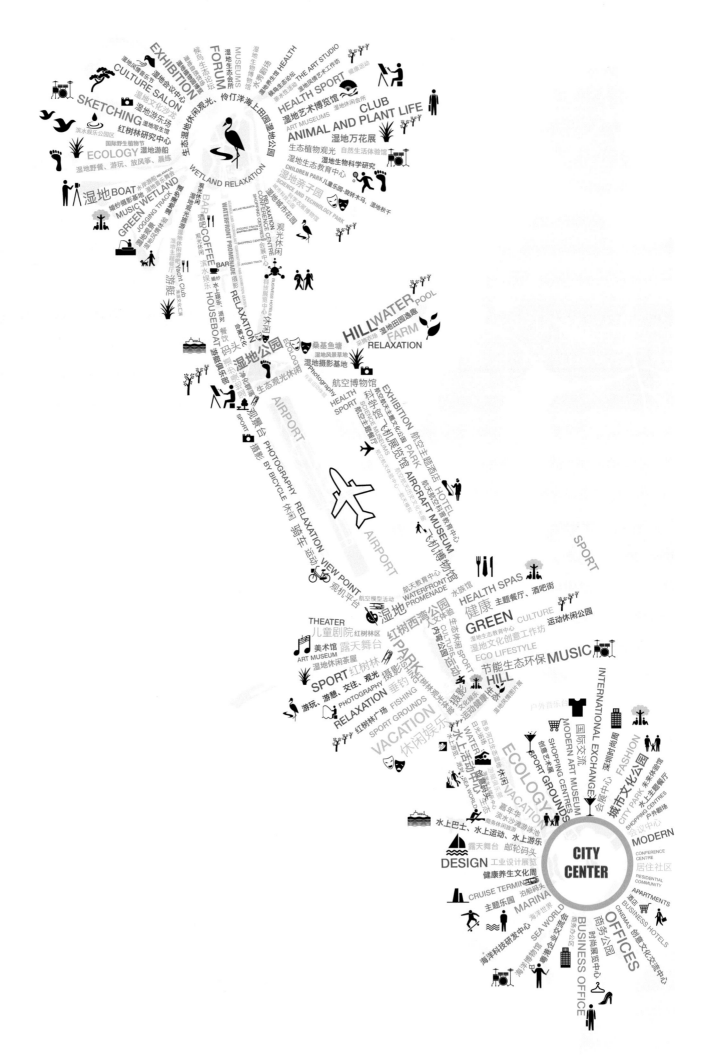

KCAP in cooperation with LAY-OUT and Atelier Dreiseitl, Baoan New Water City, Shenzhen, China, analysis (this page) and master plan concept (opposite).

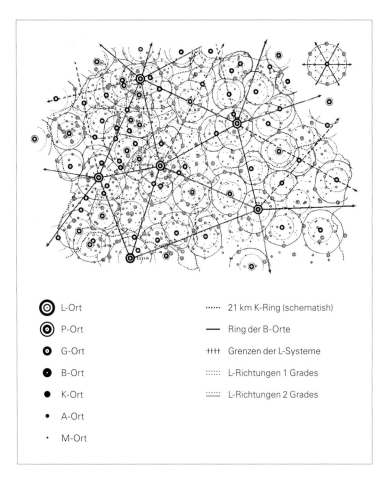

Walter Christaller, The Central Places in Southern Germany, 1933.

◉	L-Ort	⋯⋯	21 km K-Ring (schematish)
◉	P-Ort	—	Ring der B-Orte
⊙	G-Ort	+∦+	Grenzen der L-Systeme
⦿	B-Ort	⦂⦂⦂⦂⦂	L-Richtungen 1 Grades
●	K-Ort	⦂⦂⦂⦂⦂	L-Richtungen 2 Grades
•	A-Ort		
·	M-Ort		

green metropolis, where districts are given distinctive identities by green belts that accommodate exchangeable infrastructures, amenities, and ecological corridors.

"Urbanized Landscape"

According to certain statistics, more than 50% of the world's population lives in cities; the so-called "urban age" is supposed to have arrived.[8] However, looking at the distribution of population across the globe, we notice a number of mega-regions that are extremely densely populated, like the Southeast-Asian river valleys and deltas, the entire island of Java, the shores of the Ganges, the east coast of China, and parts of Japan. Importantly, these regions are at the same time those with the highest rice production per hectare in the world. Obviously, a considerable part of the alleged Urban Age population lives in productive landscapes—a mixture of urbanized and agriculturally cultivated land. The surface area of urbanized landscapes of this type is huge in comparison with the surface area of the concentrated city type, which is promoted today as the ideal model for sustainable living and said to experience a renaissance.

The steady proliferation of mobility toward productive landscapes has propelled urban sprawl beyond any limit. We may therefore assume that this form of urbanization will be as much a prevailing future urban model as the concentrated city. The compact city and the urbanized landscape are two extreme conditions in a dynamic field of human settlement, or, to repeat Maki's quotation from above: "We must now see our urban society as a dynamic field of interrelated forces. It is a set of mutually independent variables in a rapidly expanding infinite series. Any order introduced within the pattern of forces contributes to a state of dynamic equilibrium—an equilibrium which will change in character as time passes."

In general, the urbanized landscape is not considered to be sustainable, because it wastes valuable land and causes transportation challenges due to the diluted population density in catchment areas. In addition, it requires extensive and costly technical infrastructure, like energy, clean-water, and wastewater grids. It is also considered environmentally damaging due to the occupation of land, the destruction of flora and fauna, and the hardly controllable management of waste and pollution. On the other hand, it must be acknowledged that poor regions in developing countries have in themselves a relatively small environmental footprint, due to the low depletion of resources. And urbanized landscapes located in Western European social democracies have developed highly sophisticated policies and technologies that, in the long run, may allow to tackle the massive depletion of resources.

In the 1930s, the German geographer Walter Christaller developed his "Theory of Central Places," a theory of economic geography. While the theory is somewhat outdated today, Christaller's map of urban regions, comprising of the cities of Munich, Zurich, Strasbourg, and Frankfurt, describes a landscape where the towns and villages form centralities in a continuous urban network. Europe has developed several of these network city or *Netzstadt* regions, which have densified into prosperous, productive environments.

For instance, the Swiss Midlands, stretching from Lake Geneva to Lake Constance, where the majority of the Swiss population lives, accommodates at the same time most of the country's agricultural and industrial production. It consists of hundreds of villages, small towns, and some larger agglomerations, equipped with a uniquely efficient road and rail infrastructure. Spatial development is strongly regulated, protecting forests, natural areas, and farmland. A certain surface of farmland per capita is legally required, in order to guarantee self-sufficiency in food supply in times of crisis. In this landscape, households live and work easily across distances of 100 km: a family may live in Bern, the father works in Basel, the mother in Lausanne, while the children study in Zurich. As green technology is highly developed in Switzerland, households may not only be largely self-sufficient in terms of energy and biomass, but may even feed their energy surplus back into the grid, turning buildings into power plants. Of course, most people would not grow their own food, but a certain form of autonomous life is becoming *en vogue* and technically feasible.

What emerges from these considerations is that there seems to be hope for this prevailing and inevitable form of urbanization, the urbanized landscape, or "Desa-Kota" in the words of urban geographer Terry McGhee. Generally considered as very negative, this type of urban form needs sophisticated infrastructural systems, both in the field of mobility and of technical infrastructure and self-sufficient technologies. The most important challenge, however, is the acknowledgement that managing urbanization processes in this type of region is a complex affair, dealing, as Maki points out, with multiple forces of influence.

An example for the complex and paradoxical forces at work is Schiphol Airport in the Amsterdam Metropolitan Area, where the urbanization pressure exerted by the cities of Amsterdam, Haarlem, Hoofddorp, and Aalsmeer collides with the expansion of the airport, and vice versa. The resulting agriculture, sports, and leisure landscape is shaped in adaptation to the noise contours of the runways, whose orientation in turn is determined by avoiding flight-paths that run over residential quarters—an equilibrium that is not per se negative. On the contrary, this specific spatial constellation has created a "green lung" between the cities and has triggered innovative uses of greenery, like sculptural sound-protecting landscapes or a farm where de-icing liquid is neutralized with the help of algae. In the traditional flower-growing city of Aalsmeer, one of the greenhouse compounds houses a diverse stock of tropical species, where most palm trees for the boulevards of Dubai are bred. Biodiversity around the airport has increased to an extent that intensive hunting, for instance of wild geese, has become necessary.

The example of Schiphol suggests that basic strategic thinking about balancing initially undesirable or adverse developments is of great importance for planning and intervening in the urbanized landscape. It also makes us aware that intervention, in this context, is less a matter of design and more like "conducting." In Montpellier, for the master plan of the area entitled "Oz, Nature Urbaine," which will accommodate a new high-speed railroad line and a new freeway from Paris/Lyon to Barcelona, a strategy of reverse thinking is being followed. Normally in Europe, trains stop at a city's main station and trigger mixed-use development projects in connection with smart mobility concepts. In France, the high-speed rail track preferably runs past cities, thereby saving costs, reducing the number of stations, and keeping the speed of the train high. The local mobility problems that this policy causes are taken for granted. For this project, as a result of centralist planning decisions made in Paris, the high-speed train track and the new freeway are projected in a landscape zone between the city of Montpellier and the villages on the coast. Surrounding the station, a new urban district of 1,500,000 sqm has been envisaged.

At the point when KCAP was selected for the master plan, the courses of the railroad tracks and the freeway were already fixed, spaced more than 100 m apart. This would have caused a fragmentation of the landscape zone into useless residual spaces. In a successful effort to convince the central government to align the two infrastructures into a narrow bundle, we projected the railroad station on top of an elevated square that crosses the ensuing bundle in one go. We extended the tramline from the city across the square to the airport on the coast. The remaining tracks were wrapped in soundproof building blocks and landscaping. This resulted in two development areas on either side of the bundle. For these areas we created a "green archipelago," consisting of the inundation zones of the existing streams and additional landscape corridors. Within this green framework, five or six "landscape rooms" accommodate agriculture, sports, allotments, and leisure activities. These rooms can transform into urban districts in the case of mounting development pressure. Construction will be allowed only up to a certain density, maintaining a balance between the built and the green areas. The confined sizes of the landscape rooms enable incremental development and situations of partial completion after every phase. The plan can quickly adapt to changing circumstances.

The "inverse strategy" practiced here lies in the fact that the urban designer safeguards the landscape and ecological qualities of an area as a first step before allowing construction within an area. This reverse thinking is also the quintessence of the Swiss planning legislation, in which the contours of precious landscape eventually direct urbanization.

"The Ecology of Green"

In the above-mentioned publication, *Los Angeles: The Architecture of Four Ecologies*, Rayner Banham discerns four different "eco-systems" of urban and architectural culture, attributed respectively to the freeway, the beach, the flatlands, and the foothills. Similarly, in *The Ecology of Fear*, Mike Davis describes the "eco-systems" of social behavior as caused by the USA's chronic condition of crime and lack of safety, and its condensation into urban and architectural form: gates, guards, cameras, school buses. In analogy to these approaches one may sketch an "ecology of green," describing a cloud of green consciousness and behavior and its condensation into the physical environment.

A green roof or terrace with sufficient earth coverage will help a building regulate its temperature by the heat and cold storage of the earth's mass and the absorption and evaporation of rainwater. Plants on the roof will provide shade. A green roof terrace looks better than any other roof. People feel attracted to green surfaces. Roofs may be used for growing vegetables and fruit—but not for heavy crops, which means that the idea of food self-sufficiency on built surfaces is illusory, except on super-large buildings like airplane hangars.

A green facade is typically a piece of hydroponic engineering, wherein water and nutrients are distributed by a fine network of drains. This type of facade produces shade and may help to cool a building. Growing leafy vegetables or fruit may be possible. A green facade, and be it only ivy or as a cover for a sound-protection wall along a parkway, looks more attractive than any designed facade. In addition, green surfaces on buildings produce fragrances and house small animals, perform photosynthesis, and help clear the air.

The atrium as a type is widely deployed even in moderate and cold zones as a climate regulator and collective or event space in residential, office, and public buildings, as well as in shopping malls. The use of vegetation has been optimized and sometimes plays a role in a building's air and humidity household. All this is triggering the evolution of a hybrid residential typology, which, for example in the Netherlands, is positioned between generally mono-functional housing estates on the periphery of towns. As "urban catalysts," they attract secondary functions like nurseries and convenience stores. In the Gardens by the Bay in Singapore, a large public greenhouse is cooled to accommodate vegetation from the northern region as part of an educational garden—an extreme example of a sophisticated indoor culture in this tropical country, where a large part of the day is spent inside climatized spaces.

Greenhouses can be put anywhere and hardly need soil for growing tomatoes or other fruits and vegetables, because their nutrients are distributed in other ways. A shopping mall can also be a greenhouse, where part of the surface is turned into a piece of tropical jungle. Atria of senior residences in cold countries can be designed as greenhouses, where the residents attend concerts by schoolchildren while parrots fly over their heads. Equipped with the proper technology, atria will regulate their temperature and even their own rainwater supply. Greenhouses can have multiple stories and can use the solar energy of the daytime to heat and light at nighttime, so that plants can grow at all times. This, however, means that the plants are, as it were, forced to grow. Is this also part of the "ecology of green"?

Why do condominiums not have allotments, but only artificial gardens that require a lot of water and maintenance to keep up their looks? Because the lifestyle of condominium residents is not geared toward gardening: they instead buy organically grown food in the supermarket. There aren't even any fruit trees in condominium gardens. Nevertheless, allotment gardens

ETH Zurich Urban Design Research Studio, Schiphol Airport noise landscape, 2010.

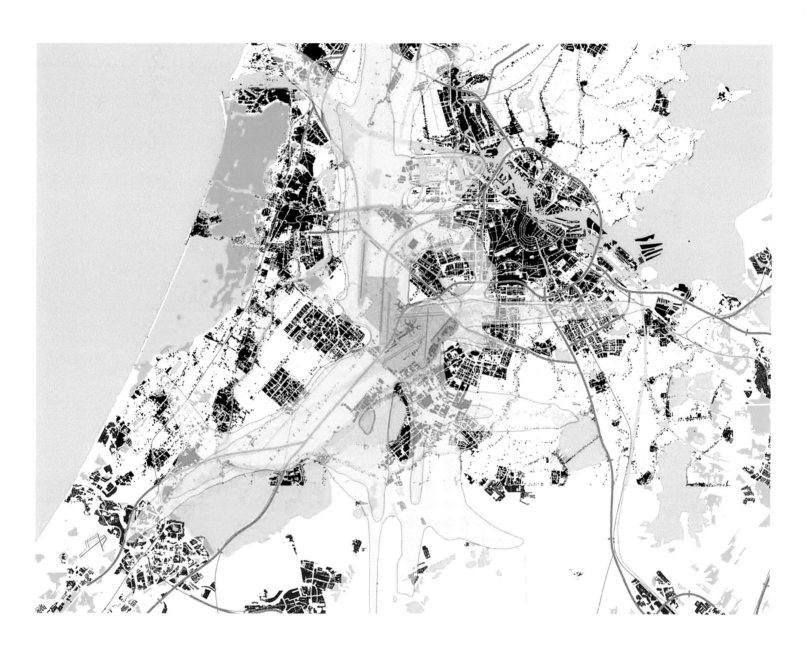

provide a much-needed additional source of food production for many urban dwellers in the world and offer moments of mindful resting that come with cultivating one's own crop. In the eco-friendly GWL quarter in Amsterdam, allotment gardens have been offered to all housing units, which has resulted in a sharp reduction in construction and maintenance costs of the public space. The allotments make sure that more people are outside more often, and as a consequence there is less burglary in the neighborhood and less graffiti on the facades—partly because these are covered with green. Security in the neighborhood is better than in the surrounding quarters. So is the residents' satisfaction.

Is a "City in a Garden," where all gardens are regularly sprayed with insecticides that accidentally kill some small wildlife along with the mosquitoes that bring malaria, dengue, and other diseases, a green city? This may at some point be replaced by more ecological technologies, as may the purely artificial way in which gardens are maintained by a mix of control and *laissez-faire* of intervention and letting nature bloom. Freeway viaducts will become part of ecological corridors—a survey on the perception of noise-protection screens along freeways[9] demonstrates that screens covered with green are most appreciated by drivers. Naturally ventilated spaces in malls may contribute to the distribution and variety of species in flora and fauna. Green corridors will serve as cold air paths, stimulating the effect of the breeze in public space. And urban farming of herbs, fruits, and vegetables may enrich the residents' diet and fulfill an important social role.

What is the difference between green, sustainable, zero-emission, self-sufficiency, and liveability? Do we still know?

1. Krakauer, Friedrich. *Strassen in Berlin und Anderswo*. Frankfurt a. M.: Suhrkamp, 1964 (1931).
2. Maki, Fumihiko. *Investigations in Collective Form*. A Special Publication, no. 2. The School of Architecture, Washington University, St. Louis, June 1964.
3. Banham, Reyner. *Los Angeles. The Architecture of Four Ecologies*. London: Penguin Books, 1971.
4. Davies, Mike. *Ecology of Fear. Los Angeles and the imagination of disaster*. New York: Vintage Books, 1999.
5. Map "Social and functional analysis of London" from *The County of London Plan* by Sir Patrick Abercrombie et al., 1943.
6. Ungers, Oswalt Mathias, Rem Koolhaas, Peter Riemann, Hans Kollhoff, Arthur Ovaska. „La Città nella città. Proposte della Sommer Akademie per *Berlino / Cities within the City. Proposals by the Sommer Akademie for Berlin*, Lotus 19 (1978). Newly published as Hertweck, Florian, Sébastien Marot (eds.). *The City in the City. Berlin: A Green Archipelago*. Zürich: Lars Müller Publishers, 2013.
7. *Ibid.*
8. UN DESA Population Division. *World Urbanization Prospects* (source: http://www.un.org/en/development/desa/population/theme/urbanization/index.shtml).
9. PBL Netherlands Environmental Assessment Agency (source: http://www.pbl.nl/publicaties/2010/De-omgeving-van-infrastructuur).

Dense and Green Building Typologies

Thomas Schröpfer

Innovative building types for high-density contexts include extensive sky terraces, sky bridges, vertical parks, roof gardens, and other green components, set in the framework of conceptual approaches where density and sustainability are not seen as contradictory but rather as mutually dependent and synergistic. In considering the dense and green paradigm primarily through building types, a formal road map emerges for recognizing general ways to combine ecological sensitivity, architecture, and urban densification.

The five building types assessed in this book—institutions, offices, residences, infrastructure, and mixed-use facilities—retain many functional and formal features that help us understand this typological evolution as one specific to the use of a particular project. In an effort to identify unique features of this approach, a sublayer of architectural strategies becomes recognizable that run through this delineation. They can be defined as: 1) the topographic ground plane, 2) the atypical section, 3) the vegetal habitat, and 4) the transgression between indoor and outdoor space.

The first strategy alludes to the relatively recent phenomenon where the ground level of a building is coterminous with, and sometimes mimetic of, natural undulating contours of the topography outside of the building volume. The second strategy identifies ways in which the increasingly unconventional section, which no longer comprises serial floor plates, has a direct impact on the dense and green paradigm through the facilitation of courtyards and otherwise enhanced vertical spaces. The third strategy identifies the programmatic and strategic integration of vegetation into the life of buildings and indicates a move beyond the treatment of plants as decoration or enlivening elements in architecture but rather as integral and contained ecosystems in and of themselves. The fourth strategy describes the extent to which the architecture-landscape hybridization has emerged from the deliberate obfuscation of the boundaries between enclosed interior spaces and open exterior spaces.

Institutions

Institutional buildings undoubtedly have a particularly visible ability to articulate the dense and green paradigm in a grand and sustained way. Although a wide range of institutional buildings—educational facilities, foundations, and civic structures of all kinds—have developed certain traits in connection with the dense and green paradigm, it is those of the museum that are often the most instructive in this context.

A good example for an innovative approach to this building type is Herzog & de Meuron's design for the Pérez Art Museum Miami, Florida, USA. Facing Miami's Biscayne Bay, the project is a genuine manifesto of both architecture as landscape and the civic ambitions of the dense and green paradigm. Comprising a dense field of columns and an intensely planted pergola canopy, the building creates an exemplar of a vegetal microcosm. The design presents a clear articulation of outside-inside blurring through a system of planted chambers, each with its own microclimate and an almost disorienting obfuscation of gallery and green spaces. Even once inside the actual museum space, a number of densely vegetated interstitial spaces stage the interplay of the natural world with the very different, contemplative space of the art gallery.

The Biosphere Pavilion in Potsdam, Germany, by Barkow Leibinger, is a second innovative example of the articulation of the institutional typology. The building's form is generated by the pre-existing earthen berms constructed on the site by the Soviet Army during their time in East Germany. The berms form an artificial valley that houses the Biosphere's varied functions and exhibits, enclosed by a simple flat roof with skylights. By being carved into the earth, the sunken garden reduces the height of the building and gives it a camouflaged appearance from the outside, inviting comparisons with the Art Museum in Miami. The berm forms, clad with oak logs, grass, slate, or poured concrete, corroborate the topographic nature of the building's various systems of circulation. The main entry to the structure is via a pathway cut diagonally over a lawn-covered berm, further enhancing the anti-monumental quality of the building's relationship with its ground plane.

A third example for a novel approach to this building type is Renzo Piano's California Academy of Sciences in San Francisco, USA. The project combines exhibition spaces, a natural history museum, an aquarium, a planetarium, as well as educational, conservation, and research facilities all beneath one massive green roof. The respective functions are expressed in the profile of the building's roofline, which echoes the form of the components beneath it. The roof is covered with an estimated 1.7 million selected plants in specially conceived biodegradable coconut-fiber containers. Piano articulates the expressive and symbolic functions of the roof: "The roof is flat at its perimeter and, like a natural landscape, becomes increasingly undulating as it moves away from the edge to form a series of domes of various sizes rising up from the roof plane."[1] The two main domes cover the planetarium and the rainforest exhibitions, while a convex

glazed roof shelters the central courtyard. Photovoltaic cells are embedded between the two glass panels that form the transparent canopy around the perimeter of the green roof. The roof's profile also echoes the rolling hill landscape of the Bay Area.

As evident in these three examples, the museum subcategory of the institutional building type is the one where the most forthright proposals about an architectural "return to nature" can be found. Architectural elements such as domes and berms take on new meaning, exploiting the program of the museum as a place for display and contemplation. While the implementation of plant life in architecture is not unique to the recent past (although its frequency has increased exponentially), it is pertinent to note that the implementation of vegetation into building types, both institutional and otherwise, has become systematized, demonstrating a rigorous conceptual model that conceives of institutional, residential, and office buildings as apparatuses of miniature ecosystems. As such, they are distinct from the applied knowledge that comes to the design professions from the traditions of landscape architecture. These ecosystems vary in their ambitions and functions—some purify air, some provide food, some modulate the microclimate—but in all of the leading examples they engage closely with their architectural "host" in order to function.

Office Buildings

Innovative dense and green design strategies for office buildings have a certain amount of commonalities but also present variation, largely depending on whether they pertain to high- or low-rise developments. A major common feature, particularly in high-rise constructions, is the atypical section. In the present context, this term refers to a section that exhibits considerable variation instead of evenly stacked repetitive floor plates. While this has no direct or symbolic bearing on the integration of landscape with nature in the way that the manipulation of the ground plane has, it does emerge as a continuous recent thread in the integration of landscape in office buildings as well as residential architecture. Atypical sections have often driven ecologically-minded programs such as vertical courtyards, features for harvesting energy, and ways of humanizing otherwise monotonous structures for work through the punctuation of dense space with open space. This has produced a broad array of typological manifestations that demonstrate the power of the atypical section and its key role in the combination of architecture and nature.

ingenhoven architects, 1 Bligh, Sydney, Australia, 2011, exterior, interior, aerial view.

For example, ingenhoven architects' high-rise office building, 1 Bligh in Sydney, Australia, details many of the innovations of the high-rise typology. The building not only surpassed the country's highest efficiency rating but also did so with a refined and novel design approach. The volumetric envelope of the 30-story building is configured entirely according to optimal solar orientation, a goal that in turn dictates the elliptical shape of the plan and the double-glazed exterior facade. The project's most significant element is a massive central atrium that penetrates the entire height of the structure. It provides daylighting and allows for natural ventilation of the offices and balconies that face the atrium, thereby considerably improving the building's air quality. The atrium draws its energy from a single, streamlined system that combines cooling, heating, and the generation of electric power through a vacuum tube solar collector, generating the necessary electricity *in situ*, off the Sydney power grid. Reflecting the particularly precarious standing of water as a natural resource in Australia, the building has its own filtration plant in the basement. A plethora of incentives to commute to the building via bike enhance its ecological profile.

While not as formally adventurous as Norman Foster's Swiss Re Headquarters in London, 1 Bligh is perhaps more prototypical for the office typology in its clear articulation of the vertical cavity as a ventilating element and source of natural daylight, its straightforward double glazing and solar orientation, and its internalized energy and resource provisions. To a large degree, the most successful high-rise dense and green office buildings use and recalibrate this formula. 1 Bligh's success lies not only in its innovative interpretation of the building type but also in the elegance that comes from its steadfast adherence to key ideas of the dense and green paradigm, departing from established formal motifs of more conventional ecological design.

T. R. Hamzah & Yeang's EDITT Tower, an office building in Singapore pending completion at the time of writing, is another excellent example of how versatility often lies in the section of high-rise dense and green building types. A highly variegated system of floor plates, which at times spiral into one another, slide backward or peel forward plays a double function. The spiraling articulation of the vertical profile provides open spaces for human use and also facilitates a diverse vegetal ecosystem and overall ecosystem stability in order to support ambient cooling of the facades. In a similar spirit, Foster + Partners' City Hall in London warps a stack of floor plates, based on sun angles, to create a spherical profile, which in turn

animates the vertical circulation in the building through the use of a helical stairwell.

A good example of the hybridized possibilities of low- and high-rise office buildings can be seen in the mid-rise ACROS Building in Fukuoka, Japan, by Emilio Ambasz. The building alludes to its site on the last significant piece of green space in the dense city center by terracing the south facade as if extending vertically the park that it faces. A large semicircular light shaft funnels light into the stepped atrium space, a concrete construction exemplifying a guiding design principle that Ambasz describes as "green over grey." The building makes a clear statement about its civic and urbanistic ambitions without rejecting the material and spatial traditions in Japanese office architecture, so plainly evident in the interior.

In low-rise office buildings, the opening up of a deep vertical core is often not necessary for the optimization of the ecological profile. Consequently, an innovative low-rise office building typology often markedly differs from its high-rise kin, tending to vary more in form and approach. Sauerbruch Hutton's Federal Environment Agency in Dessau, Germany, is a prime example for the opportunities of low-rise office buildings in the creation of a genuine second-order typology within the greater office building typology. The project is based on ideas of challenging standard office typologies by integrating the built environment with nature. Sauerbruch Hutton synthesize their trademark use of color with a technologically advanced climate-controlled garden, which connects the building complex with its site and the surrounding city. The building is organized around a landscaped public forum that serves as the public entrance. The forum seamlessly connects to a larger network of public park spaces and provides access not only to the building's public programs—an auditorium, the largest environmental library in Europe, and an exhibition area—but also to a large landscaped atrium that extends the public park network deep within the building's footprint. Covered with an operable glass saw-tooth roof, each of these landscaped voids serves as a socially vibrant node of the building.

Residential

Innovation in dense and green residential building types is very diverse and does not show specific typological morphologies that carry across a wide range. Nonetheless, the residential typology is where some of the most interesting evolutions of the dense and green paradigm can be found; a select few of them are instructive as to how potential commonalities could develop around a number of outstanding examples.

Stefano Boeri's Bosco Verticale, discussed in the first agenda of this book, employs the familiar use of plantings on its exterior in a way that transcends the conventional placement of greenery. A series of thick "regions" project off the residential core, each of them containing the equivalent of 10,000 sqm of forest. What is perhaps most provocative about Boeri's design is the unequal planting system of the residential core within the even profile of the green envelope. It alludes to the typical profile expected of a rectilinear high-rise while taking poetic licenses. Contrary to what might be expected, the deep green layering acts not as a planting system that rearticulates the building's ecological function but instead camouflages the building's program and serves in and of itself as the core of the ecological function.

The desire to meld architecture and landscape within the dense and green framework has often generated strategies that avoid literal connectivity of the two in favor of symbolic or metaphorical approaches. This has been particularly true in the realm of residential architecture. By contrast, the move toward an embrace of literal approaches is one of the characteristics of architecture's current "landscape turn." This is most obvious in the understanding of the architectural ground plane and the way in which it connects with the domicile, be it a small multi-family unit or a large residential tower. An important historical precedent for this approach is Le Corbusier's *promenade architecturale* that seeks to produce a gradual transition from the natural topography of a given site to the interior of a building. In transitioning from the topography of the earth to the topography of the interior in a slow and seamless fashion, Le Corbusier was able to avoid disruptions posed by the contrast of the variegated condition of the earth's surface and the rationalized condition of rectilinear "floor plate architecture" common to the realm of residential buildings.

In recent years, this strategy of melding the ground plane of a site and the interior has returned and has been revised in more overtly naturalistic terms. The continuous "terrain" has become quite literally a topography that continues, almost as if it does not need to be actualized by the architectural intervention. The potentially seamless procession from a natural or built landscape to an interior one builds upon Le Corbusier's notion of the *promenade architecturale* by articulating the continuous movement through architecture and landscape but also by tying this process to the particular motif of the topographic surface. Whereas Boeri's high-rise tower privileges the experience of the viewer within

his or her isolated unit within the Bosco Verticale, the resident of KWK PROMES' OUTrial House in Książenice, Poland, experiences the transition by descending into the earthen, grass-covered house from outside. Once inside, the view opens back onto the landscape, facing away from the built mound and renewing the sense of prospect.

Such a deliberate blurring of outdoor and indoor spaces is of specific relevance for residential architectural design in terms of the natural benefits it proffers for human comfort and spatial flexibility in and at home, especially in temperate climates. Yet the design of deliberately blurry outdoor and indoor spaces for their formal and representational value is a phenomenon that has only recently taken hold, in an attempt to exploit the recurrent concept of transparency in order to articulate architecture's intrinsic symbiotic relationship with the natural world.

In many regards, Frank Lloyd Wright's Fallingwater (or Kaufmann Residence) in Mill Run, Pennsylvania, USA, is an important historical precedent for this strategy and offers some operative clues into how to read it. Wright's stacked terraces intentionally mimic the horizontal schist formations beneath, creating a certain morphological continuity between nature and architecture. The sensation of this approach is enhanced by the continuous use of local stone, finely polished to the point of reflectivity, to pave interior and exterior surfaces seamlessly. The very sheen of the surface creates an optical confusion as to whether the stones are wet (as they would be outside near the waterfall) or whether they are merely polished. Columns do not resemble conventional slender columns but rather collections of stratified native stone so as to suggest that the structure may in fact not be a structure but rather the inhabitation of a natural outcropping of rock. While such visual experiments in architecture have been widely explored in the eighty years since Wright's design of Fallingwater, the original example is instructive as it ascertains a number of the guiding principles behind the contemporary typological amalgamation of residential architecture and landscape. In the time since the building of Fallingwater, optical effects between outside and inside have often returned to the theme of transparency, literal and phenomenal, in experiential and visual forms, as a means for understanding and reading space.[2] When applied in a more operative way, such as through the use of finishes, material choices, and the mimesis of nature, there emerges a sort of transparency that is based on the presupposition that architecture and nature are not conterminous but rather commingling.

Residential architecture has specific capacities and mechanisms to push this agenda. The most tangible typological implication is the increasing legibility of the unit as a unit, even in large residential buildings like Bosco Verticale. Whereas units have typically abutted one another, there is an increasing tendency for units to break free from the contiguous envelope to acquire some "breathing room," increasing the unit's ventilation and its capacity for a "greened" envelope of air and plants. Another example for this approach is Herzog & de Meuron's Beirut Terraces project in Lebanon. The building's stratified structure produces terraces and overhangs, light and shadow, places of shelter and exposure. Each unit is unique and variations in the layout of the apartments on each layer shape a vertical neighborhood.

Infrastructure

Infrastructure buildings have also been witness to a considerable amount of innovation, albeit largely dependent on the specifics of their program. Terminal 3 at Singapore's Changi International Airport, designed by the CPG Corporation in collaboration with Skidmore, Owings & Merrill, is an important example in the context of the dense and green paradigm in recent years. Beyond its superior ecological profile, Changi's Terminal 3 breathes a great deal of life into the staid airport typology by referring to the human and tactile potential of places otherwise easily written off as mere processors of people. While the structure is characterized by its considerable use of glass, a number of climatically expressive elements soften the space and locate it within Singapore in particular and a global context in general. A network of modulated, permeable skylights allow in an abundant amount of natural light, while a massive green wall with hanging creepers and a waterfall, designed by the Singapore design firm Tierra Design, is incorporated for visual interest as well as its microclimatic advantages.

The Yokohama Port Terminal for cruise ships in Japan's second-largest city creates a continuous string of new public spaces along the waterfront. While it was a given that the public plaza function was assigned to the building's roof, the architects went beyond the typical linear circulation patterns of a pier in an attempt to generate a novel and differentiated building plan and section from circulation. The result is a network of interweaving routes for passengers and workers on the pier level, which in turn articulate an undulating plaza surface whose faceted and uneven profile features large green areas, pockets of public activity in lieu of a single flat surface. The project is conceived as

Frank Lloyd Wright, Fallingwater (Kaufmann Residence), Mill Run, Pennsylvania, USA, 1935.
Herzog & de Meuron, Beirut Terraces, Lebanon, 2015, floorplates with terraces, rendering.

CPG Consultants/SOM, Changi Airport Terminal 3, Singapore, 2008, interior.
Foreign Office Architects, Yokohama Ferry Terminal, Japan, 2002, undulating plaza surface.

Michael Maltzan Architecture/The Office of James Burnett, Playa Vista Central Park, California, USA, 2010, greenscapes.

an extension of the urban topography, formed through the folding and bifurcation of planar surfaces. In structural terms, the upper surface forms a skin whose folds—dictated by the pier's circulation calculus—distribute the loads through the surface themselves, a particularly appropriate structural reinforcement given the high seismic activity of the region. Going beyond a merely formal statement, the folds of the surface create slowly ramping access routes both at the edges and in the center, which facilitate steady continuities between the pier functions below and the urban waterfront edge. The ensuing loop condition conceives architecture's role less as something to move into and more as something to move through.

The public park itself is another important type of infrastructure in the dense and green paradigm. The park, a patently un-dense space, nevertheless has an intrinsic value in supporting the principles of the dense and green paradigm by bringing a natural habitat to city dwellers. Two important innovative examples for such projects are Michael Maltzan and James Burnett's Playa Vista Park and James Corner Field Operations and Diller Scofidio + Renfro's High Line.

Playa Vista Park in Los Angeles, California, USA, is a "greenscape" that contains a number of habitable structures necessary for park programming. The structures are discretely woven into the quasi-artificial landscape through tucked mounds or caverns that in some instances mimic natural topography and in others allow the structures to occur like natural growths ("urban rooms") in the landscape. Regardless of whether they are readily visible or not, the overall effect is one of a continuous landscape, a seamless space that meanders through both outside and inside without reducing this seamlessness to a visual trick. Maltzan identifies the conflation between topography and structure as the moment of design innovation: "The boundary between landscape and architecture barely exists anymore… If you remove the traditional distinctions between what disciplines are supposed to be doing and imagine what needs to be done, then you can create real innovation." [3]

The High Line in New York City, USA, a park reusing a no longer functional elevated railway line on Manhattan's West Side, derives its specific ecosystem from the inspiration by the melancholic beauty of the wild vegetation that grew on the long-disused railway bed. The park comprises a "self-seeded" landscape of perennials, grasses, shrubs, and trees selected for their "hardiness, sustainability and textural and color variation, with a focus on native species,"[4] including many that already

JDS Architects, Premier Campus Office in Kagithane, Istanbul, Turkey, 2013, rendering.
OMA, Bryghusprojektet, Copenhagen, Denmark, 2008, rendering.

existed on the site. The High Line employs much of the same technology that is used for standard green roofs, including the reduction of stormwater, the mediation of the urban heat island effect, and the provision of a habitat for birds and insects. However, the High Line goes one step further to create a unified ecosystem, one that is actually reliant on the pre-existing structure. The railway bed provides a sort of second earth and thus modulates a self-contained ecosystem that is not coterminous with nature. The substrate placed on the industrial structure includes six distinct layers, whose sophisticated orchestration provides a highly specific alchemy of drainage, subsoil, topsoil, water retention, nutrition, and erosion resistance.

While airports, ports, and parks represent extremes of the infrastructure type of the dense and green paradigm, they also reveal some of the commonalities. All of the projects seek a warmer, naturalized environment where the quality of the human experience is paramount. They underscore, many mimetically, others through the manipulation of natural features such as light and water, the driving force of the integration of nature in both clarifying the logic and softening the feeling of structures that carry out massive functions essential to civic life.

Mixed-use

Innovative examples of mixed-use facilities blend many of the innovations mentioned earlier. As cities struggle with appropriating existing space for new use (an inherently "green" aim in and of itself), mixed-use facilities are at the forefront of the dense and green paradigm's potential to innovate a typology from the bottom up. One provocative example is JDS Architect's proposal for a mixed-use commercial project in Istanbul, Turkey. The building design is driven by the desire to have the architecture interact with its environment. The building opens up to the neighborhood and offers plazas, intimate gardens and generous terraces. The building volume is carved out to invite the surroundings in. The local hilly landscape is continued in the meandering both in plan, adapting to the site's edges, and in section, weaving into itself in a series of gentle curving slopes. On the upper levels, offices open out onto green terraces populated with lush vegetation, tempering Istanbul's hot springs and summers.

Even though this kind of topographic manipulation of the ground plane is by its very nature limited to the ground level, higher floor plates do not go uninflected by what happens on the ground. In the Bryghusgrunden mixed-use complex in Copenhagen,

Denmark, by OMA, the upper levels, while flat, are differentiated both in their span as well as their position in the building section, mimetically engaging the contour of the building's slow dip to a sunken point at ground level.

While there are excellent examples for innovative mixed-use facilities in the dense and green context, they remain, probably, the least recognizable typology. They feature mixtures of the previously described typological innovations in accordance with the respective mix of the various uses. Here may be found the capacity of the mixed-use type for some of the most creative and uncharted experimental ventures in typological innovation.

The following case studies are innovative examples for the five building types assessed in this book—institutions, offices, residences, infrastructure, and mixed-use facilities. Each one of them provides key data, descriptions, drawings, and photographs that allow for a systematic typological categorization and comparison across climate zones, building typologies, and densities. The case studies further identify key features of the dense and green paradigm that allow for an identification of larger architectural design strategies in the global trend towards dense and green building typologies.

1. Source: http://www.rpbw.com/project/68/california-academy-of-sciences/.
2. The discourse on transparency in architecture was initiated by Colin Rowe and Robert Slutzky with their publication *Transparency.* Basel: Birkhäuser, 1993.
3. Lubell, Sam. "Budding Relationship: The Merger of Landscape and Architecture is creating Fertile New Approaches to Building", in *The Architect's Newspaper,* 4 February 2011 (source: http://archpaper.com/news/articles.asp?id=5111).
4. Source: http://www.thehighline.org/design/planting.

DENISE + GREEN CASE STUDIES

Regional Chamber of Commerce and Industry of Picardie

Chartier-Corbasson Architectes

Building Type: Institutional
Climate Zone: Marine West Coast
Location: Mail Albert 1er,
80000 Amiens, France
Coordinates: 49°53'20"N 2°17'56"E
Date: 2012

Height: 18 m/6 floors, 1 basement
Gross Floor Area: 1,800 m²
Gross Green Area in Building: 383 m²
Gross Green Area to Built-Up Area: 21%

In 2007, the Regional Chamber of Commerce and Industry of Picardie organized an architectural competition to call for ideas for a 1,800 sqm, six-story extension to the existing Hôtel Bouctot-Vagniez, built as a marital home for the wealthy couple André Bouctot and Marie-Louise Vagniez in 1907. Louis Duthoit, a descendant of the Duthoit family of famous architects, artists, and sculptors, included floral motifs in the Art Nouveau style in the design. Serving changing uses, the building was classified as a French Heritage Monument in the 1990s.

The Art Nouveau motifs of the facade of the existing building are sensitively restored and the interior is redesigned as a reception area. The design for the extension on the neighboring plot, bordering sprawling gardens at the back of a series of townhouses as well as Rue Pierre l'Hermite and Mail Albert 1er, establishes a relationship with its surrounding environment that includes the extensive use of green features.

Green Features

Atrium

The extension is conceived as a dichotomy of two volumes that are combined by a green wall and a roof tapestry, the latter being seamlessly integrated with the surrounding landscape. The two volumes are separated by a void forming an atrium that, despite the narrowness of the plot, channels natural light into the core of the building. The atrium organizes the two volumes by establishing spatial and functional hierarchies. The first volume, a metal and glass structure, contains the access and service spaces of the extension. The second volume is a concrete structure covered with extensive green surfaces. Its pure geometrical forms are juxtaposed with greenery on walls and roofs to produce a subtle kind of overall shapelessness.

Glass bridges that lead from the service areas to the offices across the full-height atrium provide views of the adjacent avenues, the two volumes, and the heritage building: "All the essential features of the project are represented in a plinth of living greenery that creates a link between the new wing, the existing premises and the gardens. The offices will be situated above this greenery plinth."[1] The plinth of greenery, as the architects describe it, gradually descends into a landscaped garden that integrates both the green and the hardscape, using locally sourced stone to create a texture that evokes both traditional Japanese as well as Art Nouveau gardens.

"Living Greenery" and Rainwater Harvesting

The architects describe the green walls and undulating roof as being inspired by traditional Japanese gardens, whereas the choice of the plants was guided by the design for the original landscape. This resulted in a wondrously woven tapestry of "living greenery,"[2] comprised of climbing plants and a mixture of flowering and non-flowering vegetation. It softens the facade and produces an intertwining of organic and static surfaces. The overall fluid shape of the surfaces was made possible with the engineering of a crinoline-like steel structure. A system of purlins was integrated into the steel framework to accommodate layers of substrate suspended on the inside.

The plants are not only aesthetically appealing but are also meant to improve the surrounding air quality. A recent study by the German Karlsruhe Institute of Technology (KIT) found that green walls that are located in areas where concentrations of pollutants are highest have an exponentially greater effect on air quality than green roofs or plants located in parks, as especially climbing plants filter nitrogen oxide (N_2O) and microscopic particles such as fine dust from the air.[3] The World Health Organization (WHO) has published reports that more than one million people worldwide die from the consequences of such air pollution every year. Walls of grass, ivy, and other plants create an air filtration system that can reduce pollution by more than 10%.

A closed-circuit rainwater harvesting system is integrated in the steel structure. The water is channeled from the surfaces of the green walls and roofs to temporary storage areas below the framework and used to water the plants, creating a small self-sustaining ecosystem.[4]

Facade Technology

The facades of the new building were designed in terms of their angled solar orientations. Double screens minimize the intake of direct sunlight into the interiors on the street side while large panoramic bay windows are placed in the green wall-roof, clad in metal in a dark finish that complements the green tapestry on the courtyard side. The metal claddings are chamfered at their edges to direct more natural daylight into the interior.[5]

The southern facade of the extension is angled as a double skin of metal screens,[6] providing a sunshading system that balances optimization of natural daylighting, interior lighting conditions, and privacy. Areas behind the angled screens that receive the most direct sunlight throughout the year are optimized such that their greater material density also creates a heat shield. For programs

that require privacy, the metal mesh is further differentiated through a denser gradient. The varying porosity of the metal mesh allows for the calibration of natural in addition to mechanical ventilation. The use of metal as a material for the mesh screens, contrasting with the sinuous green of the northern facade, blends with the existing streetscape that it fronts and integrates it with its brick context.[7]

Critique

The elegant, energy-efficient extension project juxtaposes not just old and new buildings, but also traditional and modern gardens. The use of greenery is extended beyond landscaping to become a seamless architectural language that unites old and new, varying programs and porosity, as well as building and nature.

1. Travino, Santi, and Josep M. Minguet (eds.). *Bio Architecture*. Barcelona: Monsa, 2014.
2. Frearson, Amy. "Regional Chamber of Commerce and Industry." Dezeen, 2012 (source: http://www.dezeen.com/2012/10/16/regional-chamber-of-commerce-and-industry-with-green-walls-by-chartier-corbasson-architectes/).
3. Defreitas, Susan. "Meet the Chamber of Commerce for the Shire." earthtechling, 2012 (source: http://earthtechling.com/2012/10/meet-the-chamber-of-commerce-for-the-shire/).
4. Gonzalez, Xavier. "Camouflaged Commerce" in *A10.eu*, n. 49 (January/February 2013 (source: http://www.a10.eu/magazine/issues/49/camouflaged_commerce_amiens.html).
5. Hudson, Danny. "Chartier Corbasson Architectes: Regional Chamber of Commerce and Industry." Designboom, 2012 (source: http://www.designboom.com/architecture/chartier-corbasson-architectes-regional-chamber-of-commerce-and-industry/).
6. "Regional Chamber of Commerce and Industry/Chartier-Corbasson Architects." ArchDaily, 2012 (source: http://www.archdaily.com/284238/regional-chamber-of-commerce-and-industry-chartier-corbasson-architects/).
7. Laylin, Tafline. "Spectacular Japanese Vertical Garden Clads the Picardy Regional Chamber of Commerce and Industry in France." inhabitat, 2012 (source: http://inhabitat.com/spectacular-japanese-style-vertical-garden-clads-the-picardy-regional-chamber-of-commerce-and-industry-in-france/).

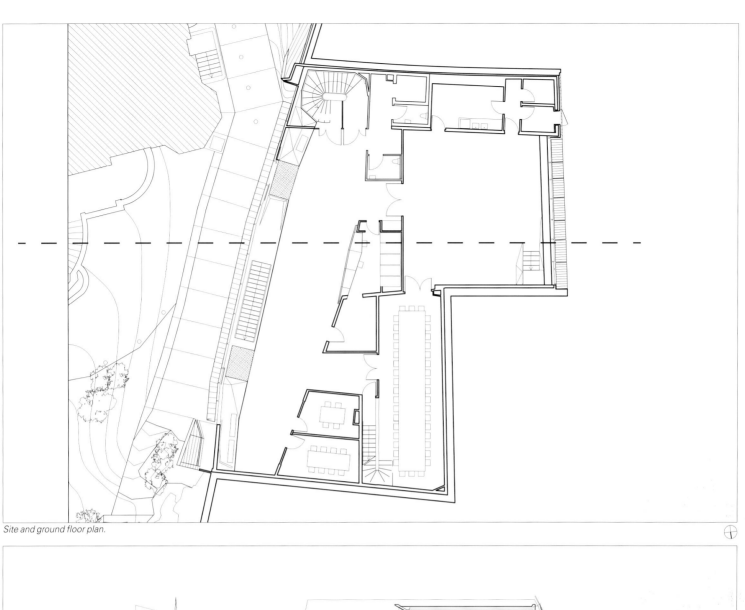

Site and ground floor plan.

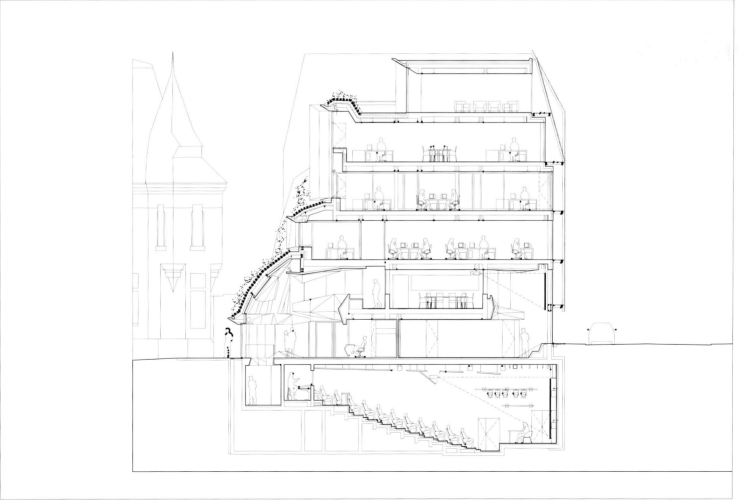

Section.

Brooklyn Botanic Garden Visitor Center

Weiss/Manfredi

Building Type: Institutional
Climate Zone: Humid Continental
Location: 990 Washington Avenue,
Brooklyn, NY 11225, USA
Coordinates: 40°40'10"N 73°57'45"W
Date: 2012

Height: 9 m/1 floor + mezzanine
Gross Floor Area: 2,044 m²
Gross Green Area in Building: 930 m²
Gross Green Area to Built-Up Area: 44%

"Being able to design a building that is as much embedded within as it is extending the systems of the pathways, discoveries and unfolding vistas—and the extent to which the building can capture those identities—is really about inverting the paradigm of a building freestanding on the landscape as an object."

–Marion Weiss, Weiss/Manfredi[1]

In designing the Botanic Garden's new visitor center, Brooklyn-based architecture firm Weiss/Manfredi Architecture/Landscape/Urbanism takes a novel approach to the building's presence in the context of plants. The center is neither a garden pavilion nor an inhabitable landscape, but rather merges the built environment with naturalistic landscapes. From the siting and massing of the project to the sequencing of spaces and use of materials, the building shifts the visitors' relationship to the surrounding city and landscape.

Shifting the Site

The 100-year-old Brooklyn Botanic Garden is located in the heart of Brooklyn, adjacent to Prospect Park designed by Frederick Law Olmsted. The triangular garden is bounded on three sides by heavily trafficked streets—on the north by Eastern Parkway and the Brooklyn Museum, on the east by Washington Avenue, and on the west by Flatbush Avenue. In contrast to the local species found in the Olmstedian landscapes of Prospect Park, Brooklyn Botanic Garden is a showcase of distinctly themed gardens from around the world, such as the Japanese Garden, the Cherry Esplanade, the Osborne Garden, the Overlook, and the Cranford Rose Garden.[2] These gardens unfold before the viewer as a series of discrete spaces. However, again compared to its larger neighbor, the Brooklyn Botanic Garden has always been a "secret garden," hidden behind the high berms and trees of its urban perimeter.

The visitor center is intended to define an entrance from the city into the garden, but also to bring the garden into the city. In an invited request-for-proposals process, the designers questioned the site as defined by the Brooklyn Botanic Garden master plan. The original site sat atop an existing berm that separates the Brooklyn Museum parking lot from the Botanic Garden.[3] In placing the building there, an existing gingko tree alley would have had to be displaced and the building would have sat awkwardly at the terminus of the main axis of the Cherry Esplanade. Instead, Weiss/Manfredi proposed that the building be relocated to enhance the garden's strong relationship with the urban context along Washington Avenue. The new location seamlessly draws visitors into the garden, while also preserving and integrating it

closely with the cherished gingko tree alley. The result is a building that simultaneously brings the public to the garden but also presents the institutional values of the Brooklyn Botanic Garden to the public.[4]

Space Woven into the Garden's Trees

In shifting the site to Washington Avenue, Weiss/Manfredi set highly restrictive site constraints to preserve existing trees and other historic landscape features, forcing them to position and shape the building within the found space of the existing garden.[5] The result is a 177-m-long building volume, providing 1,858 sqm of space woven into the garden's trees.[6] The project's three distinct masses are embedded in the adjacent berm and connected by an undulating green roof, which allows the building to unfold before the visitors in a way that immediately draws them into the garden. The sequence begins along Washington Avenue where the building presents a modest facade of concrete, steel, and glass that ties in with the other Brooklyn Botanic Garden buildings further down the street. Simultaneously, an intimately scaled paved plaza welcomes visitors off the street and directs them between the gift shop occupying the street side mass, the ticketing counters embedded within the exhibition and an administration volume. Visitors are drawn deeper into the garden beneath the dappled light of a glazed canopy, which stitches these volumes together. The glazed masses are embedded into the berm, disappearing into the dappled light of the trees and canopy and revealing exhibition spaces, among them a gingko-paneled space that occupies the final building mass. A retaining wall emerges from the hillside and leads visitors toward the garden's iconic Cherry Esplanade.

This strategy, comprised of overlapping interwoven architectural and landscape components, reinforces the slippages that move the visitor center beyond an object-based design strategy typical of garden pavilions in Olmsted's landscapes and instead toward an architecture of seamless transition between interior and exterior—an experience-based design strategy in which the building actively curates the views and experiences of the visitors and brings them in closer contact with the surrounding environment.

The Vegetation

Rather than solely minimizing its impact, the building design improves the *status quo* of the Botanic Garden. With 3,900 sqm of freshly planted landscape surrounding the structures, including 930 sqm of undulating green roof stretching across its

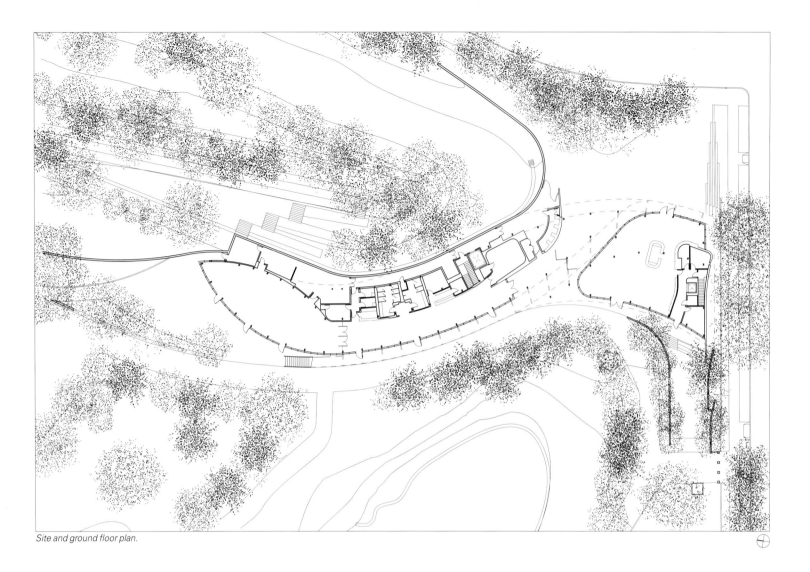

Site and ground floor plan.

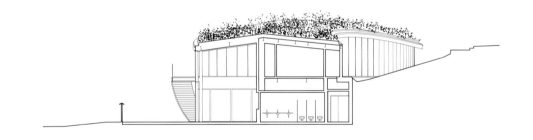

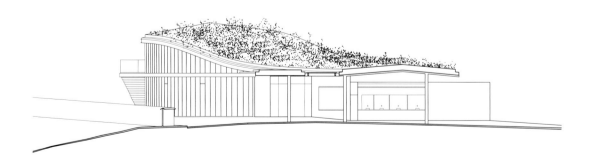

Sections.

three volumes, the building completely reorganizes the northeast corner of the garden. As part of the project's environmental strategy, Weiss/Manfredi, in conjunction with landscape architect HMWhite, developed a rainwater strategy that absorbs, filters, directs, and retains nearly 757,000 liters of water each year from the green roof alone. A complex system of green roofs, bioswales, and collection basins ultimately directs the water to the Japanese Hill and Pond Garden.[7] Throughout this system, a range of native plants was selected for specific moisture and runoff conditions. This required specifically engineered soils to meet each species' performance criteria, slope, and adjacencies.[8] These complex water systems become an educational showcase as the visitor center's exhibitions extend to include the Rain Garden basins in the plaza just outside of the double-height exhibition area.

The design and shape of the project's green roof is based on the simultaneous needs to collect water efficiently and to provide proper solar orientation for the continued growth of the plants. Given the complex shape of the building in plan, these ambitions were at times in conflict with each other, creating challenging geometric design criteria. For example, the undulating planted roof, which ranges in slope from 4° to 27°, provided structural as well as landscape engineering challenges.[9] As with other areas of the landscape, more special soils were designed, again based on the specificities of the orientation, water requirements, plant types, and roof slopes. Another example is the building construction of 29 hollow steel section rigid frames that allow for the required diversity in the geometry, but more importantly provide spatial diversity on the interior to match the range of spaces found in the gardens beyond.[10] Mediating the relationship between the interior and the exterior is the curtain wall, which is fritted to create a veiled separation between the two, minimize heat gain, and optimize natural lighting.[11]

The building is partially embedded into the southern slope of the berm that separates the Botanic Garden from the Brooklyn Museum's parking lot. This decision allows for taking advantage of the insulating benefits of the earth, underscoring the innate connection to the landscape. Furthermore, 28 geothermal wells heat and cool the building, supplemented by the utility grid only as needed.[12] The building's southern exposure provides strong sunlight into the exhibition and public spaces. Subtle fritting on the curtain wall and canopy further dapple the sunlight coming through the surrounding trees, maintaining comfortable light levels throughout the year. The working and administrative spaces are pushed to the north and are lit through clerestory windows where the building extends above the berm.

Critique

The Brooklyn Botanic Garden Visitor Center redefines the relationships between city, architecture, nature, and ecology. The building serves as an educational showpiece not only through the exhibits, but also in the way in which it is sited within the surrounding garden. Rather than integrating plants with the architecture, it is a building that integrates the architecture with plants, effectively redefining the garden pavilion from an object to a series of thresholds. These thresholds introduce the visitors to the garden as a sequence of spaces, vistas, and experiences. The project provides a potential reality of the future of the city—where plants, people, and buildings seamlessly coexist without finite boundaries but rather as a series of overlapping and intertwined systems.

1. Van Loon, Benjamin. "Edge Condition" in *Green Building & Design,* March/April 2013.
2. Brooklyn Botanic Garden Visitor Center—Architect's Statement, Weiss/Manfredi, 2012.
3. Gendall, John. "Brooklyn Botanic Garden Visitor Center" in *Architect,* July 2012
(source: http://www.architectmagazine.com/cultural-projects/brooklyn-botanic-garden-
visitor-center.aspx).
4. Iovine, Julie. "When a Ticket-Taker and Turnstile Aren't Enough" in *Wall Street Journal,*
15 May 2012.
5. Gendall, John. "Brooklyn Botanic Garden …"
6. Pearson, Clifford. "Groundswell." in *Architectural Record,* July 2012. pp. 74-79.
7. "Visitor Center Landscape." Brooklyn Botanic Garden Visitor Center
(source: http://www.bbg.org/discover/gardens/visitor_center#/tabs-4).
8. "Brooklyn Botanic Garden Visitors Center." ASLA Professional Award
(*source:* http://www.asla.org/2013awards/274.html).
9. Brooklyn Botanic Garden. "Visitor Center Landscape …"
10. Webber, Gwen. "In Detail: Brooklyn Botanic Garden" in *Architect's Newspaper,*
9 May 2012.
11. Ibid.
12. Brooklyn Botanic Garden. "Visitor Center Landscape …"

Khoo Teck Puat Hospital

CPG Consultants/RMJM Hillier

Building Type: Institutional
Climate Zone: Tropical Wet
Location: 90 Yishun Central,
Singapore 768828
Coordinates: 1°25'27"N 103°50'18"E
Date: 2010

Height: 30.9 m/7 floors, 2 basements
Gross Floor Area: 109,000 m²
Number of units: 588 beds
Gross Green Area in Building: 14,000 m²
Gross Green Area to Built-Up Area: 13%

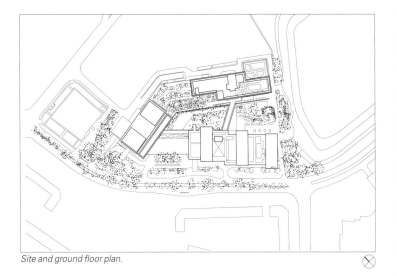

Site and ground floor plan.

The design of Khoo Teck Puat Hospital (KTPH) aims to foster physical, mental and social wellbeing in addition to providing medical care to support the institutional culture of providing a holistic approach to the healing process. One of the project's main features is its strong relationship with the urban context, which includes a lush public park and a large pond that is addressed through a whole range of careful design considerations, including building orientation, massing, and facade design. Architecturally as well as programmatically, patients, visitors, and the community at large are able to engage with the gardens, thereby providing Singapore with a diverse institution that benefits and is benefitted by the surrounding community.

"Hospital in a Garden, Garden in a Hospital"

The development of the hospital typology has been closely tied to that of medical thinking. The benefit of the integration of nature within healthcare facilities has been examined since Plato and Aristotle's early ideas of health and wellness, in which man is seen as living in unity with nature. Light and air were valued as key components of the healing process.[1] By the middle of the 20th Century, however, medical science had developed a new understanding of disease, and healthcare took a pathogenic approach to healing where disease was seen as an intrusion on our natural state of salubrity. Simultaneously, building technology such as air conditioning became commonplace, allowing for increased concerns over infections and contamination to push the evolution of hospital design toward a hermetically sealed and sterile environment planned primarily from a doctor's perspective.[2] The belief that efficiency equals effectiveness overshadowed the patients' wellness, as overall wellbeing was marginalized in favor of clinical models of efficiency.

More recently, gardens have increasingly been incorporated, be it in therapeutic settings, terminal wards, or living environments for Alzheimer patients as a means of providing well-being and enlivening the experience. This development is representative of a more nuanced view of human health, which supports the WHO's definition of health as inclusive of psychological and social factors.[3] Studies of these healing, or caregiving, environments, which take into account more holistic measures of wellbeing (physical, mental, and social), confirm the benefits of spaces that provide patients with opportunities for independent activity, social engagement, and physical activity in the presence of a natural environment.[4]

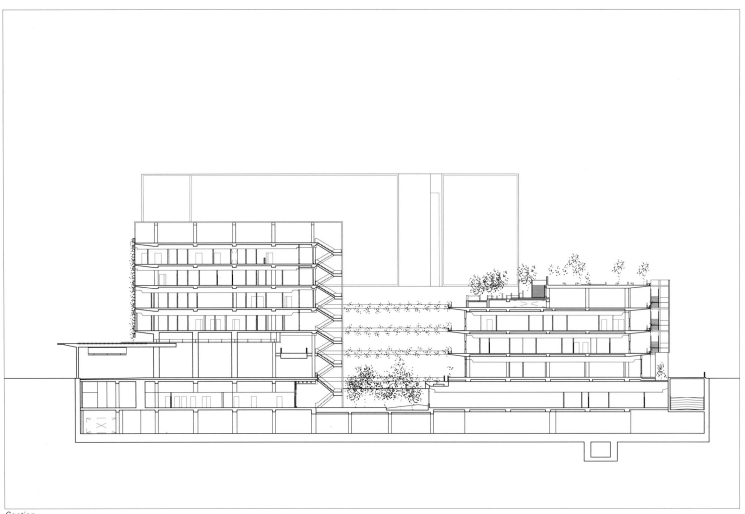

Section.

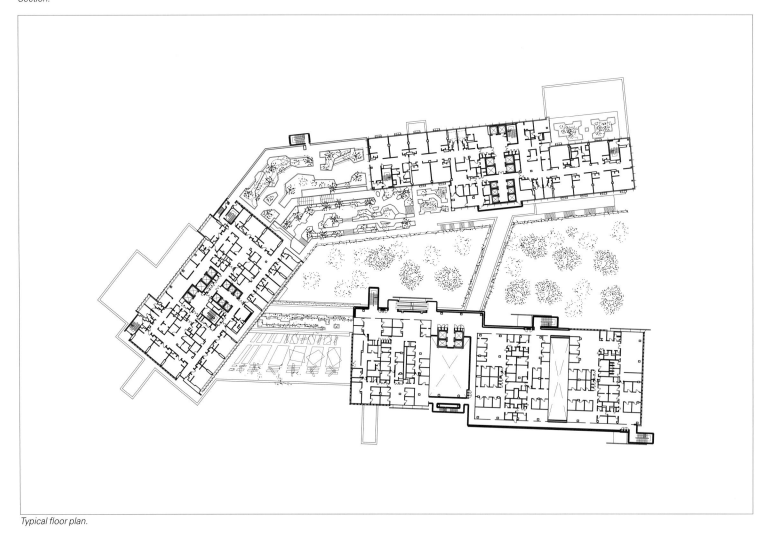

Typical floor plan.

The design of KTPH questions the reductive nature of restricting planted areas and proposes the alternative model of a "hospital in a garden, garden in a hospital." By blurring the distinction between landscape and architecture in an effort to improve healing, patients are brought into a dialogue with a healthy and sustainable environment. It is through this lens that the qualitative benefits of providing strong connections between interior and exterior and planted areas within a healthcare project can be evaluated relative to a typical facility.

Site Selection

In the context of a campaign to expand Singapore's medical facilities with a series of full-service, community-oriented hospitals, one such facility was slated to serve the northern communities of Woodlands, Yishun, and Sengkang, easing the pressure on the centrally located Tan Tock Seng Hospital.[5] The selected site was an overgrown greenfield in central Yishun, largely surrounded by public housing. In order to support the Singapore Urban Redevelopment Authority's desire to create lively full-service town centers with amenities close by, the specific site was selected directly adjacent to the existing Yishun Polyclinic, which would allow the two facilities to conveniently complement one another. Furthermore, the hospital was located within easy walking distance of the Yishun MRT Station and Bus Interchange, allowing convenient access by public transport. Most importantly, two green spaces border the site—Yishun Pond, the previously underdeveloped stormwater retention pond directly to the northeast, and Yishun Park to the east, across the main road of Yishun Central.[6] By situating the hospital at the western terminus of this greenbelt, the Singapore Ministry of Health provided a site with the potential for the adjacent green spaces to serve as a catalyst for the hospital's relationship to its surroundings and to enhance the vibrancy of its own outdoor spaces as essential elements of the design.

Layout Optimization: Enhancing Connections

The brief for the new hospital was in many ways a straightforward one: "…build a hospital … with patients unambiguously at the centre of the focus … a hassle-free hospital."[7] Requirements included subsidized and private wards as well as a full range of medical specialist and emergency facilities. CPG Consultants developed a scheme that responded to the potential of the adjacent green spaces by integrating them with key programmatic elements through the development of the concept of "hospital in a garden, garden in the hospital." Additionally, the hierarchies typically found within a hospital were redistributed to simplify and improve the user experience of the hospital.

KTPH is broken up into three mid-rise towers, ranging from six to ten stories. Tower A, located at the western edge of the site, houses the private wards. Tower B, situated at the northeast corner, is the tallest of the three towers and comprises the subsidized wards. Tower C borders on the main road of Yishun Central and contains the specialist outpatient clinics. Each of the three towers provides strong visual and physical connections to the exterior gardens as well as to the surrounding community. The buildings are connected on the lower levels by a U-shaped, terraced, and planted plinth, which provides direct access to the redeveloped Yishun Pond. In breaking away from typical hospital planning, which places centralized service areas at the heart of a large flexible floor plate, KTPH employs a more porous layout strategy that

results in a fragmented massing, allowing for stronger connections with the surrounding community while increasing the potential for natural ventilation.[8]

Forward thinking through the design of the building and development of operational practices has allowed KTPH to become a hallmark of efficiency despite its relatively small bed-count. Putting the planning of the patient wards at the forefront of the design process allows the hospital team to better deploy its resources to its patients. To undertake this task, the design team along with the hospital administration explored Toyota's lean manufacturing process. By placing the product at the center of the assembly line, Toyota seeks to empower those on the ground to eliminate inefficiency. This idea has been employed at KTPH in a number of ways. Key adjacencies and configurations were rethought from the ground up. A principle was that patient services were co-located within each department—the x-ray facilities were located adjacent to orthopedic surgeons and the pharmacy was placed adjacent to the exit.

Integration of Green Space—Connect with Community

The dispersed massing of the building allows for a variety of relationships between architecture and landscape. The gardens take the form of roof gardens, exterior corridor planters, and planter boxes built into the facade. Gardens range from densely forested canopies, orchards, and flowers to a community-supported fruit and vegetable farm.[9] Their implementation is guided by three principles: gardens should be practical and self-sustaining, be created with people and nature in mind, and be energy- and resource-efficient.[10] These principles are manifested in a variety of ways throughout the project. A diverse arrangement of gardens relative to the architecture provides patients and visitors with a range of opportunities. They can make choices, seek privacy, and experience a sense of control; gather together and experience social support; move around and exercise; and engage with nature.[11]

In addition to the direct health benefits provided by the gardens, three features serve to extend the building's impact on the surrounding community—increased biodiversity, water reuse, and food production. In order to create more self-sufficient gardens, which are able to flourish with little human interference, the majority of the gardens were planted at a natural density with local species of plants. As the site is understood as part of a larger green belt, this strategy promotes biodiversity on the site. Additionally, KTPH's water balance acknowledges and engages these larger ecologies, as Yishun Pond is utilized as a source of irrigation water for all of its gardens during dry periods. Conversely, during Singapore's torrential wet periods, the hospital's gardens allow to absorb and retain far more water than a typical building of this kind would be able to do, which eases the pressure on Yishun Pond. Before KTPH was built, Yishun Pond was solely an infrastructural component of the community. By drawing the pond into the hospital's ecology, it was further developed with a more extensive planting program as well as running and biking trails that create seamless connections between the hospital and its surroundings.

The extent of the planting at KTPH had a remarkable influence on the surrounding community and established the hospital as a civic institution that the neighboring residents take pride in. The community was brought in to assist in planning and maintaining the rooftop vegetable gardens and some of the other key green

features. The produce is consumed by those working in the gardens but is also used in the hospital cafeteria. Such outreach programs serve to improve the familiarity and comfort levels of the community with the hospital. [12]

Facade Design

The facade of KPTH is designed in a way that creates meaningful connections between interior and exterior spaces while responding to specific programmatic and climatic requirements of the hospital wards. The facade design varies between the three main building volumes for functional reasons, while formally this differentiation serves to break down the scale of the complex, providing distinct identity to its parts. The hospital projects a welcoming atmosphere to the surrounding community, minimizing the often-imposing nature of hospital complexes. Furthermore, the facades play a key role in improving the patients' thermal comfort and they also reinforce the concept of "nature as nurture" throughout the building by improving visual as well as physical access to green spaces.

While the subsidized wards are naturally ventilated, the private wards and clinical specialist block are mechanically conditioned spaces. They therefore employ a more straightforward, yet equally thoughtful approach. Fixed screens modulate direct sunlight and glare, while maximizing views to the exterior gardens. Operable windows, with a switch system connected to the air conditioning, allow for natural ventilation on cool days, or when there is strong airflow. [13] These techniques also serve to break down the scale of the private ward as seen from the outside. Furthermore, on the clinical specialist block, the vertical circulation and corridors are pushed to the exterior, which engages the public with the gardens and activates the facades. The vertical circulation stairs are enclosed with a vertical louver system, which further articulates the block along the street.

In order to provide physiological comfort in the naturally ventilated subsidized ward, the design team employed a number of simple but very effective techniques, which come together to form a cohesive strategy. Layouts and orientation maximize cross-ventilation while retaining patient privacy and comfort. The design team determined that a wind speed of at least 0.6 m/s would provide adequate thermal comfort for the patients, while providing a reduction in mechanical ventilation consumption of up to 60%. This wind speed was achieved through the use of an operable and modular jalousie window system that reduces glare, improves airflow, and minimizes rain penetration. Additionally, wing walls are designed on the facade to increase pressure build-up between the interior and exterior, maximizing airflow even when there is no wind. Light shelves are integrated into the wing wall system in order to reduce glare and improve the quality of light transmitted to the interior, reducing solar heat gains associated with direct sunlight as well as the energy required for lighting. [14] As the subsidized ward is the largest in terms of height, planter boxes are integrated into the depth of the wing walls in the facades, which brings the gardens directly into the ward and reinforces their impact on the hospital setting.

Critique

In adopting a patient-first attitude, novel relationships emerged from a complex layering of design features in KTPH: relationships between building and landscape, institution and community,

site and surroundings, as well as staff and patient. In a time when civic buildings exhibit an increasing tendency to utilize symbolic means to engage with the surrounding community, the project relies on more strategic approaches that allow for a large number of diverse and varied interactions. As such, KTPH provides a model for rethinking healthcare facilities from a patient perspective as well as the role of the institution within the community. In the end, the project's ability to engage the continued evolution of the hospital as a place of healing will be evaluated based on the improvements it provides to the quality and efficiency of healthcare. In the case of KTPH, the extensive inclusion of green elements plays a key role in achieving this goal and has produced an exemplary building typology innovation. While the project can be seen as a culmination of site, context, client, climate, and brief, it sets a new standard in terms of its ambition.

1. Dilani, Alan. "A New Paradigm of Design and Health." Paper presented at the 3rd World Design and Health Congress and Exhibition, Montreal, 25-29 June 2003.
2. Marcus, Clare Cooper. "Gardens and Health." Paper presented at the 2nd World Design and Health Congress and Exhibition, Stockholm, 2000.
3. Dilani, Alan. "A New Paradigm …"
4. Marcus, Clare Cooper. "Gardens and Health …"
5. "Northern General Hospital (Yishun) to open before 2010 to help ease patient load at TTSH." Channelnewsasia, 15 August 2005.
6. "400-bed Hospital for the North in Yishun Central" in The Straits Times, 23 March 2004.
7. Boon Wan Khaw, Singapore Parliamentary Debate, 17 March 2004.
8. "President's Design Award 2011 Project Write Up." Design Singapore (source: http://www.designsingapore.org/pda_public/gallery.aspx?sid=844).
9. A Healing Space: Creating Biodiversity at Khoo Teck Puat Hospital. Singapore: Corporate Communications Department, Alexandra Health System, 2013.
10. "Khoo Teck Puat Hospital: Healing Gardens" in FuturArc, vol. 22, 3rd quarter 2011.
11. Marcus, Clare Cooper. "Gardens and Health …"
12. Dilani, Alan, "A New Paradigm …"
13. "Khoo Teck Puat Hospital: Healing Gardens." in FuturArc, vol. 22, 3rd quarter 2011.
14. Ibid.

School of the Arts

WOHA

Building Type: Institutional
Climate Zone: Tropical Wet
Location: 1 Zubir Said Drive,
Singapore 227968
Coordinates: 1°17'57"N 103°50'55"E
Date: 2010

Height: 57 m/8 floors
Gross Floor Area: 52,945 m²
Site Area: 10,657 m²
Gross Green Area in Building: 8,893 m²
Gross Green Area to Built-Up Area: 17%
Gross Green to Site Area: 83%

The School of the Arts (SOTA) is Singapore's first specialized and independent pre-tertiary-education arts school. Situated in the heart of the Civic District, at the gateway to the Arts and Entertainment District, the building combines a high-density, inner-city school with a professional performing arts venue. The site is located along Bras Basah Road in the south and Prinsep Street in the west and faces the Cathay Building, a historical landmark and Singapore's first skyscraper, which initially served as the headquarters for the British Malaya Broadcasting Corporation.[1]

A Dialogue Between Indoor and Outdoor Environments

As the winner of the competition for the project, WOHA designed the building as a large, dense, yet perforated volume that establishes a dialogue between indoor and outdoor environments in a tropical urban context. The duality of its internal and external spaces is derived from the design brief[2] that asked for the school to be a place for exchange between students, between teachers and students, the school and the surrounding urban fabric, and the school and the wider community. This is manifested architecturally by two visually connected horizontal strata, which the architects refer to as "Backdrop" and "Blank Canvas."[3]

The Backdrop is a large podium containing a concert hall, a drama theater, a black box theater, and several small informal performing spaces. It is against this backdrop, designed as a faceted sculptural space that highlights views to the surrounding city, that the School communicates with the public urban realm through a number of spaces. High-volume, naturally ventilated, informal spaces between the performance areas surround an "urban shortcut," with meandering pedestrian flows abstractly inscribed to varied stone floor patterns. A civic amphitheater is created next to a number of conserved trees; this space has become very popular since the opening of SOTA, with curious pedestrians who find themselves veering off from the public pavements to the cool and shaded plaza. The Backdrop entails retail shops and a covered public walkway that references a typology reminiscent of the distinctive five-foot ways of Singapore shophouses that resided at this site in the early 20ᵗʰ Century.

The accentuated and lushly landscaped West Plaza features tiered planters complementing two large conserved trees. The space provides a public linkage to another large plaza in front of the Cathay Building across Bras Basah Road. West Plaza is mirrored on a smaller scale by East Plaza, establishing an internal public street. Two lecture theaters are located along the diagonal axis on the building's second story, which fronts the concourses.

The two triple-volume concourses connect between the horizontal stratification of Level 2 and 3, providing visual porosity while maintaining axial relationships. A mechanical transfer level at Level 4 subtly buffers between the two horizontal strata of the Backdrop and the Blank Canvas. The accommodation and thereby concealment of all mechanical services here frees up the roof level for a landscaped recreational park.[4]

The Blank Canvas is introduced on Level 5 and upwards, housing the more simple spaces of the secured school areas. The metaphor chosen by the architects suggests the intended flexibility in terms of use. Three long rectangular volumes have a secured point of access. Gantries are located strategically along the circulation pathways and visually connected through the porosity of the overall massing. Bridges on Level 7 connect classrooms and activity rooms, which are separated by a void to allow for quiet and loud zones. Sky terraces from Levels 8 to 10 offer indoor-to-outdoor extensions of the classrooms and studios *vis-à-vis* the learning environment.

As classrooms, studios, and circulation areas are all naturally ventilated, open corridors along the facade allow for the classrooms to be set back and avoid heat gains and glare. The open corridors are interspersed with planters and vertical greenery that create a relaxing backdrop to the high level of activity of the city below. Green facades function as environmental filters, cut out glare and dust, and keep the building's interior cool. In addition, they help to reduce the traffic noise of the surrounding city. The circulation sequence culminates in a large recreational park featuring an integrated running track. While the building's orientation follows that of the site, organized along the east-west axis to minimize heat gains, the volumes on the upper levels are manipulated such that they can catch prevalent winds to allow for a maximum of natural cross-ventilation. This leads to comfortable climatic conditions throughout the building.

Greenery weaves through the entire building, from the horizontally tiered lush landscapes of the street-level plaza to the vertical facade greenery and through the core, with interconnected sky terraces and complemented by a balanced palette of materials that range from light grey powder-coated aluminum mesh screens to regionally sourced dark brown timber panels, and from patterned metal screens to prefabricated concrete planter beds.

The spatial arrangement of the breezeways allows at the same time for natural lighting of classrooms and studio spaces. The facades of the breezeways are splayed three-dimensionally

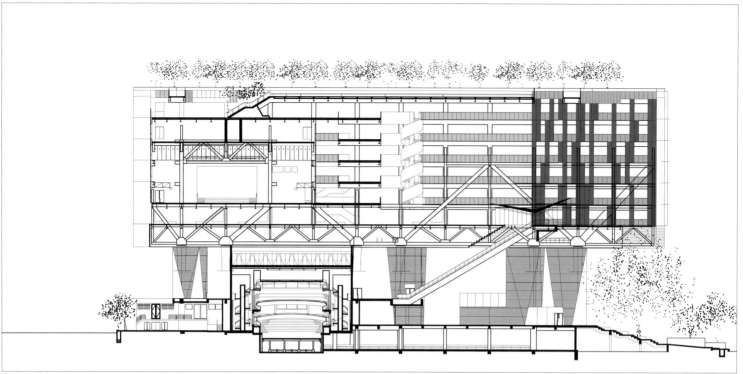

Sectional view.

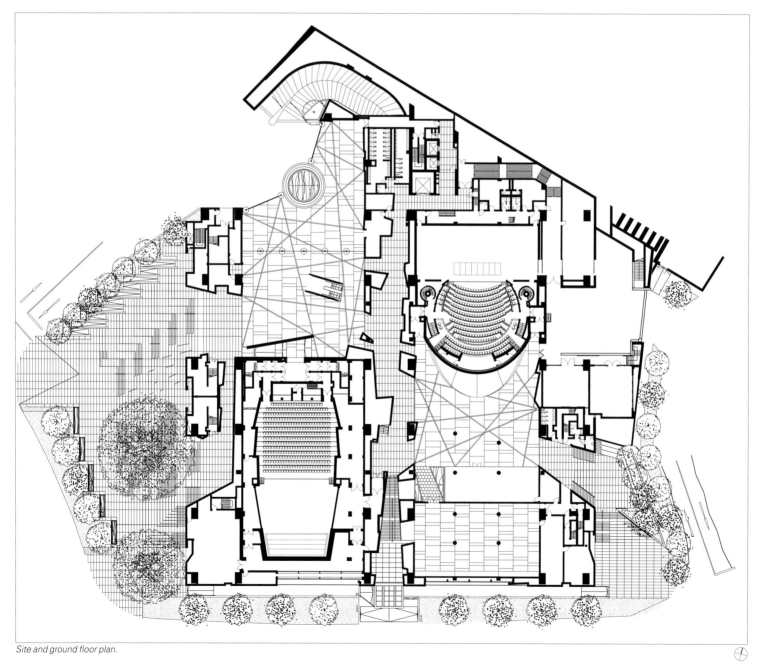

Site and ground floor plan.

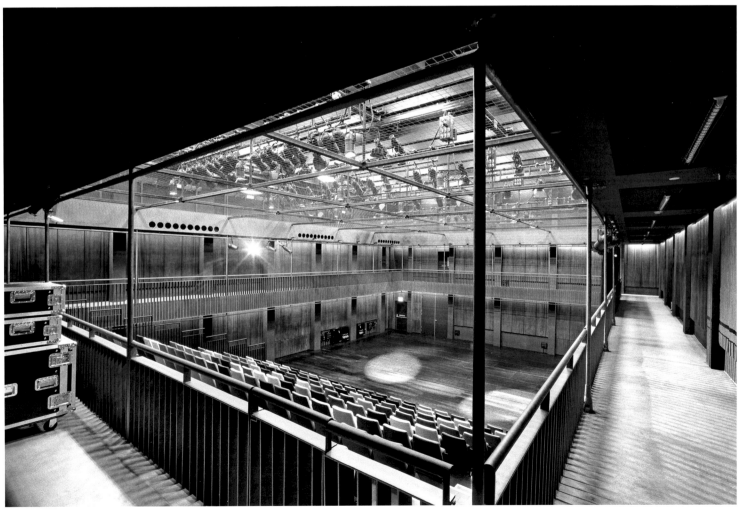

to allow for better cross-ventilation. The breezeways are framed by green facades that are part of the facades facing Bras Basah Road and Prinsep Street from Levels 4 to 10. The diagonal derivative from the urban fabric axes is the basis for a formal language of wooden panels that shield the Level 2 concourse from direct solar radiation and provide shading for the triangulated tinted glass facade along Prinsep Street. The glass and timber elements work in tandem to mitigate rain ingress to the interior triple-volume spaces.

The facade articulation is completed with custom-galvanized iron railings that, together with the lush foliage of the vertical greenery, reduce heat gain and produce beautiful shadow patterns over the course of the day. The vertical green foliage, *Epipremnum Aureum*, is an apt selection of an evergreen vine that climbs up the prefabricated modular wire mesh panels positioned between the railings. These panels are distributed in a seemingly variegated vertical pattern that offers a green relief from the harsh urban concrete-and-glass environment surrounding the building. This detail reappears on the sky terraces located within the center of the building. It allows for easy maintenance and watering of the plants, doing away with the need for complicated and expensive gondola systems or building maintenance units. Located behind the vertical green foliage are precast planters that line the common corridors, planted with broad-leaved shrubs. The generous breezeways on Levels 9 and 10 are designed as pocket gardens for students to meet among beautifully framed views of the city along the east and west facades.

Breezeways, bridges, sky terraces, and sky gardens together provide a system of open spaces that reduce heat gain and help absorb pollution through a selection of lush, broad-leaved plants and vines. Sky bridges at the roof level, located above the garden terraces between the academic blocks, provide circulation access as well as a 400 m running track for students and staff. [5]

Critique

WOHA's approach to sustainability is largely based on passive design strategies and shows interesting similarities to those of architects Kerry Hill and Geoffrey Bawa, albeit with a contemporary selection of materials and a different formal language. This approach is continued in WOHA's subsequent projects such as the Iluma on Victoria Street and PARKROYAL on Pickering.

1. Bingham-Hall, Patrick. *WOHA*. Vol. 1: *Selected Projects*. Singapore: Pesaro Publishing, 2011.
2. "Our History." School of the Arts, 2013 (source: http://www.sota.edu.sg/TheSchool/OurHistory/tabid/65/Default.aspx).
3. "School of the Arts, Singapore - Architect's Statement." WOHA, 2013 (source: http://www.woha.net/#School-of-the-Arts).
4. "URA's masterplanning efforts for Bras Basah.Bugis district win prestigious Urban Land Institute Award for Excellence 2008: Asia Pacific." URA, 11 July 2008 (source: http://www.ura.gov.sg/pr/text/2008/pr08-73.html).
5. Busenkell, Michaela, and Peter Cachola Schmal (eds.). WOH*A: Breathing Architecture*. Munich: Prestel, 2011.

Nanyang Technological University Learning Hub

Heatherwick Studio/CPG Consultants

Building Type: Institutional
Climate Zone: Tropical Wet
Location: 50 Nanyang Avenue,
Singapore 639798
Coordinates: 1°20'35"N 103°40'57"E
Date: 2015

Height: 39 m/8 floors
Gross Floor Area: 14,000 m²
Gross Green Area in Building: 950 m²
Gross Green Area to Built-Up Area: 7%

In recent years, as increasing amounts of information become available universally through technology, the role of the university is shifting from a holder of knowledge to an attractor of people. People—faculty, researchers, and students—are a major component of a university's capital. Universities are therefore asking architects to develop new types of spaces, programs, and buildings that promote and provide spaces for encounters between the various groups. The design of the Nanyang Technological University (NTU) South Spine Learning Hub addresses these developments through the integration of green elements that serve as both environmental and social mediators, interconnecting large communal spaces with small intimate ones.

NTU's 2011 campus master plan is based on Kenzo Tange's original idea of a "university in the garden." The master plan calls for updated academic, residential, and social spaces while retaining the overall feeling of the original campus abutting a large forested area in the western reaches of Singapore. It seeks to define particular relationships between the soon-to-be-constructed buildings and the existing landscape through the preservation and restoration of key ecological features throughout the campus. The integration of planted areas with the built environment blurs lines between interior and exterior spaces. It also assists in replacing the landscaped area lost in the building campaign. A significant densification of the campus is intended to increase social interaction.[1]

An Innovative Learning Environment

In Heatherwick Studio's scheme, these two ambitions—the integration of greenery with the built environment and social interaction—are intertwined and actually serve to support one another in the creation of a naturally lit and ventilated as well as socially active educational space.

The Learning Hub is located near the center of a campus zone defined as the South Spine, which houses diverse Schools. The building will be open 24 hours and provide 55 classroom and tutorial rooms to host formal class meetings as well as informal meetings of students and campus organizations. Responding to the project's location among a variety of academic disciplines, the scheme keeps the spaces open, with access at ground level at 12 points. Visitors enter directly into a large interior communal atrium space, where they can visually survey the range of activities within the building.[2] The academic meeting spaces are distributed into 11 small inverted conical towers, which define the exterior of the building. These spaces, clad in precast concrete on the exterior and glass on the interior, bound the open-air central atrium. On each of the upper levels, a generous open-air balcony connects the towers and provides informal gathering spaces. Views into the classrooms from the interior of the building are left unobstructed in order to promote chance encounters between their occupants. The building is capped by a stepped roof garden, which also provides a range of gathering spaces.

The building's 55 teaching spaces are designed as "flipped classrooms," which redefine the experience of the typical four-sided space and break down the top-down hierarchy of a typical university classroom. Technology and group work are prioritized[3] in these technology-filled round spaces that facilitate student collaboration around shared tables. Professors serve as facilitators more than masters. This model of learning space is in line with recent research into the design of environments that best foster collaborative learning. For example, Susan J. Wolff defines six primary spatial factors that impact a learning environment:[4] group size, psychological/physiological supporting, furnishings, adjacencies, functional spaces, as well as flexible aspects. Spatial attributes that Wolff associates with these factors are, for example, spaces that provide a sense of ownership, "get-away" spaces, display spaces, access to community, adjacent, nested, or layered spaces, and informal learning space. The Learning Hub physically manifests many of these conclusions. For example, the creation of small towers of variable size with meeting rooms effectively breaks down the size and scale of the building, but also creates layered and nested spaces with optimal adjacencies between active and passive zones. Also, Wolff specifically references a naturally lit cave in close proximity to a "home base" or communal space as being ideal. Correspondingly, the Learning Hub provides many small rooms with a wide range in size and arrangement, surrounding and opening into a series of large interconnected social and communal spaces.

Combining Mineral and Organic Elements

Typically the design of learning environments composed of repetitive spaces tends toward the generic and sterile, without taking into account the specific types of activity taking place within them. To support the spatial hierarchies and varieties created by the organization and massing of the project, the design provides tactile differentiations of the spaces at the human scale. To favor a "hand-made futuristic"[5] language that adds human qualities and

engenders visceral feeling and response, each of the conical towers is clad in banded precast concrete elements that integrate pigments and textures.[6] This type of durable and naturally finished material seamlessly integrates with the planted areas of the building, creating a dialogue with the building's verdant facades and the surrounding campus. Furthermore, by minimizing the finishing of the concrete and other materials, such as phosphor bronze and solid timber, the chemical off-gassing of the building is greatly reduced, resulting in a healthier working and learning environment.[7]

In the same spirit, the design of the NTU Learning Hub seeks to minimize the volume of air-conditioned space. Instead, the massing and the materiality are put to work in tempering the environment within the building. The shape of the inverted cone towers shades and shelters the smaller lower floors, carefully controlling the amount of natural daylight entering the atrium.[8] Simultaneously, the lower levels taper to maximize the openings for both people and natural airflow to enter the building. In addition, the thermal mass of the precast concrete keeps the meeting spaces relatively cool while also inducing vertical movement of air through the open-air atrium.

As all of the interstitial spaces between the towers are open-air, the scheme provides ample opportunity for the introduction of green areas, which actively differentiate and characterize the various spaces. Each level incorporates plantings on the interior atrium balustrades, supporting the creation of a cooling semi-outdoor environment.[9] Furthermore, between each of the conical masses, the balconies are pushed to the exterior, creating more outward-facing planted terraces and gardens. While the gardens and plants that ring the internal and external balconies are distinctly tropical, a number of different planted ecologies are introduced as well, ranging from a tropical floral to a succulent garden.[10]

Critique

The inclusion of plants throughout the interior and exterior of the project signals a shift in the way architecture is conceived, particularly in the context of tropical environments. No longer does a distinction between interior and exterior need to be clearly defined. The building mass can allow exterior spaces to be drawn into the depth of the interior. This approach has many environmental benefits including the possibility of a significant reduction of air-conditioned space. More importantly, this approach draws the occupants of the building in closer contact with their surrounding natural environment.

1. "Yunnan Garden Campus Master Plan." August 2010 (source: http://www.ntu.edu.sg/odfm/campusmasterplan/Documents/CampusMasterPlanPrincipalIdeas.pdf).
2. Chan, Chrystal. "No Doubting Thomas." *Hey!*, issue 20 (*February 2015*).
3. Keat, Heng Swee. "Singapore Minister of Education at the Campus Master Plan Groundbreaking Ceremony of Nanyang Technological University." NTU News Hub, 12 October 2012 (source: http://news.ntu.edu.sg/Pages/NewsDetail.aspx?URL=http://news.ntu.edu.sg/news/Pages/Speeches2012_Oct12.aspx&Guid=554905b2-7413-4246-97ab-8d6f46e6b217&Category=all).
4. Wolff, S. *Design Features for Project-Based Learning*. Oregon State University, 2002.
5. Chan, Chrystal. "No Doubting Thomas ..."
6. LWC Alliance (source: http://www.lwc.com.sg/Track.aspx).
7. "NTU South Spine Learning Hub." *FuturArc* (source: http://www.futurarc.com/index.cfm/web-exclusive/online-projects/ntu-south-spine-learning-hub/).
8. *Ibid.*
9. *Ibid.*
10. "Landscape Design." CPG Consultants and Perfect Sense (source: http://www.perfect-sense.net/default.aspx?uc=29).

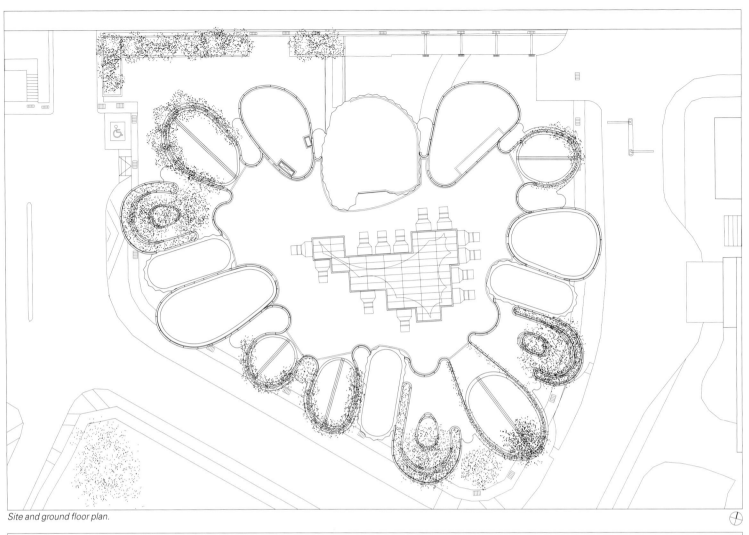

Site and ground floor plan.

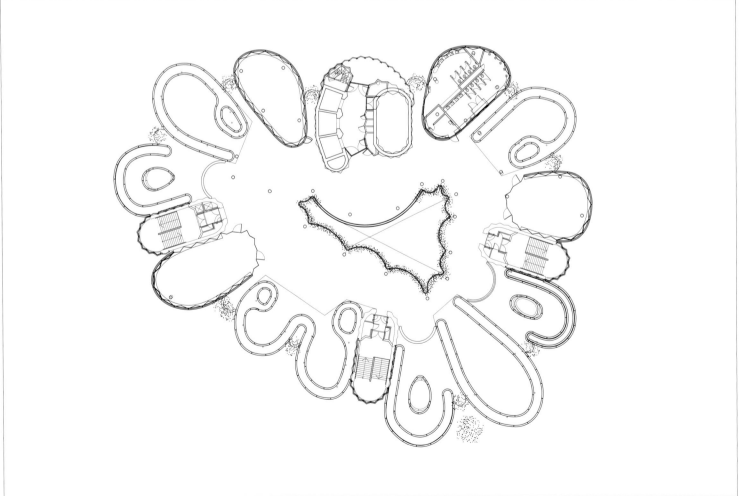

Typical floor plan.

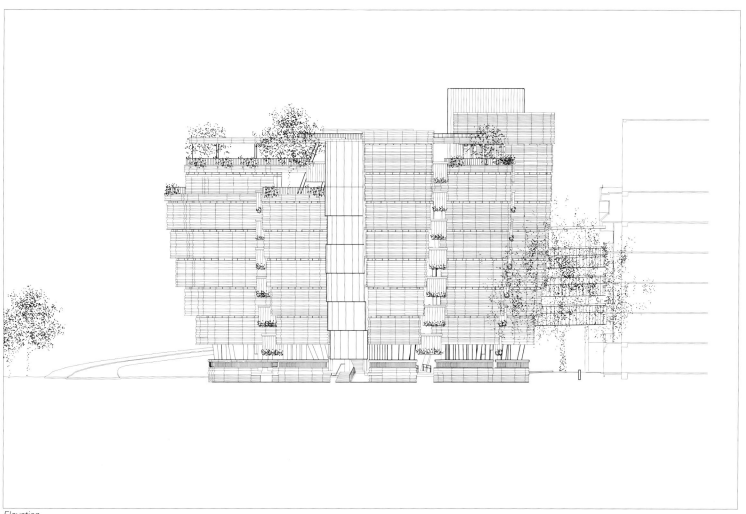

Elevation.

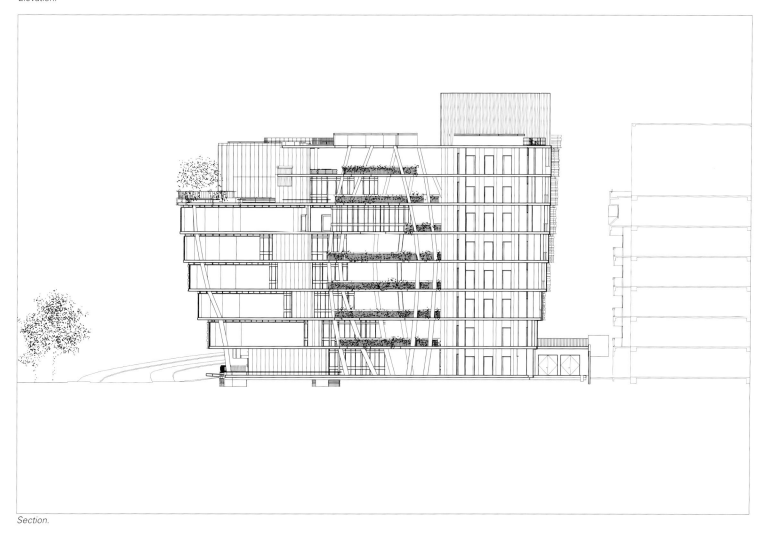

Section.

Ministry for Urban Development and the Environment

Sauerbruch Hutton

Building Type: Office
Climate Zone: Marine West Coast
Location: Neuenfelder Strasse, 21109 Hamburg, Germany
Coordinates: 53°29'46"N 10°0'34"E
Date: 2013

Height: 48 m/13 floors, 2 basements
Gross Floor Area: 61,000 m²
Gross Green Area in Building: 4,000 m²
Gross Green Area to Built-Up Area: 7%

Site Plan.

The Ministry for Urban Development and the Environment is located as the new centerpiece of urban development in the long forgotten Hamburg district of Wilhelmsburg.[1] Wilhelmsburg occupies a large isle, well served by major transport routes in close proximity to one of Europe's largest ports. The re-urbanization program, labeled "The Leap Across the Elbe," expands on the successful development of HafenCity Hamburg—the conversion of a former harbor district close to the city center. In order to kick-start the urban transformation of Wilhelmsburg, the City of Hamburg organized an International Building Exhibition in conjunction with an International Garden Exhibition. Both exhibitions explored specific forms of landscape urbanism through the integration of over 70 acres of green spaces in the redevelopment of the site.[2] The integration of those spaces within the overall master plan was intended to allow for new directions in the redevelopment of de-industrialized sites, the challenges of climate change, and the district's tentative social environment characterized by enormous cultural and social diversity.[3]

The new ministry brings together multiple state planning agencies, which had previously been housed across the city, into one single building complex.[4] Sauerbruch Hutton's trademark use of color is applied to heighten the effect of the project's integrated green spaces, which foster cross-agency collaboration. Serving as the public face of the new urban development, the project proposes a hopeful building future for the area—a future that balances environmental and technological advancement with social aspects of collaboration in close dialogue with the surrounding environment.

The building is located in the immediate vicinity of the Wilhelmsburg S-Bahn Station, at the crossing of a major north-south railway track and a major east-west boulevard cutting through the district. There are plans to develop a north-south expressway alongside the rail tracks in the near future. In 2009, at the time of the competition for the project, the site and its surroundings were undeveloped.[5] However, in preparation for the International Building Exhibition (IBA) and International Garden Exhibition in 2013, construction of nearly one billion Euros of value took place in the immediate surroundings of the site. The Ministry accounted for one fifth of the overall cost of the IBA construction.[6]

The L-shaped building consists of two five-story wings running parallel to the rail tracks and the boulevard, which frame a courtyard protected from the noise and traffic of the adjacent infrastructure. A 12-story tower rises above the intersection of

Site and ground floor plan.

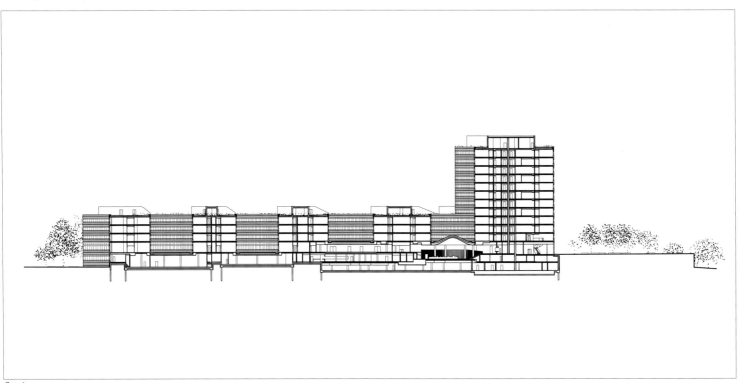

Section.

the boulevard and the railway. Roughly diamond-shaped in plan, the tower relates to the triangular geometry of the building's wings below. Its massing subtly varies when viewed from passing cars and trains, offering a changing identity that never reveals the true size of the building volume (61,000 sqm of floor area on a 23,200 sqm site).[7] The project's two long wings are composed of triangular volumes, which are connected along one side, creating a building mass that is serrated along one side and smooth along the other. The east-west wing pushes its articulated side towards the main street in response to the smaller residential buildings to the south of the project.

Color and Greenery

The open areas within the overall building mass create opportunities for the integration of green spaces, which are easily viewed from the offices. Additionally, they work with the master plan's overall goal of an integration of green spaces in the urban environment. The north-south wing, which is composed of three triangular volumes and whose flat side echoes the adjacent railway, faces the building's more intimate courtyard with an articulated side, framing a series of small gardens in its open area.

To break down the scale of the volume, the two wings are composed of seven smaller "houses" connected by an interior street, matching approximately the various departments within the Ministry. Each house is organized around a small atrium, which brings in natural light and promotes natural airflow. Additionally, each atrium connects vertically through the entire section of the complex and provides an open staircase linking directly to the internal street for easy inter-departmental collaboration.[8] Each atrium provides subtle distinctions through the creation of unique design features as well as the use of color. Here, Sauerbruch Hutton's trademark use of color creates a fun and lively atmosphere that adds a sensory experience to the subtle variations of the atria. The ground level, entirely dedicated to public programs, provides a public interface for the Ministry to suggest to the public transparent planning processes. Visitors enter the complex at the bottom of the tower, where a central foyer provides access to the public programs and most importantly houses a large-scale model of the City of Hamburg to present the overall vision for the city.

Sauerbruch Hutton's use of color is not only deployed on a functional level to differentiate and humanize the large building mass of the Ministry's new headquarters. On a more fundamental level, Sauerbruch Hutton see color as a means of drawing people into closer dialogue with their surroundings. This takes on social as well as environmental interests as the office takes "a certain pleasure in the fact that color is such an applied material that you can completely change the perception of space or an object with just a minimum."[9] The patchwork of the building's skin changes in hue as one walks around the complex: a range of reds (from purple to orange) at the sunny high-street elevation turns into blues, greens, and yellows at the shady backside. In relating the use of color to its form as well as environmental and urban conditions, the building creates a range of exterior spaces. For example, the exterior open spaces formed by the massing face both the busy street to the south as well as the intimate interior courtyard. These spaces include gardens, which provide an additional public interface for the Ministry. While the gardens naturally take on different qualities based on their urban context, the color creates further subtle differences

between them. Green roofs covering the entire project minimize surface water runoffs and improve overall thermal insulation. However, they are inaccessible except for maintenance purposes.

Sustainability

In order to reduce energy consumption, the building employs a range of passive measures such as enhanced thermal insulation, careful control of the transparency of the facade, a compact building volume, and cross-ventilation that is achieved through natural convection in the atria. These passive measures are combined with a number of active technologies such as the use of geothermal energy to condition the spaces through radiant heat, and the use of an on-site biogas-powered electricity production facility that supplies the entire redeveloped district.[10] Additionally, the windows are equipped with daylight refraction, external solar shading, and dedicated ventilation openings that allow night cooling. This energy concept attains standards of operation that allow the building to be run on less than 70 kWh/sqm primary energy per year.[11]

Most components of this concept are simple and user-controlled in an effort to minimize the use of a central building management system. However, in order to maximize the users' involvement in the control of their environment, the central building control system sends out recommendations to the users on how to modify various building devices according to the respective weather and daylight conditions. This system is a purposeful and meaningful departure from typical building management system, which automatically adjust the building's environment for maximum comfort and efficiency.

Critique

The Ministry for Urban Development and the Environment provides an intriguing image of the current state of the design of office buildings. Efficient and flexibly planned, the project aims to create a relationship between public space and human sensation through the dynamic use of color, program, and the integration of green spaces. While the building clearly engages the senses and produces iconicity through its use of color, the interior planning, while efficient, does not push the integration of green space to the fullest. The massing creates a dynamic facade, well-lit and activity-filled atria, green spaces, and green roofs. However, the interior spaces are largely conventional and the gardens, although well-defined by the undulating facade shape, are only seen from the interior and cannot be experienced or even accessed easily.

1. Architect Statement. Sauerbruch Hutton. 2013.
2. Edelman, Thomas. "Pleasing an Entire Island." Stylepark, 30 April 2013 (source: http://www.stylepark.com/en/contributions/internationale-bauausstellung-iba).
3. IBA Hamburg (source: http://www.iba-hamburg.de/en/projects/wilhelmsburg-central/new-building-of-the-state-ministry-for-urban-development-and-the-environment/projekt/new-building-of-the-state-ministry-for-urban-development-and-the-environment.html).
4. *Ibid.*
5. Architect Statement …
6. IBA Hamburg …
7. *Ibid.*
8. Architect Statement …
9. Serra, Juan. Color and Space, Practice and Theory. Reflections with Matthias Sauerbruch and Mark Wigley.
10. IBA Hamburg …
11. Architect Statement …

Phare Tower Project

Jacques Ferrier Architectures

Building Type: Office
Climate Zone: Marine West Coast
Location: 12 Place Gravet, 92800
Puteaux, France
Coordinates: 48°53'38"N 2°14'19"E
Date: Unbuilt – Design in 2006

Height: 324 m/78 floors, 7 basements
Gross Floor Area: 140,000 m²
Gross Green Area in Building: 10,000 m²
Gross Green Area to Built-Up Area: 7%

Jacques Ferrier Architectures' proposal for the 2006 Phare Tower competition in La Défense, Paris, couples the office's research interests with innovations in material science that allow for a transformation of the high-rise typology. Ferrier's scheme posits that density enables high degrees of variation within the urban landscape. For example, New York City's Central Park only exists in its current form because of the density of the surrounding city. Paris offers a contrasting canvas—a seemingly endless field of mid-rise buildings. La Défense, the city's only hyper-dense zone, stands as an alternate model for the French capital and Ferrier's proposal aims to push its potential closer to reality.

Ferrier's Phare Tower was the office's entry to a competition launched by Unibail for an iconic tower in the heart of La Défense as part of the Public Establishment for Installation of La Défense's (EPAD) 2005 plan to redefine the district as a dynamic contemporary mixed-use neighborhood[1] and reimagine the stagnant image of the corporate office tower.[2] This new beacon for La Défense was to stretch 297 m tall and provide 147,000 sqm of office space for over 8,500 employees. In total, ten architecture firms were invited to participate in the competition. Nine firms were from Europe, five of whom were French, including Jacques Ferrier Architectures. Morphosis Architects won the competition and was awarded the commission.

A Collaborative Office Environment

Jacques Ferrier's proposal for the Phare Tower competition is a site- and program-specific hybrid of two former research schemes devoid of specific site and program constraints.

Concept Office, launched in 2002, aimed to define the future of office space at the leading edge of sustainable development with regard to energy, but also addressed the lifestyle within the building and its relationship to public space.[3] In collaboration with the French national electricity supply agency, Electricité de France (EDF), Ferrier developed an architectural scheme for a 20,000 sqm building that supported an open and collaborative office environment and outperformed EDF's thermal and energy standards.[4] The scheme underscored the idea that sustainable architecture can be embedded with novel spatial and social experiences.

Hypergreen built upon the social, organizational, and environmental aspects of Concept Office and deployed them at the scale of a mixed-use tower. In collaboration with Lafarge's research and development department, Ferrier proposed a structural exoskeleton that freed the building's internal organization to incorporate a vertically organized collective space, while also integrating novel environmental responsiveness.[5] The Phare Tower scheme fine-tunes Hypergreen's strategies for an environmental high-rise to navigate the complex nature of its La Défense site.

Diagrid Structure

In order to enable this new-found freedom in the organization of a contemporary high-rise, the design team, in collaboration with structural engineer Jean-Marc Weil and the research and development group at concrete manufacturer Lafarge, departed from the typical core-and-column-grid system. Drawing cues from 19th-Century Russian engineer and inventor Vladimir Shukov's studies in steel lattice tower structures, the design team developed a diagrid exoskeleton that transferred more than half of the building's vertical load path to the exterior, freeing the interior spaces to accommodate any number of uses and organizations.[6]

The external load-bearing diagrid lattice can vary in density through a simple subdivision logic. Variations in density are mapped onto the facade as a direct response to structural, wind, solar, and even programmatic inputs. Additionally, the building's massing is stretched to the northeast and southwest in order to provide additional stiffness.[7] The result is a structural and environmental buffer that provides even distribution of light and air for the building's interior.

During the Hypergreen research program, Ferrier began working with Lafarge to develop a lattice-like exoskeleton of Ultra-High Performance Fiber-Reinforced Concrete (UHPFRC). UHPFRC is an advanced cementitious material characterized by non-linear structural behavior. Instead of metal reinforcement bars, the mixture incorporates extremely fine steel fibers, which absorb all the stresses and impart ductile behavior on the material.[8] This technical innovation allows for the architectural separation of the filigree exoskeleton from the transparent skin, resulting in a lightness and translucency that conveys a novel image of an environmental tower. The Phare Tower diagrid pattern provides the greatest flexibility and adaptibility within the manufacturing criteria for the material.

Hyperconnectivity

The earliest plans for La Défense of the late 1950s and early 1960s were based loosely on Le Corbusier's concept for a *Ville Contemporaine*. The plans defined a strict separation of

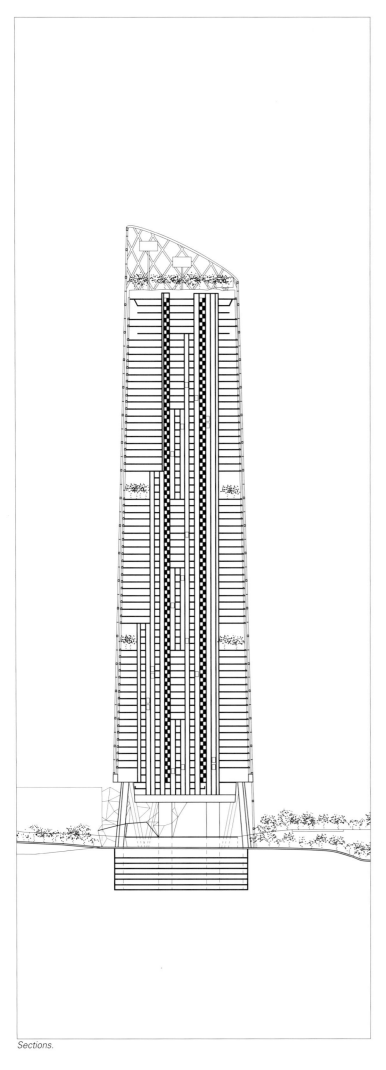

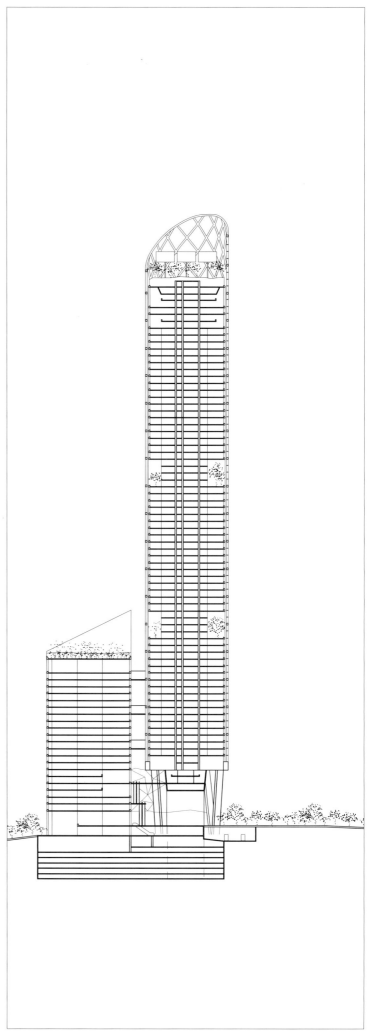

Sections.

vehicular and pedestrian traffic through the construction of a continuous 1.5 km pedestrian plaza elevated above road and rail infrastructure. Later development, influenced in part by Archigram and Team X, shifted from the static formalism of the original plan in favor of an open and flexible field condition capable of supporting a more dynamic and varied lifestyle.[9] The 2005 master plan focuses development on the densification and revitalization of La Défense as a 24-hour, mixed-use community.[10]

The selection of the Phare Tower site supports the ambition of this most recent plan, as the tower rises from a complicated site between the Grande Arche, which sits to the southwest, and CNIT directly to the south. The site is bounded on the north by the N13 Expressway (Boulevard Circulaire de La Défense), while a pedestrian bridge extends the original pedestrian esplanade across the expressway to the Université Léonard de Vinci further north. Strong links to Paris' public transportation networks require that any scheme must plug into the existing infrastructural systems, which stretch multiple levels beneath the existing esplanade.[11]

Ferrier's response to the complexity of the existing urban networks was to conciously separate the tower portion above the ground plane to allow infrastructure and landscape to pass continuously below as a multi-dimensional subterranean plinth.[12] The massing has been lifted above the ground on six large *pilotis*, which allow the public landscape to continue under the building. By engendering the base of the tower with visual and literal porosity, Ferrier's scheme allows for a kind of hyperconnectivity both horizontally through the building and vertically to the rail platforms and the tower lobby.[13] Public space extends vertically throughout the building to support Ferrier's assertion that because office buildings are only occupied one third of the time and represent a massive factor in the built environment, the contemporary city should provide a more integrated lifestyle.[14]

Green Components

Plants become a key component in the creation of enjoyable, pleasant spaces for gathering.[15] At the ground level, gardens serve to blur transitions between the interior and exterior. They are specifically integrated into the spatial experience of entering the building and connecting visually and physically to various locations within the complex.[16] Planted areas stretch vertically through the project to provide visual cues to the public spaces dispersed throughout the tower. Two double-height atria break the monotony of the striated tower, while small green vestibules are carved out of each floor. Collective spaces stretch from the basement to the upper floors, incorporating lounges, gardens, conference rooms, and interactive spaces where public and private come together, providing a type of urban experience that might be understood as a variation of the *Unité d'Habitation*.

The most pressing concerns for typical office towers are the provision of natural light and ventilation for the building interior. One of the main issues with naturally ventilating towers is the increased speed of winds at the top of the structure. For the Phare Tower, the massing and patterning of the exoskeleton were designed in response to local wind conditions to reduce the speed of the wind entering the building. Furthermore, specifically designed air inlets and window mechanisms reduce the wind pressure down to an acceptable less than 10%.[17]

Site plan.

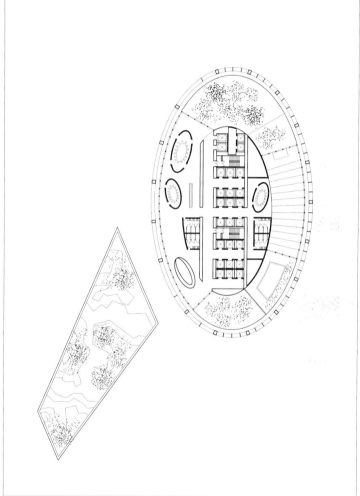

Typical floor plan.

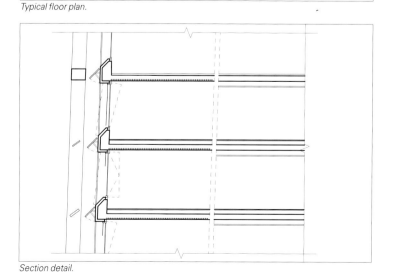

Section detail.

The patterning of the exoskeleton is further derived from solar analysis to create naturally daylit conditions that are free from glare. The elongated shape of the building maximizes the floor area with access to high levels of natural light. Areas at the two elongated ends that do not fall within 5 to 6 m of the facade are used for less frequently occupied spaces, such as meeting rooms or waiting areas. Additionally, the patterned exoskeleton adapts to the environmental requirements of the plants in the public areas. Solar panels incorporated into the double-skin facade take advantage of the solar exposure of the tower, which in conjunction with wind turbines on the roof creates a new image for the sustainable tower.

Critique

While Ferrier's proposal relies heavily on technological and material innovation, the architects do not intend it to be understood as technically driven. Instead, the Phare Tower and Hypergreen present transparency, lightness, and accessibility as a new image of sustainability. If Alejandro Zaera-Polo asserts that architecture is a capable and responsible tool in the production of societal change,[18] then Jacques Ferrier Architectures' Phare Tower pushes to be at the forefront of changing the way we inhabit, view, and experience our cities. From afar, the building's envelope conveys an image of depth, which also subtly traces the passage of time. The load-bearing structure's detachment from the elevation behind it allows to create an in-between space composed of light, shadow, and reflection. As one moves closer, this depth presents a paradox of concrete—the typical massiveness has been replaced by sensuality and delicacy. This visible shift in experience encourages active participation in the evolution of our urban environment.

1. "Le Nouveau Visage de La Defense: History." Etablissement public de gestion du quartier d'affaires de La Défense (source: http://www.ladefense.fr/en/history-place).
2. "La Tour Phare. Consultation Internationale: Le Programme"
(source: http://www.tour-phare.com/#!architecture/consultation_internationale/2).
3. Ferrier, Jacques. The Making of Phare and Hypergreen Towers. Brussels, Paris: AAM Editions, 2007. p. 51.
4. Ibid.
5. Ibid., p. 54.
6. Jacques Ferrier, contribution to: Bell, Michael and Craig Buckley (ed.). Solid States: Concrete in Transition. New York: Princeton Architectural Press, 2010.
7. Ferrier, Jacques. The Making of …, p. 54.
8. Spasojevic, A., D. Redaelli, and A. Muttoni. "Thin UHPFRC Slabs without Conventional Reinforcement as Light-weight Structural Elements." Proceedings from fib (Federation Internationale de Beton) Symposium 2009. London, 2009.
9. Roberts, Nick. "La Defense: From Axial Hierarchy to Field Condition." Proceedings from ACSA National Conference 2011. Montreal, 2011.
10. Le Nouveau Visage …
11. Mayne, Thom. "Consultation pour La Tour Phare." November 2006
(source: http://www.youtube.com/watch?v=Xn8O7SzLJg8).
12. Ferrier, Jacques. The Making of …, p. 6.
13. Ibid., p. 14.
14. Ibid., p. 53.
15. Ibid.
16. Ibid., pp. 80-84.
17. Ibid., p. 27.
18. Zaera-Polo, Alejandro. "Politics of the Envelope" in Log, n. 13. pp. 193-207.

Federal Environment Agency

Sauerbruch Hutton

Building Type: Office
Climate Zone: Marine West Coast
Location: Wörlitzer Platz 1, 06844
Dessau-Roßlau, Germany
Coordinates: 51°50'31"N 12°14'22"E
Date: 2005

Height: 18 m/4 floors, 1 basement
Gross Floor Area: 41,000 m²
Gross Green Area in Building: 2,400 m²
Gross Green Area to Built-Up Area: 6%

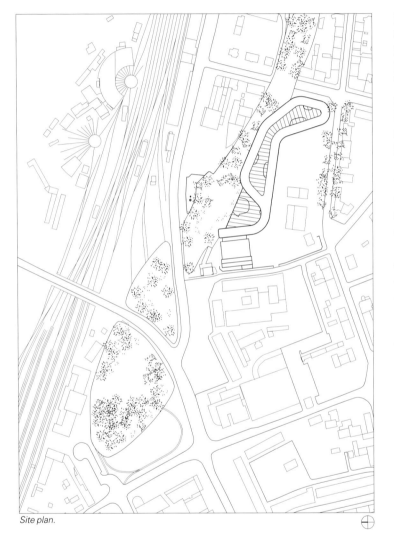

Site plan.

In 1992, two years after the German reunification, the Federalism Commission decided to relocate the majority of the Federal Environment Agency (Umweltbundesamt, UBA) from Berlin to Dessau, in the German Federal State of Saxony-Anhalt.[1] The institution's relocation was symbolic of a larger desire to reinvigorate the city of Dessau, home of the historic Bauhaus. In the early 1990s, the city had seen a steady decline in employment until just prior to the competition, when it had the highest rate of unemployment in Germany at nearly 40%.[2] In need of new headquarters to house more than 750 employees, the agency, which oversees environmental regulation and conservation, took the project as an opportunity to create a symbolic statement for all of Germany. Sauerbruch Hutton won the competition for the project in 1998. Their scheme combines this interest with more fundamental concerns of integrating a federal agency's headquarters with the close-knit surrounding community as well as redefining the design and arrangement of the contemporary office block. The project explores architectural design in terms of history, planning, form, color, and an integration of landscape that "combines spatial and material economy with the deliberate stimulation of the senses."[3]

A main driving force for the selection of the site was its industrial past. Previously occupied by a small railway station and a factory for gas appliances, it was seen as an opportunity for a showcase project to demonstrate the challenges, best practices, as well as the opportunities of working in a former industrial area. In the five years leading up to the construction of the new building, the land was treated to eliminate pollution while the existing architecture of the railway station was rehabilitated and integrated into the new design.

The building's long and narrow site borders a low-rise residential neighborhood that merges with the Dessau-Wörlitz Garden Realm, the iconic 18th-Century cultural landscape listed as a UNESCO World Heritage Site, further to the east. Located across the rail tracks, which bound the site on the west, is Walter Gropius' modernist masterpiece Bauhaus Dessau. Located directly between these two significant contextual elements, the Federal Environment Agency draws on the pastoral aspects of the famed landscapes while openly acknowledging and learning from Gropius' embrace of technology in the Bauhaus. Designed and constructed in a very short period between 1925 and 1926, the Bauhaus building famously and defiantly engaged the industrial technology of the time to communicate "unbroken dominance over nature."[4] 80 years

later, technology is no longer deployed as a means to overcome nature, but instead is used to bring us closer to nature and to bring nature closer to our cities.

Integration of Nature and Building

The design of the Federal Environment Agency is based on ideas of integrating the built environment with nature to challenge standard office typologies. In this project, Sauerbruch Hutton synthesize their trademark use of color with a technologically advanced climate-controlled garden, which connects the building complex with its site and the surrounding city. The building is organized around a landscaped and public forum that serves as the public entrance to the building. The forum seamlessly connects to a larger network of public park spaces extending north and south along the rail tracks on the west side of the site. It provides access to the building's public programs—an auditorium, the largest environmental library in Europe, and an exhibition area—as well as a larger landscaped atrium that extends the public park network deep within the building's footprint. Covered with an operable glass saw-tooth roof, each of these landscaped voids serves as a socially vibrant node of the building. Defined by a snaking form of office volumes, both void spaces bring together the agency, the public, and nature.

Sauerbruch Hutton's design challenges the typical organization of an office building. The project brief asked for offices for approximately 800 employees. German government workplace requirements demand that each employee have an office with access to natural light and a minimum area of 12 sqm.[5] Lining up all offices in a row stacked four stories high would have resulted in a volume 600 m in length. Instead, Sauerbruch Hutton conceived a long curving building volume, with offices organized along a double-loaded corridor, enclosing the central courtyard. Along the ground level, the public programs protrude from the extruded mass above, further defining various smaller landscaped zones within the courtyard while breaking down the overall large scale of the building and atrium.

The atrium, the social center of the building, can be understood as a critique of Gropius' dismissal of nature mentioned above. Technology in Sauerbruch Hutton's project allows for the careful control of light and air within the atrium, which serves to condition the office spaces within, but also allows for a year-round landscaped garden space for interaction and collaboration. Furthermore, the atrium functions as a natural thermal buffer throughout the year as it can also be operated in a naturally ventilated mode through the use of openings in the roof that control the flow of air in and out of the building. Additionally, with the exception of those on the western facade, all offices are fitted with operable and user-controlled windows, allowing personalized access and connection to the surrounding environment and atrium. The mechanical ventilation of the spaces supports a feedback loop between interior and exterior: when outdoor temperatures fall below 5°C, the air drawn from the exterior is channeled to an earth-to-heat exchanger and is pre-heated before entering the air-conditioning system. The reverse happens when the exterior temperatures exceed 22°C.[6] Overall, the UBA outperforms the already strict German energy-efficiency standards for public buildings, with an energy use of 30 kWh/sqm per year.

Glass in eight main colors distinguishes the various parts of the facade, creating a powerful composition that engages the

Site and ground floor plan.

Section.

senses of the users and passersby, heightening their awareness of the surroundings and the landscaped features that are carefully integrated into the building. Adjacent glass colors are chromatically related, ranging from madder red and saffron yellow via orange and cobalt blue to mint green and lemon yellow.[7]

Critique

Germany's Federal Environment Agency uses technology to integrate architecture and landscape elements in multiple scales. At the scale of the city, the building creates literal and conceptual connections with larger networks of surrounding parks and greenways. At the smaller scale, the building uses these green networks as a formal, functional, and environmental driver for the integration of public green spaces that run through the building. These spaces serve as an interface with the public, which is able to pass through the building. Within this verdant space, multiple overhead bridges link the different departments, while public exhibitions, galleries, and lecture halls protrude into the garden. The offices maintain their relative distance from the gardens below; there are no plants within the building's office interiors. The mass of the offices literally encloses and defines the building's landscaped area, establishing a symbiotic relationship between building and landscape.

By enclosing the landscape with an operable and responsive roof, the gardens are brought into a subtle dialogue with the office interiors, creating an inversion of a typical office building organization. Here, the least tempered space—the landscaped atrium—is at the center, allowing for complex environmental and spatial exchanges to take place and providing the users and the public with a space of interaction and engagement.

1. "New Building for the German Federal Environment Agency in Dessau." EnOB, Research for Energy Optimized Building (source: http://www.enob.info/en/new-buildings/project/details/new-building-for-the-german-federal-environment-agency-in-dessau/).
2. Finch, Paul. "Pure and simple: Sauerbruch Hutton's headquarters building, for Germany's Federal Environment Agency, is a model of integration" in *The Architectural Review*, July 2005.
3. Sauerbruch Hutton. Architects Statement (source: http://www.sauerbruchhutton.de/images/UBA_environment_agency_en.pdf).
4. "Modernism without Dogma." Lecture by Matthias Sauerbruch, 2002.
5. Stephens, Suzanne. "Federal Environment Agency" in *Architectural Record*, August 2006.
6. "New Building …"
7. "Colorful Ribbon Federal Environment Agency in Dessau." Mapolis architecture + BIM (source: http://architecture.mapolismagazin.com/content/colorful-ribbon-federal-environment-agency-dessau).

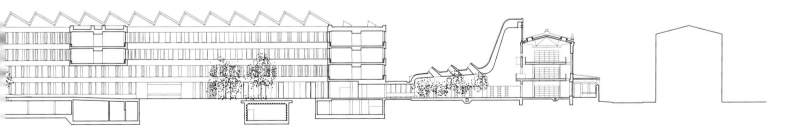

Solaris

T. R. Hamzah & Yeang/CPG Consultants

Building Type: Office
Climate Zone: Tropical Wet
Location: 1 Fusionopolis Walk,
Singapore 138628
Coordinates: 1°7'59"N 103°47'16"E
Date: 2012

Height: 79 m/14 floors, 3 basements
Gross Floor Area: 51,200 m²
Gross Green Area in Building: 8,363 m²
Gross Green Area to Built-Up Area: 17%

The Solaris is part of the One North master plan by Zaha Hadid Architects (ZHA) that commenced in 2001 and is expected to be completed by 2021. Commissioned by the Science Hub Development Group (SHDG) and Jurong Town Corporation (JTC), two of Singapore's research and suburban development groups, it projects a built area of about 5 million sqm and is expected to host a working population of 138,000. The site lies in the western part of Singapore, in a suburban area outside of the city's Central Development District dedicated to research and development in a variety of fields and in close proximity to three of Singapore's universities.

The master plan is conceived as a morphology of natural landscape formations that would mould into its own skyline. ZHA conceived it as "… a morphological system which allows for infinite variation within the bounds of a strong formal coherence and lawfulness. In contrast to exacting and vulnerable Platonic forms—squares, circles, strict axes et al.—One North's form is 'free' and therefore malleable at any stage of its development."[1]

Solaris has taken cues from the master plan by taking on a curvilinear form that flows and connects with its neighboring buildings and by integrating the surrounding environment. T.R. Hamzah & Yeang won the competition that was organized by the Jurong Town Corporation for an office building to house multi-national corporations from the infocommunications, media, science and engineering research & development (R&D) industries, with a proposal that is a distinctively "green" articulation of the idea of a fluid building envelope.[2] The building design consists of two tower blocks that rise above three basement floors of car park. The design endows the site with a self-sustaining ecosystem through the use of both passive and active sustainable design features with a low level of maintenance. The towers, nine and 15 levels in height, are combined formally via a diagonally glazed 13-level atrium with a diagonal light shaft within the 15-level tower. Roof gardens harvest both solar energy and rainwater. A landscaped continuous perimeter ramp surrounds the complex and extends to the basement car park levels below.[3]

Green Features

Ecological Armature
One of the key and most visually prominent design features of Solaris is a continuous landscaped perimeter ramp that wraps seamlessly around the entire complex and blends harmoniously with the adjacent One North Park at ground level. It extends uninterrupted for a length of 1.5 km from the basement with a cascading sequence of roof gardens at the top of the two tower blocks. The ramp varies in width as it coils around the building, with a minimum width of 3 m to ensure comfort and maintainability of the peripheral landscape elements.[4]

A parallel pathway allows for the servicing of the continuous planter boxes without requiring access from the internal tenanted spaces. This pathway also serves as a linear park, stretching all the way from the ground level to the top roof areas, and interconnects all external planted areas in a way that is significantly different from the typical pockets of sky gardens or planter boxes that rely on small-scale ecological systems as they are often seen in similar projects. Through its significantly larger scale, the continuity of the ramp encourages biodiversity. The ramp is further designed to provide passive and ambient cooling through its extensive and deep overhangs in combination with large concentrations of plants selected mainly for their shade-generating properties.

Eco Cell
The Ecological Armature connects to the so-called Eco Cell at the ground and basement levels of the building. This part of the building allows vegetation, daylight, and natural ventilation to infiltrate the car park levels below. The lowest level of the Eco Cell consists of the mechanical services of the rainwater harvesting system.

Solar Shaft
The volume of the taller Tower A is cut diagonally by a light shaft that intersects the upper floors and allows for daylight to penetrate deep into the building's interior. The building as a whole is equipped with a lighting management system that provides optimum lighting levels for its occupants.

Grand Atrium
The two tower blocks are connected via a multi-level grand atrium functioning as a covered public plaza. This mixed-mode zone, both mechanically and naturally ventilated, is climatically controlled with an operable glass-louvered roof that enhances ventilation while providing protection from Singapore's tropical monsoons.[5]

Facade Louvers
The extensive system of sunshading louvers that double as light shelves is responsive to the sun's path, which is almost exactly east-west and has also been considered for the project's massing. The system is further enhanced by the landscaped ramp where the fenestration is set back significantly from the actual exterior to reduce heat transfer to the interior. This holistic shading strategy

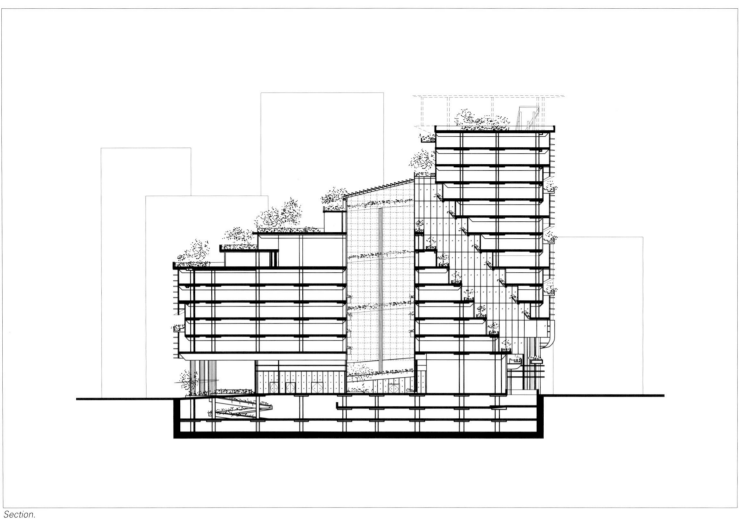

Section.

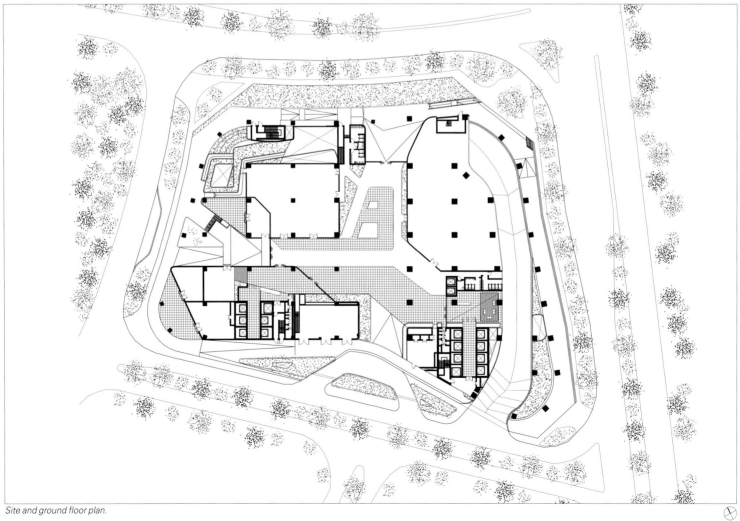

Site and ground floor plan.

results in a comparatively low External Thermal Transfer Value (EETV) of 39 W/sqm that is supported by the overall low-e double-glazed perimeter facade. The sunshade louvers, whose aggregate linear length runs in excess of 10 km, support the establishment of comfortable microclimates in the habitable spaces along the building's exterior.

Green Terraces
The ecological armature serves to connect the many terraces that proliferate the project's massing. The pocket park/plaza at ground level links to One North Park across the street and allows for cross-ventilation of the ground floor plaza. The green terraces continue on the roof gardens and corner sky terraces. The ecological armature culminates in a double-volume sky terrace at each corner of the building, altogether resulting in an overall 95% of the project's greenery above the ground level.

Rainwater Harvesting/Recycling
The building's extensive green spaces are irrigated through a large-scale rainwater recycling system. As the design of the massing produces a naturally sloping gradient from the taller to the lower tower block, rainwater is collected through siphonic drainage as well as from the drainage pipes of the ramp. The project's combined storage capacity of over 700 m³ is able to irrigate almost all of the building's green areas. The automated system is integrated with a fertigation system that helps to maintain organic nutrient levels throughout the irrigation cycle, enabling the micro-ecosystems to be self-sustaining.

Critique

Solaris continues T. R. Hamzah & Yeang's progressive research into creating self-sustaining high-rise green ecosystems that reinterpret dense, urban living in tropical environments.[6] The project has won multiple accolades for its integrated green design, including the Singapore Building Construction Authority's Green Mark Platinum Award (a local equivalent of the USGBC LEED Standard),[7] the Skyrise Greenery Award from the Singapore Institute of Architects and National Parks Singapore, and the Green Good Design Award for Architecture in 2010 from the Chicago Athenaeum: Museum of Architecture & Design and the European Center for Architecture Art Design and Urban Studies.

1. "One North Masterplan." Zaha Hadid Architects, 2013 (source: http://www.zaha-hadid.com/masterplans/one-north-masterplan.)
2. "Large Building—Solaris, Fusionopolis." T. R. Hamzah & Yeang, 2013 (source: http://www.trhamzahyeang.com/project/large-buildings/solaris_01.html).
3. Yeang, Ken, and Arthur Spector. *Green Design: From Theory to Practice*. Black Dog Publishing Limited, 2011.
4. Bierig, Alexsandr. "Ramping up Green." Green Source, 2009 (source: http://greensource.construction.com/people/2009/05_Ramping-Up-Green.asp).
5. "Solaris Singapore." Council on Tall Buildings and Urban Habitat, 2013 (source: http://www.ctbuh.org/TallBuildings/FeaturedTallBuildings/FeaturedTallBuilding Archive2012/SolarisSingapore/tabid/3854/language/en-GB/Default.aspx).
6. Yeang, Ken. *The skyscraper bioclimatically considered: a design primer*. Academy Editions, 1996.
7. Tan, Puay Yok. *A Vertical Garden City*. Singapore: Straits Times Press, 2013.

National University Health System Tower Block

DP Architects

Building Type: Office
Climate Zone: Tropical Wet
Location: 1E Kent Ridge Road,
Singapore 119228
Coordinates: 1°7'41"N 103°46'58"E
Date: 2010

Height: 67 m/15 floors
Gross Floor Area: 35,458 m²/54,147 m²
(built-up)
Gross Green Area in Building: 20,393 m²
Gross Green Area to Built-Up Area: 37%

This administrative tower is an addition to the National University Health System (NUHS) facilities, one of Singapore's leading hospital and medical services providers and part of the National University of Singapore's (NUS) medical research and training facilities. DP Architects' competition proposal for this project was selected for its innovative interpretation and integration of the site and the adjacent dense forest as well as its holistic sustainable features, making the tower "an extension to the adjacent ecological habitat." [1]

Located adjacent to the National University of Singapore in the Kent Ridge suburban area, the site is surrounded by a hilly landscape, unusual for Singapore's otherwise largely flat topography. It is covered with lush tropical *Adinandra Belukar* greenery. [2] The term describes secondary forest growth that comes into place after human settlements and interventions, which often result in a very deep erosion of the ground soil. [3]

In order to integrate the building with its environment, a series of landscapes was created. For that, vegetation was carefully chosen from the regional flora. The greenery extends from the entrance to the internal courtyard of the building, which features a soaring vertical green wall that covers the entire 12 levels of the project (an eight-level office tower placed over an at-grade four-level car park podium). [4]

Green Features

The design process of the NUHS Tower Block employed a plethora of green design strategies and construction methods, with the purpose of integrating the office building with a site characterized by a pronounced topography adjacent to the national public park.

Building Orientation
The building design maximizes north- and south- and minimizes east- and west-facing facades. The orientation of the long building edge features expansive views of the natural greenery of Pasir Panjang Park as well as the greenery in the west and the sea to the south.

Sustainable Building Materials
Many of the construction materials used in the project are accredited by the Singapore Green Label Scheme (SGLS) and administered by Singapore's Building Construction Authority Green Mark Scheme, a local building regulatory body equivalent to the United States Green Building Council's LEED scheme.

The Concrete Usage Index, computed with the division of the concrete volume by the constructed floor area, was kept as low as possible. Modular dry wall systems with a high bio-degradable content were employed extensively throughout the project to reduce energy consumption during construction.

Lighting, Ventilation, Sanitation
Acknowledging the challenges of the client's request for a fully glazed building in Singapore's tropical climate, the building's air-conditioning system was optimized to achieve an indoor temperature range of 22.5°C to 25.5°C and a relative humidity of less than 70%. The air-conditioning and mechanical ventilation system incorporates variable screw chillers and speed drives that are automated and calibrated by an integrated Building Management System (BMS). The BMS also assures the calibration of the interior artificial lighting that complements the natural lighting from the building's facades and interior air well. Energy-efficient fixtures such as T5 fluorescent lighting tubes and electronic magnetic ballasts automatically switch off when natural lighting fulfills the interior lighting requirements. Separate digital sub-metering is employed for major electrical consumers as part of the BMS. Photo-electric cells on the roof harness Singapore's abundant solar energy and power external lighting fixtures as well as the staircase lighting. Major water users are provided with individual water sub-metering, which is monitored to quickly detect leaks. Separate tank systems are used to store rainwater, which is used for landscape irrigation. This significantly reduces the consumption of fresh water, which is precious in Singapore.

As part of the overall design concept and to maximize natural cross-ventilation, the four-story car park podium is wrapped with a layer of perforated metal screens. The perforation produces a facade image of foliage reminiscent of the numerous tembusu trees and their lush canopies in the surroundings.

Low-e Facade
The curtain wall system of the glass facades features horizontal aluminum shading fins that mask the panels of the floor slab edges. Large-scale prototypes of the facade and the glass spandrels were put up on site during the construction phase to iteratively test the resultant emittance, transmittance, and reflectance of the glass on site. The modular 28-mm-thick double-glazed low-e glass facade employs two variations in shading coefficients to optimize variable interior lighting conditions while providing a uniform external appearance. The innovative facade design results in a cumulative reduction

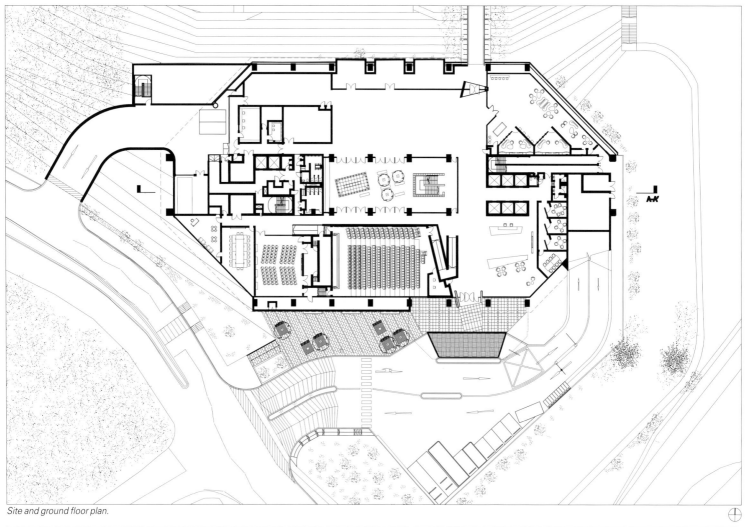

Site and ground floor plan.

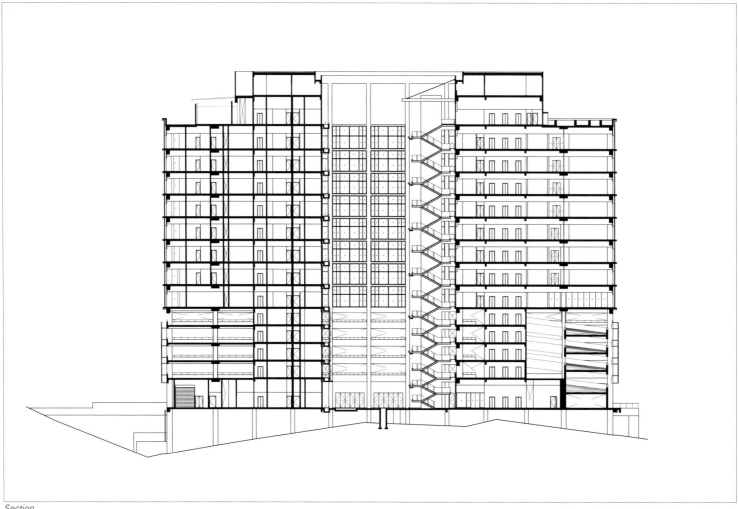

Section.

of heat gains of 11 W/sqm and a 29.5% reduction in total energy consumption of the building.

Green Wall

The 12-level green wall is lit naturally through an open air well that runs through the full height of the building. Covering an area of nearly 600 sqm, the green wall is divided into two parts. The lower one extends over four levels and features 16 local plant species, among them *Aglaonema*, locally known as Pride of Sumatra, and *Homalomena rubescens*.[5] Both were selected for their aesthetic qualities (the flowering *Guzmania lingulata*, for example) and their lower natural light requirements regarding the relatively low solar penetration at the courtyard base. The upper portion of the green wall is comprised of two species, *Thunbergia grandiflora* and *Philodendron scandens*, which are hardier and easy to maintain, making them ideal plants for the placement on this part of the wall that is difficult to access for maintenance.[6]

The green wall consists of a modular system of 600 x 600 mm panels, each with its own compost bag. The compost was recycled from horticultural waste harvested from the National University Hospital building as well as from the landscape contractor's other ongoing projects. The panels are provided with individual door systems, integrated in the steel frame panel support system, that can be opened for access and maintenance. An automated drip irrigation system is extended to each one of the panels and synchronized with the BMS. As the interior landscaped courtyard is open to the sky, the irrigation system is calibrated to account for Singapore's monsoon season to avoid over-watering as well as to conserve water.

Rooftop Garden

A rooftop garden with sports facilities is located on top of the building's vertical green wall. The efficient planning of mechanical spaces on the roof allowed for the addition of a large rooftop garden. With an area of approximately 350 sqm, the green feature substantially increases the building's overall green plot ratio. The planting of the rooftop garden continues the plant species of the engineered ecosystem that starts on the building's ground level.

Sustainable Construction

Environment-friendly construction practices were applied throughout the implementation of the project. For example, rainwater was collected on site and used for a number of construction processes. A water treatment plant was deployed on site to reduce the silt content of the collected rainwater prior to its discharge to the existing external drains. A centralized placement of tap points with installed regulators controlled the amount of water dispensed.

Critique

The project received a Singapore Building Construction Authority (BCA) Green Mark Gold Plus Award. It created an extension of the existing ecological habitat by being built responsibly and sustainably. The NUHS Tower Block shows the emergence of buildings in the region that are holistically green, starting from conceptual design all the way to their management.

1. Anderson, Collin. *The Master Series: DP Architects*. Images Publishing, 2012.
2. Sim, J.W.S., H. T. W. Tan and I. M. Turner. "Adinandra belukar: an anthropogenic heath forest in Singapore" in *Vegetatio*, vol. 102, n. 2 (1992). pp. 125-137.
3. IES Academy and GeoSS. "Geology of Singapore." July 2012 (source: http://www.srmeg.org.sg/docs/N13072012_2.pdf).
4. DPA. E-mail interview. 2 December 2013.
5. Seah, Brandon. "Kent Ridge - Introduction" in *Habitat News*, 2001 (source:http://habitatnews.nus.edu.sg/heritage/pasirpanjang/ridgeplants/intro.htm).
6. Kwee, Chew Thiam. "Improving WAH Safety for Landscaping & Horticulture Works." Workplace Safety and Health Council, 2011 (source:https://www.wshc.sg/wp s/themes/html/upload/event/file/2_%20Improving%20WAH%20Safety%20for%20Landscaping%20&%20Horticulture%20Works_Mr%20Chew%20Thiam%20Kwee.pdf).

Mountain Dwellings

BIG /JDS Architects

Building Type: Residential
Climate Zone: Marine West Coast
Location: 2300 Copenhagen S, Denmark
Coordinates: 55°39'26"N 12°36'34"E
Date: 2008

Height: 37 m/12 floors
Gross Floor Area: 33,000 m²
Number of units: 80
Gross Green Area in Building: 3,950 m²
Gross Green area to Built-Up Area: 12%

Mountain Dwellings is an important example of what the Bjarke Ingels Group (BIG) likes to refer to as "architectural alchemy," i.e. the "combining [of] elements to turn architectural lead into gold."[1] A parochial brief for a car park and an apartment tower has been transformed into a special typology that offers benefits for both programs. The car park is organized as a sloping volume, which results in spectacular spaces of a quality that is rarely seen in this functional typology. The apartments are arranged in a stair-like formation on top of the sloping car park, turning them into a cascade of suburban single-story houses, each complete with its own terrace and small garden—thereby creating, according to the architects, the image of a "Cambodian temple ruin, completely covered in green."[2]

Mountain Dwellings is situated in Ørestad, a newly developed borough of Copenhagen on the island of Amager, to the east of the city center. The west of Amager Island is characterized by natural areas that, as part of the development of Ørestad, are being consolidated into Amager Nature Park, a new recreational outdoor area.[3] Largely residential suburban communities and Copenhagen's Kastrup Airport occupy the island's east. Amager Island as a whole is a node for international traffic, hosting both the airport and the Øresund Bridge, which is part of the only road connection between the European mainland and Sweden.

Ørestad, under development since 1997, is 5 km long and 600 m wide. It runs approximately in a north-south direction between the Amager Nature Park and the residential areas.[4] The borough is divided into five districts, which are connected by Ørestad Boulevard. This important traffic artery runs along the length of Ørestad, together with a newly constructed elevated metro line to the center of Copenhagen. Ørestad City, the district where Mountain Dwellings is located, is situated roughly halfway along Ørestad Boulevard and is characterized by a mix of residential blocks and large-scale commercial developments. The two defining volumes of Ørestad City, the Bella Convention Center and the Field's Shopping Mall, are each Scandinavia's largest buildings of their type.[5] Directly adjacent to the Convention Center is Scandinavia's largest hotel, the Bella Sky Comwell.[6] Located between these large commercial volumes is an area with a park and apartment buildings. Mountain Dwellings is situated close to the southwestern corner of the Convention Center, between Ørestad Boulevard and the existing suburb of Amager. Its neighbor to the south is the residential VM Building, also designed by BIG and JDS, completed in 2005.

The municipal master plan foresaw two buildings on the almost square 8,000 sqm site: a residential tower of about 10,000 sqm and a much larger parking garage of 20,000 sqm, to serve as a shared parking facility for the neighborhood.[7] In the realized project, this program resulted in 80 residential units with a total floor area of 8,000 sqm and 480 parking lots on eight levels, one of them under ground. About half of the residential units are identical, with a size of 80 sqm.[8] Those located on Mountain Dwellings' edge negotiate between the diagonal grid of the apartments and the largely orthogonal perimeter of the building, resulting in larger and varying sizes of up to 150 sqm.[9] The project further features a number of commercial programs, including 1,600 sqm of shared creative office space, an Indian restaurant, and a children's cultural center.[10] Mountain Dwellings' total floor area is 33,000 sqm.[11]

The slope of the overall building volume runs diagonally across the square site, with the lowest southwest corner touching the ground, and the highest northeast corner standing 32 m and 11 stories tall. Following the contour of the neighboring VM Building, the otherwise rectangular perimeter of Mountain Dwellings has a large zigzag on its southern side. The slope of the car park directly translates into the arrangement of the residential units, which are staggered in diagonal rows across the largely rectangular volume below, resulting in a stair formation of "penthouses"[12] that are uninterrupted by circulation areas. The residential units are suspended three floors above the car park, generating a generous open space in between that allows for daylight and fresh air to come in from the sides of the building. The resulting void spaces, with a maximum ceiling height of 16 m, are typically not seen in car parks.[13]

Residents enter their units via hallways that are connected to the car park via concrete footbridges as well as via a central staircase that runs diagonally across the car park. An additional staircase wraps around the car park on the building's perimeter. Alternatively, pedestrians and Copenhagen's ubiquitous cyclists can ride the Swiss-made funicular that runs parallel to the central staircase.[14]

The design of the car park and the voids features an almost surreal mix of textures, colors, and patterns, evoking a contemporary, urban sensibility that can be associated with MTV and hip street culture. As a contrast, the straightforward design of the apartments features only three finishes (wood, white walls, and glass) and an almost simplistic typical plan, a bar of smaller servicing spaces is

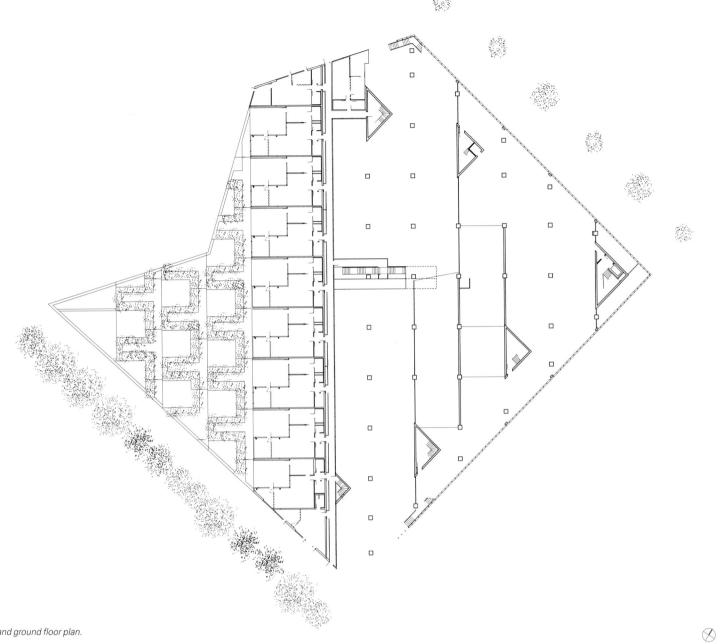

Site and ground floor plan.

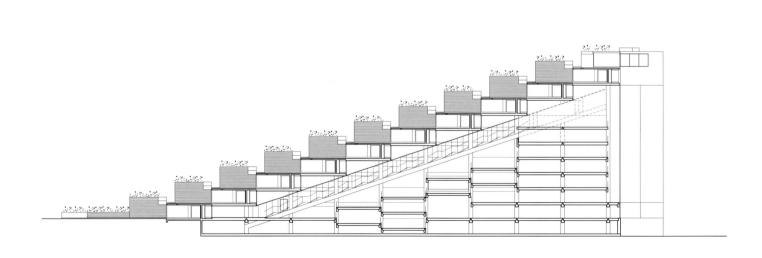

Section.

located at the back of the L-shaped units, with a large open space and bedroom opening onto a generous terrace.

According to architect Bjarke Ingels, Jørn Utzon's prototypical Kingo Houses were the inspiration for the design of the residential units.[15] Constructed between 1957 and 1960, the Kingo Houses are a residential community of so-called atrium houses near the Danish city of Helsingør. Each single-story unit covers a square of 15 x 15 m, with the L-shaped volume of the house arranged around an enclosed courtyard.[16] Over time, these courtyards have often developed into lush enclosed gardens. Taking full advantage of the forested and gently undulating site, the units are arranged in waving rows that follow the contours of the landscape and take views and solar orientation into account.[17]

Contrastingly, Mountain Dwellings' apartments are laid out in a diagonal grid of 10 x 10 m and on an artificial topology. As Ingels puts it, "because Copenhagen is completely flat, if you want to have a nice, south-facing slope with a view, you basically have to do it yourself."[18] Accordingly, the grid of the apartments is rotated 45° with respect to the overall volume, so that the "penthouse" terraces and rooms face toward the southwest. In this way, all apartments have excellent views over the lush, almost pastoral, suburb of western Amager.

AstroTurf on a Temple Ruin

Beyond the individual wooden terrace, each apartment has a grassed balcony with a planter box railing, amounting to what can be considered as a small garden, similar to the gardens of the Kingo Houses. However, the grass is AstroTurf, an artificial turf,

apparently due to budgetary constraints, since real grass would have been too heavy for the parsimonious building structure.[19] Yet the AstroTurf could also be a deliberate design move in line with the sophisticated artificiality of the car park. The planter boxes are mechanically irrigated with conserved rainwater,[20] making them almost as maintenance-free as the AstroTurf. Ingels promised in 2009 that the planter boxes would transform the building "into a sort of a Cambodian temple ruin, completely covered in green,"[21] and more recent photographs approximate that vision.[22]

An important concern in terms of the design of the terraces and balconies is privacy. In the earlier VM Building, large protruding balconies encourage interactions between the residents but offer little visual protection.[23] By contrast, the wide planter boxes of Mountain Dwellings' terraces shield residents from the views of their neighbors above and below. Ingels explains that "you should be able to walk around naked when you're on [the terrace], but when you're on the [artificial] grass you should expect to be seen."[24]

While the perforated metal facade of the car park points toward the parking lot of the Bella Convention Center, the overgrown cascade of the apartments is oriented toward the southwest, with views over the pastoral suburb of Amager. Perhaps the tension between the traditional, green residential suburb and the early-21st-Century mega-developments has resulted in a tectonic shift, pushing the car park into a slope and spreading out the apartments.

Critique

BIG's flippant rationality has pushed the one-dimensional dichotomy between grass and asphalt to its seemingly inevitable conclusion. The car park not only embraces the logic of car-based developments like the Bella Convention Center or Field's Mall, but also celebrates it with the poetic hyperbole of candy-colored aluminum and Piranesian perspectives. However, the murals depicting a wilderness of car wrecks drive home an important point: car culture already seems to be a phenomenon of the past, more relevant for the 20th Century than for the 21st. Copenhagen is a city well known for its cycling culture. It has won the title of European Green Capital of 2014, and has set itself ambitious goals, such as achieving carbon-neutrality by 2025 and having 50% of commuters ride bicycles by 2015.[25] In short, the car park's unabashed celebration of car culture is somewhat tongue-in-cheek and its graphic monumentality refers to a cultural moment that seems to have already passed.

Similarly, the apartments are greened in a symbolic, almost cartoonish way. Clearly, their generous terraces, views, and solar orientation vastly improve their quality. However, the terraces' planter boxes seem to serve more the softening of Mountain Dwellings' appearance than to improve the residents' outdoor experience. To this extent, the apartments fall short of the stated aim of combining "the splendors of the suburban backyard with the social intensity of urban density."[26] The lush appearance of the neighboring district of Amager and the compelling precedent of the Kingo Houses are telling reminders of the potential qualities of suburban outdoor spaces, admittedly hard to replicate in denser residential typologies.

In terms of urban intensity, as residents proceed directly from their parking lots to their apartments, there is little opportunity for interaction. Mountain Dwellings' few commercial programs are arranged in a strip on the eastern facade, with its ground floor dominated by parking and residential programs. The project's immediate surroundings are characterized by anonymous housing blocks and the enormous shopping mall. Beatrice Galilee writes that "the Mountain Dwellings [create] an image of modernity towering over mundane little boxes" but that the "pacey urban lifestyle that the Mountain Dwellings promise is not to be found here."[27]

Of course, some of these issues relate to the overall master plan of Ørestad City, whose juxtaposition of large-scale commercial programs and apartment buildings seems problematic. In that sense, Mountain Dwellings also shows that the integration of architecture and nature and the creation of intense urbanity depend on a framework of urban planning and building regulations.

1. "Think Big" in *dwell*, September 2009.
2. TED Talk: *Bjarke Ingels: 3 warp-speed architecture tales*. Video, July 2009 (source: http://www.ted.com/talks/bjarke_ingels_3_warp_speed_architecture_tales.html).
3. Source: http://www.orestad.dk/byliv-oplevelser/orestad_natur/naturpark_amager.aspx
4. *Godt Begyndt*. By & Havn, December 2011 (source: http://www.orestad.dk/~/media/ByOgHavn/Pdf/Godt-begyndt2011.ashx; www.orestad.dk/orestad-fakta/orestad-beliggenhed.aspx).
5. Sources: http://www.linkedin.com/company/bella-center; http://www.visitdenmark.co.uk/en-gb/denmark/fields-gdk412275.
6. Source: http://www.linkedin.com/company/bella-center.
7. "The Mountain Dwelling" in *ICON*, 064 (October 2008).
8. *Ibid*.
9. Source: http://www.dac.dk/en/dac-life/copenhagen-x-gallery/cases/mountain/.
10. *Status på byggerier i Ørestad*. By & Havn. April 2013 (source: http://www.orestad.dk/~/media/_NewOrestad/Status_Orestad_maj13.ashx).
11. Source: http://www.dac.dk/en/dac-life/copenhagen-x-gallery/cases/mountain/.
12. TED Talk …
13. Source: http://www.archdaily.com/15022/mountain-dwellings-big/
14. "Think Big ..."
15. "The Mountain Dwelling .."
16. Ejerlauget Romerhusene (2006, June). *Romerhusene*. Source: http://www.romerhusene.dk/dokumenter/folder_eng_030606.pdf
17. *Jørn Utzon 2003 Laureate Biography*. The Hyatt Foundation (source: http://www.pritzkerprize.com/sites/default/files/file_fields/field_files_inline/2003_bio.pdf).
18. TED Talk …
19. "The Mountain Dwelling ..."
20. Source: http://www.archdaily.com/15022/
21. TED Talk …
22. Source: http://ssl.panoramio.com/photo/61125774
23. Source: http://www.big.dk/#projects-vm
24. "The Mountain Dwelling ..."
25. Source: http://ec.europa.eu/environment/europeangreencapital/winning-cities/2014-copenhagen/
26. Source: http://www.dezeen.com/2008/02/17/mountain-dwellings-by-big/
27. "The Mountain Dwelling ..."

Vertical Garden House

Office of Ryue Nishizawa

Building Type: Residential
Climate Zone: Humid Subtropical
Location: Tokyo, Japan
Coordinates: 35°40'27"N 139°46'46"E
Date: 2011

Height: 13 m/5 floors
Gross Floor Area: 66 m²
Gross Green Area in Building: 20 m²
Gross Green Area to Built-Up Area: 30%

"An architecturally successful living unit does not just represent a piece of enclosed air, but rather a psychosocial immune system that is capable of regulating the degree to which it is sealed from the outside on demand." [1]

–Peter Sloterdijk

Hidden from view down one of the many 3 m alleyways in Tokyo's densely packed city center, Ryue Nishizawa's Vertical Garden House occupies a previously undeveloped site with a footprint of only 4 x 8 m. The project provides a green counterpoint to its surrounding modernist apartment towers that are tightly sealed from the outside world. [2] The architect re-appropriates familiar Western architectural tropes for his interest in reinterpreting the relationship of architecture and landscape. Such a process of synthesis can be seen as deeply rooted in Japan. As Tsuyoshi Hirooka notes in the introduction to a book on contemporary Japanese graphic design: "We have always adopted ideas and materials from overseas, always superficially because of a lack of interest in understanding the background of other countries. But we have developed those ideas according to our own interpretations and brought them to a completely different destination from the original ones." [3] For Nishizawa, the integration of plants and architecture within the densely packed confines of central Tokyo enables the building to operate as "a loose script, one that includes multiple and open-ended scenarios. Its inhabitants are offered a free range of options and trajectories, passing through realms of varied degrees of activation." [4]

The project functions as a residence and workspace for two female writers and editors in the heart of the city's bustling publishing district. The clients, dissatisfied with the stagnancy of their dark old house on the periphery of Tokyo, requested a more open and flexible space for living and working. [5]

Blending Home and City

As per Tokyo's zoning regulations, setbacks with the adjacent buildings are minimized in order to maximize the utility of the site. [6] Given the limited size and closed-in nature of the site, Nishizawa deploys a familiar Corbusian idea—the Domino Frame—to allow for a *plan libre*, which effectively extends the physical spaces of the house and the city as far as possible into one another. [7] The building's relationship with its urban surroundings is mediated, not by a particular treatment of the facade, but by its complete removal. Five concrete slabs, supported by large, strategically positioned columns relating to the openings in the adjacent buildings, form a series of vertical thresholds and provide the basis for creating a range of relationships with the city at large.

Organizationally, each floor contains a series of enclosed or partially enclosed spaces that facilitate a variety of activities—living, eating, meeting, resting, sleeping, washing. Enclosures are set back from the slab edge under deep overhangs in order to create open space at the perimeter of the structure for a variety of densely planted gardens, which provide loose definition to informal activities. In doing so, the more public functions of the home—living, meeting, and eating—are allowed to blend with the city. Sectionally, the plantings and screens are carefully distributed to mix moments of isolated reflection with experiences of community engagement within the home and its interaction with the city. The integration of plants defines each level as its own unique landscape, effectively shifting the typology of the single-family urban home from a place in which to observe one's surroundings, to a place in which to live with them.

Redefining the Program of Home and Garden

Vertical Garden House's 66 sqm of floor area are distributed over four floors. As the five nearly identical concrete slabs measure about 25 sqm each, the ample remaining space is comprised of an occupiable roof garden and extensive exterior spaces. [8] The site is oriented east to west, such that one of the 4 m sides connects directly to a 3-m-wide alley to the west.

Veiled behind a screen of potted plants, the ground floor of Vertical Garden House is fully enclosed, housing the kitchen and dining spaces at the back of the building and working and seating areas closest to the alley to the west. From here, a small open-tread metal stair winds upwards through the entire house, landing within a bedroom, with the bed screened from the stair by a simple open rack of hanging clothes. Outdoor space, which connects to a basin at the back, adds engagement with nature and the city to the nightly ritual of cleaning the dishes after dinner. A small meeting room situated at the western edge of the slab reaches out to the city, enclosed only by a translucent curtain and a raised planter-cum-railing. The loosely programmed spaces of the landscape are deployed in careful conjunction with plants and minimal curtains to screen more intimate activities within the "deep" interior.

Winding up to the third floor, the stair lands within a space only large enough to move outside to a lushly planted landscape with a packed dirt floor. At the back of this level is a fully enclosed

bathroom with a raised tile floor. Located at the front of the house, set amidst a thick veil of potted plants, is a small bench balanced precariously along the edge of the floor slab. The bench, removed from the activities of the house, sits at the vertical threshold of the garden and the city, effectively turning the house inside out.

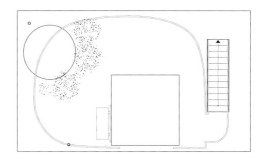

The fourth floor contains the second bedroom, which is, apart from the ground level, the largest single enclosed space in the building. A small desk at the western edge of the slab overlooks the city from above, separated only by an elevated planter and a few potted plants. A stair at the back of the house connects to a roof terrace with an enclosed storage room and an opening to below, allowing views of the sky from the desk onto the fourth floor. A railing rings the roof, defining an area for human occupancy, while potted plants are loosely arranged to suggest the use of the space.

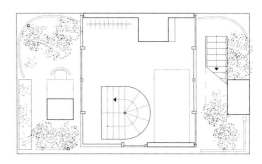

Nishizawa's architectural design palette for the project is straightforward. Internal partitions are non-existent. Instead, full-height glazed partitions and curtains delineate interior spaces from exterior gardens. In plan, space is clearly inside or outside, not both. The materials reinforce these thresholds. Treated concrete slabs on the exterior provide a substrate for the floor finishes that are found only within the interior spaces. There is no attempt at material continuity from interior to exterior; on the contrary, materials are used to heighten and clarify the distinction between the two. However, the way Nishizawa distributes the building's programs clearly subverts this distinction.

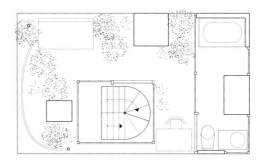

Meeting rooms, work spaces, and living rooms, functions typically associated with the interior, are placed within the surrounding garden. In placing interior programs at the periphery of the building, these spaces simultaneously belong to and exist within the space of the garden and also the city. According to Nishizawa's notion of "verb-like architecture," "there is no concrete line of demarcation between one sequence of actions and the next."[9] By subverting the notion of program relative to what is understood to be interior and what is exterior, Nishizawa is able to shift the residents' relationship to the city—bringing them into sync with the rhythms and idiosyncrasies of a particular place.

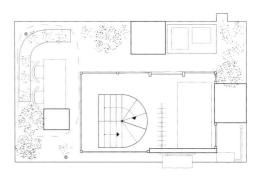

Other Nishizawa projects also capitalize on the potential of defining spatial relationships between landscape and architecture. In Moriyama House on the outskirts of Tokyo, Nishizawa atomizes the programs of a typical house as a series of boxes connected by a single exterior urban landscape. Each room opens to this landscape, generating new communal spaces and social structures. Vertical Garden House, with its comparatively restricted site, can be understood as arranging pavilions of this kind within its own vertically striated landscape. Each of these projects becomes a "space-time where building interior, exterior, and environment are all unified and continuous."[10]

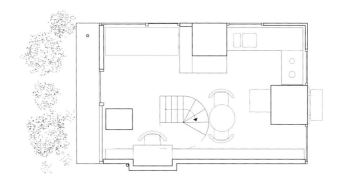

The plants play a crucial role in the creation of these multiple thresholds within a seemingly singular open space. They allow for spaces and programs that provide a looser fit with one another, allowing inhabitants to find spaces appropriate to any desired activity at any given time. As summer turns to fall and into winter, these thresholds experience a slow change, altering the inhabitants' habits and usages of spaces, but also bringing them in tune with the passage of time and the city around them—the experience of architecture, nature, and the city "through extended time."[11]

Floor plans.

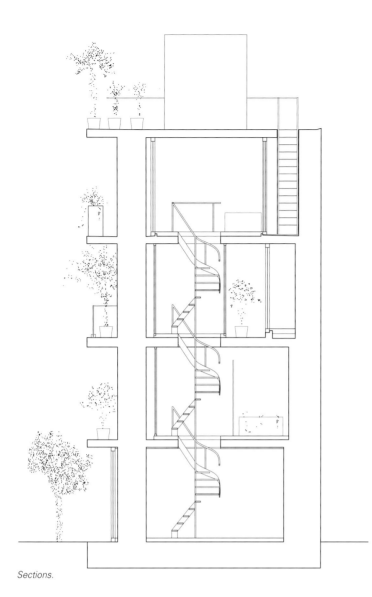
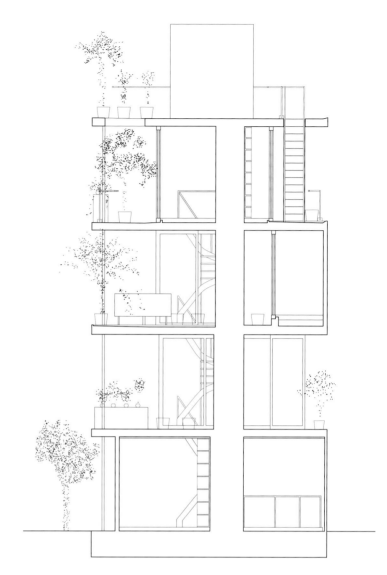

Sections.

Critique

Vertical Garden House provides a model for compact living in which the garden as flexible communal space serves a foremost role. In stark contrast, Kisho Kurokawa's Capsule Tower, composed of and articulated as individual living units, speculates on a reality in which individual self-sufficient units can be replaced and shifted as they are seemingly "plugged" into and "unplugged" from a larger infrastructure. In reality, this model proposes a suffocating lack of interaction with people and the city,—"cellular" living indeed.[12]

German philosopher Peter Sloterdijk proposes an alternative scenario in which residents are provided with the ability to seek "psychic ventilation."[13] Juxtaposed against suffocatingly tall stacks of apartments towering overhead, Vertical Garden House channels Sloterdijk by creating a layered and hybridized spatial envelope as a means of dissolving the boundary between interior and exterior—between city and home. The architectural envelope is no longer thought of as a singular line, or a series of offset lines, but instead as an entire voluminous landscape occupied by people and nature. This landscape includes the inside of the building in order to further regulate its deep interior spaces. In essence, the envelope disappears in favor of space.

In this sense, Vertical Garden House serves to reset our comfort levels. The project redefines city living by providing an infrastructure that can be occupied by humans and plants simultaneously. Passing by, one cannot imagine what it feels like to sleep behind a curtain of plants 20 m above the city, mere inches from the windows of the neighbors' air-conditioned flats. However, one can imagine watching these very same neighbors pass by the next day while sipping the morning coffee in the fresh air, feeling the soil underfoot, waving hello and watching on as they then take a seat at the cafe across the street to do the same.

1. Sloterdijk, Peter, trans. by Daniela Fabricius. "Cell block, Egospheres, Self-Container: The Apartment as a Co-isolated Existence" in *Log*, n. 10 (2007). pp. 88-108.
2. Zancan, Roberto. "Tokyo's Vertical Thresholds #2: Ryue Nishizawa" in *Domus*, 16 December 2011 (source: http://www.domusweb.it/en/architecture/2011/12/16/tokyo-s-vertical-thresholds-2-ryue-nishizawa.html).
3. Prat, Ramon, and Tomoko Sakamoto. *JPG: Japan Graphics*. Actar, 2001.
4. Idenburg, Florian. *The SANAA Studios 2006-2008: Learning from Japan: Single Story Urbanism.* Lars Müller Publishers, 2009.
5. Dimmer, Christian. "Garden & House" in *Australian Design Review*, Asia Pacific issue 127 (source: http://www.australiandesignreview.com/architecture/25787-garden-house-2).
6. Zancan, Roberto. "Tokyo's Vertical Thresholds …"
7. "Interview: Experience of Architectural Concepts, Ryue Nishizawa" in *A+U*, n. 512 (2013). pp. 66-72.
8. "Ryue Nishizawa: Garden & House" in *A+U*, n. 512 (2013). p. 19.
9. Nishizawa, Ryue, trans. by Brian Amstutz. "Essay: Landscape-like architecture, verb-like architecture" in *A+U*, n. 512 (2013). p. 8-9.
10. *Ibid.*
11. *Ibid.*
12. Peter Sloterdijk, trans. by Daniela Fabricius. "Cell block …"
13. *Ibid.*

Via Verde

Grimshaw Architects/Dattner Architects

Building Type: Residential
Climate Zone: Humid Continental
Location: 700 Brook Avenue, Bronx, NY 10455, USA
Coordinates: 40°49'9"N 73°54'45"W
Date: 2012

Height: 65 m/20 floors
Gross Floor Area: 27,000 m²
Number of units: 222
Gross Green Area in Building: 3,700 m²
Gross Green Area to Built-Up Area: 14%

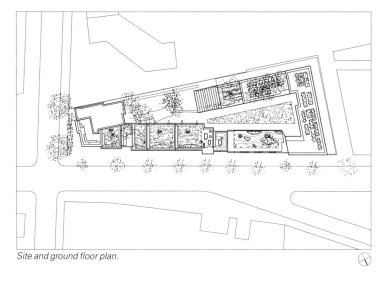

Site and ground floor plan.

"Where the Bronx once burned, we are building gardens in the sky." [1]

–Ruben Diaz Jr., Bronx Borough President

Via Verde, a subsidized affordable housing project in the South Bronx, New York City, was conceived, designed, and built as a model for similar projects within New York City and beyond. The project positions sustainability as more than environmental performance, but rather as the ability to provide a healthy lifestyle in an enriching community—to reopen the discussion of the role and potential of public housing in the USA. By engaging the local design community, the city has developed a project that casts its effects beyond the typical scope of architecture. By overlaying health as a primary concern of the project, green spaces are woven through the building in order to create specific relationships with, and enhance the value and utility of, community spaces. Similarly, the massing and organization of the complex as well as the distribution and arrangement of the units projects a scenario for public housing that deviates from past failures.

Development of Public Housing Types

Historically, changes to New York City's housing and zoning regulations had the goal to increase access to natural light and air to improve the health and well-being of the inhabitants. The earliest public housing tenements housed between 20 and 22 families each and consisted typically of four apartments per floor, with three rooms per apartment and only one of them having a window. Growing social concerns led to public health reforms, so that later regulations required windows for every room as well as fireproof partitions. [2]

Later developments included a variety of "model tenements" scattered around the growing metropolis, supported by a small number of wealthy and benevolent businessmen. Built in the late 19th Century, these new tenements provided sanitary and fireproof housing for the masses. The units were small, but naturally ventilated and equipped with running water and toilets in each unit. Often, the buildings filled entire urban blocks, which allowed for the provision of open spaces for children to play safely away from the street. However, relying on support from New York City's philanthropic community, the model tenements were never able to conquer the scale of the housing problem in New York City at that time. In subsequent years, similar attempts were made by the local labor unions and the New York City government but none could provide the required large quantities of housing.

Not until the mid-1930s did the federal government step in and begin constructing public housing. The first two projects of this type in the USA were constructed in Brooklyn and Harlem. Relative to the problem at hand, these first attempts were quite small, four-story blocks set in a landscaped park-like "superblock" with well-designed playgrounds, benches, and recreation spaces. However, these community-driven projects did not solve the issue of scale and high numbers. The ensuing vertical extension of the early projects led to the "towers in the park" type, which became the model for future public housing in the USA. While the provision of light and air, and space for recreation, was a driving force, the government failed to predict the range of social issues that would arise from the sheer quantity of dwellers without adequate social and community amenities in close proximity to their homes.[3]

More recently, public housing has been provided by public-private partnerships, wherein developers receive subsidies that make this type of construction economically rewarding. Over the years, this model has proven effective in providing large quantities of privately funded housing. However, any visions of how these buildings would be transformative were quickly forgotten. And while Via Verde falls into this model of public-private partnership, it also represents former mayor Michael Bloomberg's vision for the future of public housing. Thus, it is no surprise that beyond the historical mantras of light and air, Via Verde injects the South Bronx with important aspects of community and health.

A Model for Future Developments

The Bronx is one of the areas that saw a huge influx of public housing in the 1950s to 1970s. Once a thriving residential community in the first half of the 20th Century, the Bronx underwent a rapid downfall in the 1960s and 1970s. While the culminating event was the wave of arson that ravaged the borough in the 1970s, a series of other factors, including Robert Moses' Cross Bronx Expressway, the influx of public housing, and a number of controversial real estate policies, likely contributed to the borough's difficulties. As the area's reputation worsened, amenities in the borough were reduced or eliminated. While the Bronx has seen a recent resurgence due to increased investments in social, economic, and environmental infrastructure, health issues still abound; asthma-related illnesses in the Bronx remain much higher than in other parts of the city,[4] and obesity is a widespread problem among the population. These health issues are attributed in part to the poor air quality and lack of amenities, as these neighborhoods tend to be near areas of industry, and far from the city's parks and green spaces.

It is from this rather dire situation that Mayor Bloomberg and the NYC Department of Housing Preservation and Development (HPD) launched the New Housing New York Legacy Project competition in 2007. It was part of the ambitious New Housing Marketplace Plan, which originally called for the construction or preservation of 68,000 affordable homes for New Yorkers and was later expanded to create an additional 97,000 homes by 2013.[5] The competition called for architect-developer teams to design an innovative housing prototype that considers ideas of affordability, sustainability, transferability, and viability.[6] Thus, design was an important component of the project, but given the complexity of funding, building, and operating public or subsidized housing, the other aspects were given equal weight such that the project could stand as a model for future developments.

The site is well-connected to Manhattan via public transport.[7] The close-by "Hub," a bustling commercial district with shop-lined streets, has historically served as the social and commercial heart of the South Bronx and provides a strong community base from which the Via Verde community can grow. The 5,575 sqm, long and narrow triangular former industrial site runs north-south, with an abandoned railroad line running along the eastern edge. It is bounded by East 156th Street on the north, Brook Avenue on the west, a subsidized housing tower to the east, and a city-owned playing field to the south, which has provided increased Floor Area Ratio by virtue of applying its air rights to the Via Verde site.[8]

In addition to 3,715 sqm of green roof, the project includes 25,375 sqm of residential and 700 sqm of commercial space. 222 apartments are distributed among three distinct building types. A 20-story tower at the north end of the site relates in scale to the adjacent 18-story Bronxchester housing tower. The massing steps down from there, providing a six- to 13-story mid-rise duplex component running along Brook Avenue, which is punctured at ground level by the main entrance that leads to the inner courtyard. Two- to four-story townhouses accessed directly from this central space extend to the southern edge of the site, and wrap the southeastern corner to further enclose the courtyard. By providing a range of unit types, the design team acknowledges the need for a departure from typical repetitive apartment layouts.

Light, Air, Community

The massing of the building complex developed out of the desire to inject Via Verde with opportunities for healthy living. The project maximizes southern exposure by stepping down from north to south. Wrapping around the edge of the site, the building creates an inner garden courtyard insulated from the busy city around it. The terraced building form steps up from this central courtyard, spiralling as a series of gardens from the center to the south and finally to the north side of the site, thereby creating intimate and grand spaces while maximizing natural light and open vistas to the south. The dynamic gardens host a variety of uses.

Active gardening spaces provide the opportunity for fruit and vegetable cultivation. Spaces for recreation and fitness are coupled with sustainable systems such as stormwater control and solar energy collection. The gardens draw the community of the building together in productive and meaningful ways. In order to maximize access to natural light and air in all units, the design team developed creative ways of unitizing the project. The building's low-rise section to the south provides two-story townhouses with a private garden and one or two floor-through apartments above. Each of these apartments is accessed directly from the exterior, again increasing community engagement and access to fresh air and gardens. Ground floor live-work units open to Brook Avenue, providing further diversity while maintaining a certain amount of "eyes on the street" (Jane Jacobs).[9]

The mid-rise section loosely references Le Corbusier's *Unité d'Habitation* to increase access to natural light and air. Given the narrowness of the site and the desire to fully use the size of the ground-level courtyard, the design team reduced the typical width of a New York City mid-rise housing block. In order to maximize the efficiency of this narrower-than-normal block, double-height units are interlocked around a double-loaded corridor located on every other floor. Each unit is accessed from the corridor and occupies a floor-through area one level below the corridor.[10] In this way, each unit enjoys the benefits of cross-ventilation as well as the provision of double-height space. Eventually, the tower portion provides a range of units on each floor, from studios to three-bedrooms.

Without turning its back on the surrounding community, the project focuses on creating an intimate community within its confines. The inclusion of balconies, sunshades, and a richer and warmer palette of materials on the internal building skin help break down the scale and allow for an activated setting in which residents can monitor children at play in the courtyard below.

The green spine becomes the focus of these efforts. For example, the ground-level play area and courtyard are within view of the building's laundry room (a space typically located in the basement).

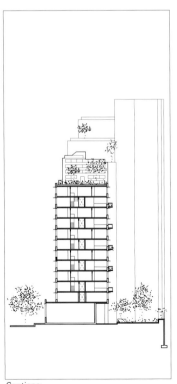
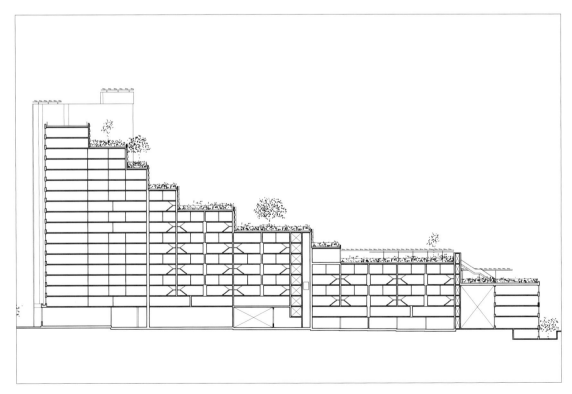

Sections.

Large amphitheater steps overlooking the central courtyard provide space for impromptu performances, gatherings, or simple conversation. Where they rise up to the community garden on the south end of the site, the planters, brimming with fresh fruits and vegetables, provide a place to come together to produce food. GrowNYC, an environmental organization that builds and supports community gardens, assists in the management and distribution of the fruits and vegetables.[11]

As the roof steps further up the building to the north, it connects to a fitness center open to all residents. The outdoor terrace of the green roof, shaded by a glistening trellis of PV panels, displays the on-site stormwater retention system used for irrigation of the green roofs. Stepping further up, the green roof is capped at the top level of the tower by a community space for residents' social functions, complete with sweeping views of the South Bronx and extending south to Manhattan.

Critique

By redefining sustainability to include community-strengthening and healthy-living measures within an affordable housing project, the architects of Via Verde have gone beyond designing for improved environmental performance. By extending the "bottom line," in economic terms, beyond the cost of the project to its overall success and longevity, this approach provides savings in other areas, most notably in healthcare. The success of the project will not only be measured by how it provides a healthy and vibrant residential community, nor how it assists in the Bronx's ascension back to respectability—on these merits, it has already succeeded. Intended to set "a new standard for affordable housing design and development,"[12] the project's true legacy will be how it transforms the typology of affordable housing in New York City and beyond. The effects of Via Verde can already be seen elsewhere in the Bronx with the construction of the Arbor House, a 124-unit apartment complex with a rooftop hydroponic farm and a living green wall in the lobby.[13] Via Verde shows the benefits of qualitative aspects of design—community, healthy living, and longevity.

1. Kimmelman, Michael. "In a Bronx Complex, Doing Good Mixes with Looking Good." *New York Times*, 26 September 2011 (source: http://www.nytimes.com/2011/09/26/arts/design/via-verde-in-south-bronx-rewrites-low-income-housing-rules.html?_r=1&ref=michaelkimmelman).
2. Dolkart, Andrew S. *The Architecture of New York City: Living Together*. Columbia University Digital Knowledge Base (source: http://ci.columbia.edu/0240s/0243_2/0243_2_fulltext.pdf).
3. *Ibid.*
4. NYC Department of Health and Mental Hygiene. "Preventing and Treating Childhood Asthma in NYC" in *NYC Vital Signs*, vol. 11, n. 4 (July 2012).
5. "Mayor Bloomberg Announces Expanded Affordable Housing Plans" in *NYCHA News*, March 2006 (source: http://www.nyc.gov/html/nycha/html/news/affordable-housing-announcement.shtml).
6. American Institute of Architects, New York. "New Housing New York Legacy Project" (source: http://www.aiany.org/NHNY/).
7. Scott, Janny. "Working Class Housing Complex Will Rise as Part of the Greenery" in *New York Times*, 17 January 2007 (source: http://www.nytimes.com/2007/01/17/nyregion/17housing.html).
8. American Institute of Architects, New York. "New Housing …"
9. Jacobs, Jane. *The Death and Life of Great American Cities*. New York: Random House, 1989.
10. Kubey, Karen. "Via Verde" in *Domus*, 14 June 2012 (source: http://www.domusweb.it/en/architecture/2012/06/14/via-verde.html).
11. Gonchar, Joann. "Affordable's New Look" in *Architectural Record*, July 2012. pp. 97-101.
12. American Institute of Architects, New York. "New Housing …"
13. Hickman, Matt. "A Bronx kale: Affordable housing meets hydroponic farming in Morrisania." Mother Nature Network, 12 March 2013 (source: http://www.mnn.com/your-home/remodeling-design/blogs/a-bronx-kale-affordable-housing-meets-hydroponic-farming-in).

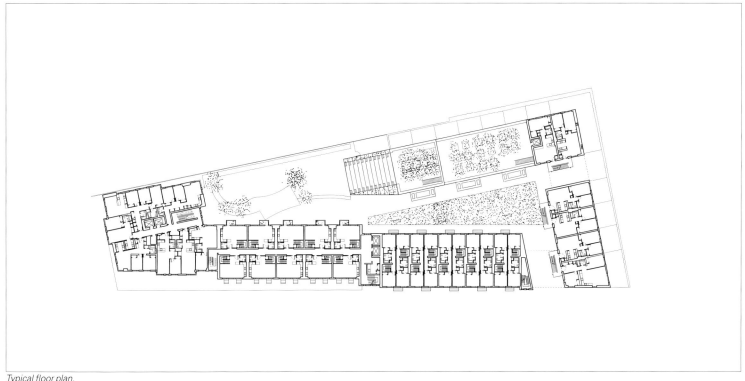

Typical floor plan.

Newton Suites

WOHA

Building Type: Residential
Climate Zone: Tropical Wet
Location: 60 Newton Road,
Singapore 307994
Coordinates: 1°19'5"N 103°50'31"E
Date: 2007

Height: 121 m/36 floors
Gross Floor Area: 11,835 m²
Number of units: 118
Site Area: 3,843 m²
Gross Green Area in Building: 4,122 m²
Gross Green Area to Built-Up Area: 35%
Gross Green Area to Site Area: 110%

Newton, District 11, is located in the central region of Singapore, in a high-rise planning zone adjacent to the city center that is considered one of the prime residential areas of the land-scarce city state. The condominium typology in Singapore is predominantly market-driven, with maximizing saleable area often being the primary goal of developers. With their first high-rise condominium project, WOHA were able to push the boundaries of high-density residential architecture.

The site offers beautiful and unobstructed views over the adjacent height-controlled MacRitchie Reservoir central nature reserve zone. However, it is bounded by Newton Road and Thomson Road, main traffic arteries connecting northern Singapore to the city center. The massing concept of Newton Suites elevates the residential portion of the project above the entrance drop-off and a car park podium.[1] The building effectively mitigates noise from the adjacent streets from the residential tower six stories above the ground level to the communal environmental deck level. The design allows for even the lowest residential units to enjoy views of the communal landscape deck at the back and views out to the central nature reserve to the front of the block.[2] This ensures that a maximum real estate value is retained for the developer.

Car Park Podium

Unlike most residential high-rises in Singapore at the time when the project was conceived, Newton Suites features an at-grade car park podium, which is formally treated as a "green box."[3] This solution lowered energy consumption during construction and is beneficial for the operation of the completed building. Labor-and energy-intensive excavations would have been required below ground level for this site, which is located on Singapore's hardest bedrocks, known as Bukit Timah Granite and Gombak Norite.[4] Metal screens flanking the building elevations serve as a support for leafy creepers that blanket the entire car park block. This design effectively screens the concrete car park block while fulfilling the requisite statutory ventilation requirements for the podium. The passive cross-ventilation reduces energy consumption for lighting and in particular mechanical ventilation. The creepers on the metal screens not only create an aesthetically appealing green screen but also absorb emissions from traffic within the car park itself.

Environmental Deck

Located on top of the car park podium, an environmental deck provides shared amenities for the residents of the tower such as jacuzzis, pools, a yoga terrace, and a gym. The deck's linear arrangement creates interesting views for the adjacent residential units, framed by a lush landscape with plants of varying heights and densities. The landscaped tree plantings surround a swimming pool that cantilevers 2 m from the adjacent floor slab, producing the image of a floating volume. The trees are rooted in 900-mm-deep planter boxes that allowed for them to be planted with semi-mature trees immediately upon completion of the project's superstructure. Plumeria trees line the central swimming pool, juxtaposed with palm trees that flank the north and south elevations to create a tapestry of vertical green. This design articulates the podium as a horizontal stratum and accentuates the verticality of the residential tower block, which features a stunning full-building-height vertical green wall. The result is an impressive continuity of green space from the car park block via the podium to the tower above.

Residential Tower Block

The residential tower rises 30 levels above the six-story car park podium and is crowned with double-volume penthouse units. The stacking of typical units over a common floor plate allowed for taking advantage of economies of scale in terms of prefabrication. There are four units per floor with two typical unit types: two-bedroom and three-bedroom units that range from approximately 80 to 120 sqm. The two penthouse units on top mirror each other in terms of their layout. They share a square sky garden of 6 x 6 m lined with timber seating for the residents to mingle or entertain guests. A large tree with an extensive canopy located slightly off center provides shading.

The massing of the otherwise tall and repetitive residential tower is interspersed on every 4th level with large and lushly planted sky gardens that cantilever 8 m from the main floor slab. Together with small, intimate 3-m-deep sky gardens that are part of the individual units' balconies, they create an interesting architectural rhythm on the facade. The habitable balconies are treated as outdoor living rooms that are oriented toward views of the nearby nature reserve and city center. When the screens are drawn, the balconies become spatial extensions of the generous indoor living rooms, framing the views to the nature reserve and pockets of green around the site.

The passive environmental design strategies for the tower range from its spatial and formal arrangement to the facade detailing. The tower is rotated on the north-south axis to mitigate glare from the morning and afternoon sun. It is also set back from the busy

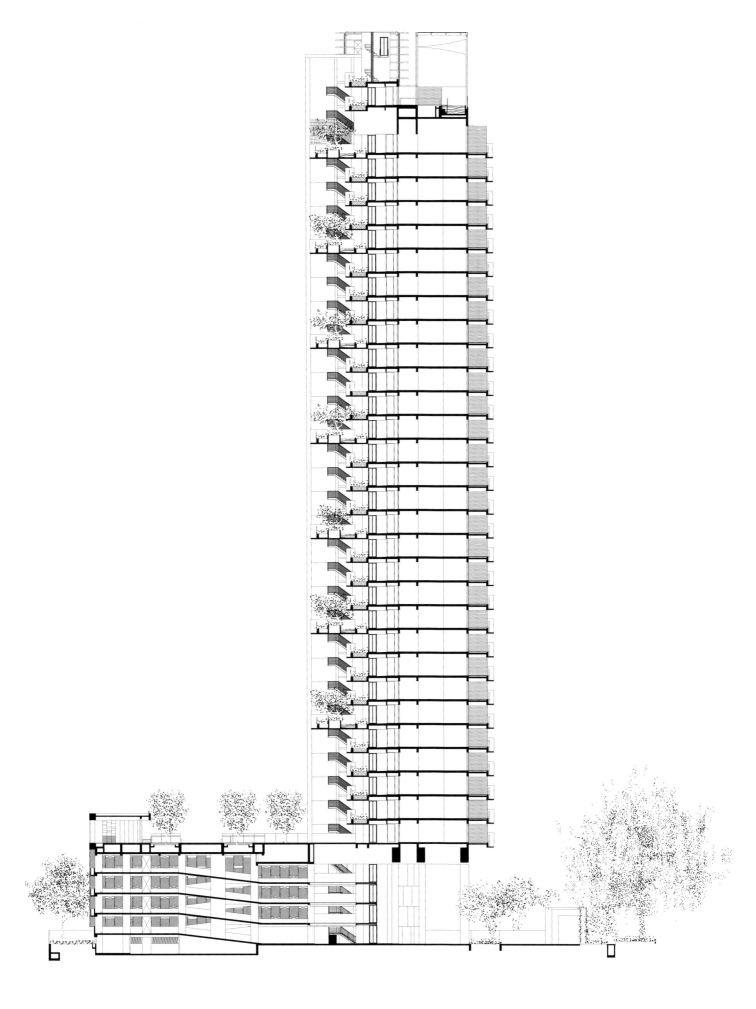

Section.

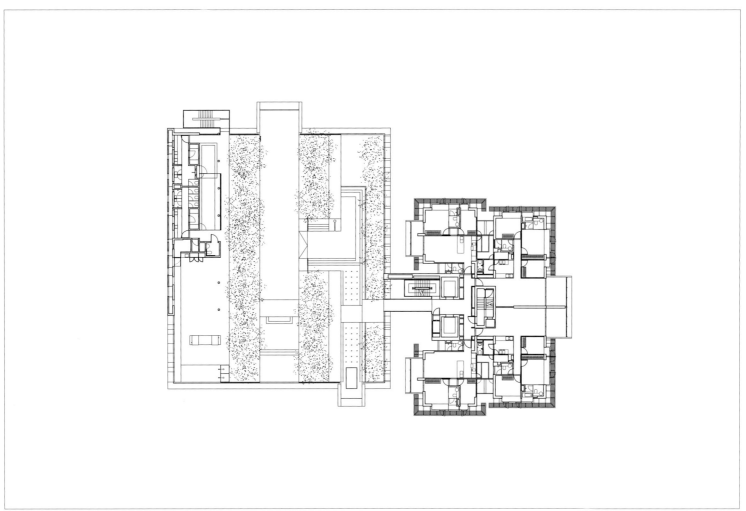

Typical floor plan.

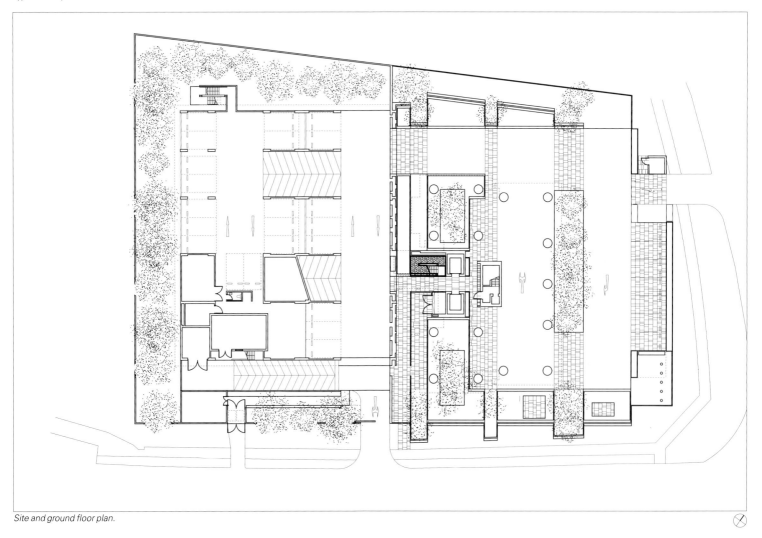

Site and ground floor plan.

streets below, with trees preventing emissions and noise from reaching the residential units. The stacked and cantilevered balconies on the northwest facade allow indirect sunlight to reach the interior spaces while reducing glare and heat gain. Shading is further enhanced by 1-m-deep horizontal metal screens with meshes that permit visual links to the ground. The variations of the meshes create changing patterns depending on the viewpoint, resulting in an interesting mixture of opaque and translucent textures on the facade. Bay windows fronting the east and west facades increase area efficiency and create a variety of patterns on the elevations, together with the varying gray prefabricated concrete panels that line the lobby and extend across the podium. The combination of the meshes and the concrete panels create interference patterns that produce a changing appearance of the building over the course of the day.

Landscape as Material

WOHA worked closely with Cicada, the landscape architects of Newton Suites, from the very beginning of the project. The ambition to "green" the building translates into a 130% planting ratio for the overall site.[5] Landscape elements are used extensively throughout the project as design materials, covering the architectural form as part of the roof and sky gardens, the green walls, and the creeper screens. The screens soften the harshness of the concrete and contribute to the shading of the building as well as the filtering of emissions. The tapestry of the green wall starts at the entrance lobby and rises a stunning 36 stories all the way to the roof, producing the tallest continuous vertical green wall in the world to date. Trees cover the podium, project out from the large sky gardens and crown the penthouse roof decks. The common sky gardens bring the tropical outdoors right into the lift lobbies and hallways of the project, creating an interesting weaving together of interior and exterior spaces.[6]

Critique

Upon completion, Newton Suites received the 2007 Silver Emporis Skyscraper Award. Since then, the concerted efforts of the architects and landscape architects have been widely recognized. The project was awarded by the Chicago Athenaeum and received the International Architecture Award in 2008, as well as the Green Good Design Award in 2009. The project was further the 1st Runner Up in the residential category for the FIABCI Prix d'Excellence Awards.

1. Bingham-Hall, Patrick. *WOHA*. Vol. 1: *Selected Projects*. Singapore: Pesaro Publishing, 2011.
2. Busenkell, Michaela, and Peter Cachola Schmal (eds.). *WOHA: breathing architecture*. Munich: Prestel, 2011.
3. "Newton Suites, Singapore—Architect's Statement." WOHA, 2013 (source: http://www.woha.net/#Newton-Suites).
4. Cai Jun Gang, Tritech Consultants. Geology of Singapore, Geotechnical Engineering Appreciation Course, jointly organized by IES Academy and GeoSS. ore. July 2012 (source: http://www.srmeg.org.sg/docs/N13072012_2.pdf).
5. "Newton Suites." Cicada (source: http://www.cicada.com.sg/cicada_main.htm).
6. WOHA. E-mail interview, 16 August 2013.

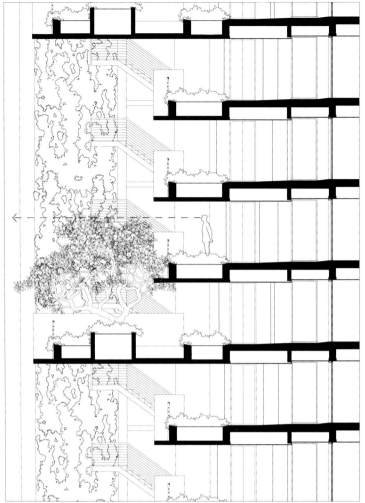

Section detail.

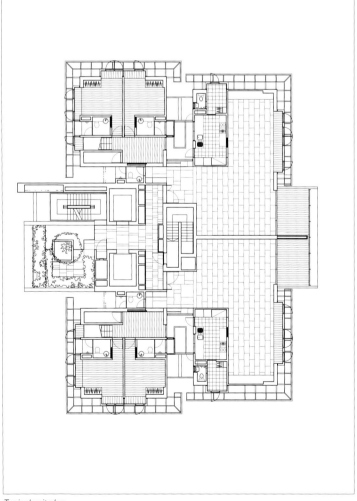

Typical unit plan.

The Interlace

OMA/Büro Ole Scheeren/RSP Architects Planners & Engineers

Building Type: Residential
Climate Zone: Tropical Wet
Location: 180-226 Depot Road,
Singapore 109684
Coordinates: 1°16'57"N 103°48'10"E
Date: 2015

Height: 83 m/24 floors
Gross Floor Area: 170,000 m²
Number of units: 1,040
Gross Green Area in Building: 34,141 m²
Gross Green area to Built-Up Area: 20%

The Interlace redefines recent residential typologies in Singapore in many ways. As the density of standard straight extrusion with vertical clusters of high-density living is increasing at an exponential rate, there is often little variety in typologies. The typical extruded tower has been discussed critically both in terms of a push for formal ingenuity as well as the required provisions for social cohesion and human living comforts. Following the example of some of the local pioneers of tropical high-density architecture, such as Chua Ka Seng and Tan Cheng Siong in some of their seminal Singapore projects including Pearlbank Apartment Tower, Pandan Valley Condominium, and Arcadia Gardens, OMA/Büro Ole Scheeren/RSP Architects Planners & Engineers revisit some of their common themes with the Interlace, such as natural ventilation, spacious gardens, and community-based developments.

The site is connected to the Southern Ridges, a historical outdoor trail that includes about 10 km of green open spaces with abundant flora and fauna. The Southern Ridges connect within walking distance to Mount Faber Park, Telok Blangah Hill Park, HortPark, Kent Ridge Park, and Labrador Nature Reserve, thereby positioning the Interlace in one of the greenest parts of the city-state. The project is located at the junction of large urban infrastructure and exotic natural greenery, with the Ayer Rajah Expressway. It is bounded by Alexandra Road and Depot Road to the north. Residents can access amenities provided by older neighborhoods in close proximity to the site, such as Gilman Village, within walking distance, as well as the small-scale conurbation[1] of HDB Town estates of Bukit Merah, Redhill, and Queensway.

With 170,000 sqm of gross floor area rising up to 24 stories above ground, the residential development provides over 1,000 condominium units with a range of two-, three-, and four-bedroom apartments, penthouses, and duplex garden units; areas vary from 75 sqm for a two-bedroom unit to 586 sqm for a penthouse with private roof garden. The Interlace is to date one of the largest residential developments in Singapore, with generous 81,000 sqm of site area. Compared with the amount of green spaces allocated to a typical residential project in Singapore, the Interlace stands out as one of the "greenest" developments.

Development of Housing Typology

Singapore's Housing Development Board (HDB) was established in 1960 to become the major driving force responsible for the overhaul of the city's pressing housing problems, at a time when the city-state was considered to be at one of its most fragile moments in history. The task of constructing Queenstown, envisioned as a "total environment," a complete town planned for 160,000 inhabitants, began soon after. A few years later, in 1966, Toa Payoh, a second new town, was launched as a city for 180,000 inhabitants. "Built on virtually virgin land, the whole town was conceived in its entirety: the road system, neighborhood precincts, the shopping, town centre, sports complexes, and a town park."[2]

As Singapore transitioned from an emerging city-state struggling to survive in the 1960s to a nation with rising economic power in the 1970s, the residential market saw a similar development: from the former high-rise, "slab as time machine"[3] utilitarian containers to more luxurious stacks of private condominium living. Considered as one of the pioneers for high-rise luxury condominiums, Pearlbank Apartment Tower's architect, Tan Cheng Siong, sought to create "panoramic views, private yet neighborly, open natural fresh air circulation, wind catching and sun screening, multi-generation, split-level design…"[4] as well as "community friendly, spacious garden environments, complete with amenities…"[5] in the Pandan Valley Estate. As the country's wealth increased from the 1980s to the early 2000s, the building trend started to shift toward high-rise, high-density units that were driven primarily by market forces, price, as well as a "chic factor." Previous notions of comfort-as-luxury started eroding as quickly as the speed at which the country was accumulating economic power. Condominiums like Chuan Park (completed in 1985 with 452 units), Bayshore Park (completed in 1986 with 1093 units), and Ava Towers (completed in 1993 with 124 units) are all examples of high-density extruded towers.

Today, ongoing residential projects pay little attention to some of the fundamentals of tropical residential design—the provision of open, natural, spacious gardens and community-friendly environments. For example, Orchard Residences, completed in 2010, is a 56-story, 218 m high-rise residential condominium with high-end luxury units in a prime location. Such developments primarily follow market trends. The recent introduction of a new regulation—a plot as small as 4,000 sqm can now be considered for condominium development—is further pushing residential developments into the taller-and-smaller category. The massing strategy of vertical extrusion has thus become the default design approach for residential typologies. Any strategy not following this approach has become challenging in the context of the dynamic high-density development in Singapore.

Site and ground floor plan.

Increasing Massing and Green Spaces

Typologically and economically, the Interlace is considered an exception to the rule due to the ingenious way of its massing. Instead of vertically stacking apartments one on top of another, the architects stacked 31 apartment blocks in a hexagonal arrangement to form community courtyards that are large and porous. This formal strategy allows each six-story block to have its own roof garden, lavish cascading terraces, and balconies. The multi-level stacking of the volumes produces large-scale voids in the massing that allow for natural light and airflow throughout the development. The angled, stacked placement of the six-story apartment blocks not only allows for an increase of surface for green roofs, it also frees up the ground plane for the provision of additional green spaces, thereby increasing the overall green ratio of the project. Building regulations in Singapore allow developers to receive higher allowances for Gross Floor Area (GFA) if the project provides more green spaces. The Interlace is a prime example for taking advantage of this regulation and for achieving a delicate balance between architectural ambition and economic logic.

Critique

Reminiscent of Le Corbusier's "fifth facade,"[6] the design introduces multiple private and public roof gardens on each of the roofs of the hexagonal stacks that constitute the Interlace, thereby extending the courtyard to each of the blocks. The roof gardens provide spaces for social interaction by embedding communal facilities within the lush vegetation, much in the way of Le Corbusier's *Unité d'Habitation*. By connecting the six-story volumes, a lush green network is created within the natural terrain. This simple but highly effective strategy is not only successful in terms of expanding green spaces; it also provides innovative new solutions for their combination with key architectural components such as floors, roofs, and balconies.

1. *AVP PictureBase Encyclopedia of the National Curriculum*, s.v. "conurbation."
2. Singapore Housing and Development Board. *Toa Payoh: Our Kind of Neighbourhood, Koh, Munshi and Mealin*. Singapore: Times Media for Housing & Development Board, 2000.
3. Koolhaas, Rem, Bruce Mau, and Hans Werlemann. *S, M, L, XL*. Monacelli Press, 1995.
4. Wong, Voon. "1970s Condominiums in Singapore" in *Viewport Magazine* (source: http://viewportmagazine.com/1970s-condominiums-in-singapore/).
5. *Ibid*.
6. Sharp, Dennis, David Jenkins, and James Steele. *Twentieth-century Classics*. Introduction by Beth Dunlop and Denis Hector. London: Phaidon, 1999.

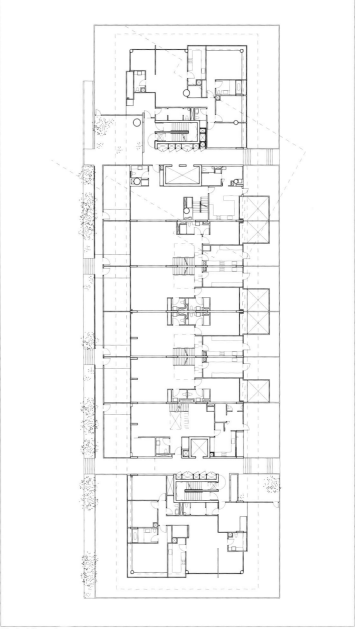

Typical floor plan.

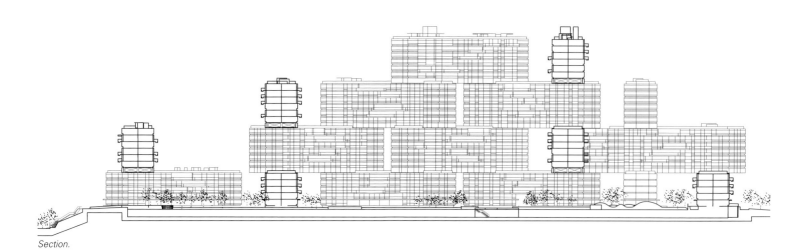

Section.

The Amager Bakke

BIG

Building Type: Infrastructure
Climate Zone: Marine West Coast
Location: Kraftværksvej 31,
2300 Copenhagen S, Denmark
Coordinates: 55°41'2"N 12°37'14"E
Date: Under construction

Height: 100 m
Gross Floor Area: 95,000 m²
Gross Green Area in Building: 37,000 m²
Gross Green Area to Built-Up Area: 39%

Power plants typically require large internal volumes to house technical equipment. BIG used this requirement as a starting point for their design and proposed one of the tallest buildings in Copenhagen and one of the most unusual waste-to-energy plants in Europe. Amager Bakke is an example of what the office of BIG calls "hedonistic sustainability—the idea that sustainability is not a burden, but that a sustainable city in fact can improve (our) quality of life. The Waste-to-Energy plant with a ski slope is the best example of a city and a building which is ecologically, economically, and socially sustainable."[1]

Amager Bakke is the first project to be realized from a bi-national, urban regional plan (conceived by BIG) called Loop City, encompassing the Øresund Region coastlines of Denmark and Sweden, connected by a short bridge.[2] Located next to Copenhagen's 45-year-old energy plant Amagerforbraending, Amager Bakke is located on Amager, an island east of the city center and north of Amagerfælled,[3] a nature park that is part of the development plan for the area as a whole. Straddling the two cities Copenhagen and Amager, the project is located between two distinct areas: a residential and an industrial one. At a smaller scale, the state-of-the-art waste treatment plant has another unique relationship with the two contrasting programs; it will be located between Denmark's oldest concrete structure, the Prøvestenen Fortifications, where the city's largest yacht harbor is currently under construction,[4] and the new activity center Copenhagen Cablepark, where multiple watersports and open-air activities are anticipated to take place.[5]

It is in part due to these contrasts that BIG proposed a plant that will be a destination in its own right and that people will visit for the purpose of leisure, as opposed to a traditional energy plant whose architecture is often reduced to the building facade and unrelated to both, the building's program and its relationship to the city.[6]

"Hedonistic Sustainability"

The design of Amager Bakke questioned the role that architecture typically plays in the creation of a power plant by asking how such a building could be iconic and integrated with its urban context.[7] In their proposal, the team at BIG tasked themselves with the development of what they referred to as the "Wrapper." The Wrapper not only considers the functions of the facade for the building itself, but also its surrounding context. The architects used the "fifth facade" of the building to connect to the surrounding recreational landscape and integrate the plant with its context. BIG proposed to turn the roof into an artificial ski slope that can be used all year round. The proposal is based on the fact that Danes are known to be big skiers despite the fact that the country does not have any skiing resorts.

An incineration plant requires a smokestack, so BIG lifted one end of the building to integrate a stack into the overall architecture. Combined with the rest of the volume, this created a slope that is used for skiing. To integrate the administration and visitor center, the architects expanded the envelope facing the slope. Here, visitors to the project can observe skiers coming down the artificial slope.

To allow for public connection rather than having a massive high wall, one end of the building is pushed down to minimize the volume so that the public can be easily connected to the plant at the human scale. This design move produces an additional slope for skiers. The building features a total of three slopes with a length of 1,500 m in total as well as a terrain park that accommodates skiers of different skill levels, from novices to professionals.

Smoke Rings

Beyond its novel interpretation of the power plant typology, what makes Amager Bakke an unusual project is that it continuously engages the public by visualizing energy consumption. Together with realities:united, an architecture and art practice based in Berlin, Germany, BIG makes a spectacle out of what is traditionally treated at locations out of sight and far away from the city and its inhabitants. The smokestack, with its 30 m diameter, features a modification enabling it to blow a smoke ring every time one ton of fossil carbon dioxide is released—according to BIG, a gentle reminder of the environmental impacts of consumption for the city.[8] As Bjarke Ingels states, "One of the problems with emissions is that they are so abstract and intangible. You can see there is smoke coming out of the chimney but you don't really know whether this is a significant amount. In Copenhagen in 2016 you will simply have to count the smoke rings. You are turning a factory into a public park and the chimney, which traditionally is a symbol of the problem, is now becoming something playful."[9]

Camouflage

Instead of making an energy plant that is disguised, BIG has enclosed the building with a vertical green facade made up of planter modules stacked like bricks: from afar, the energy plant looks like a green mountain with a white top .[10] The surrounding park is created by Topotek 1 and Man Made

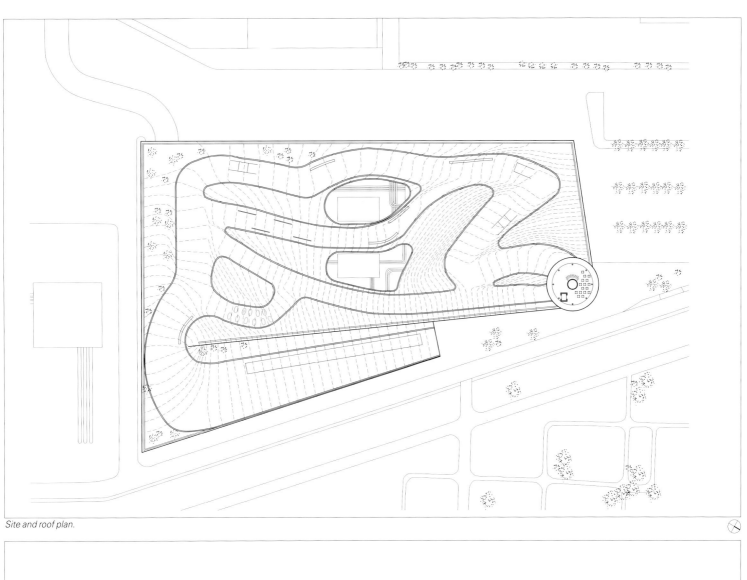

Site and roof plan.

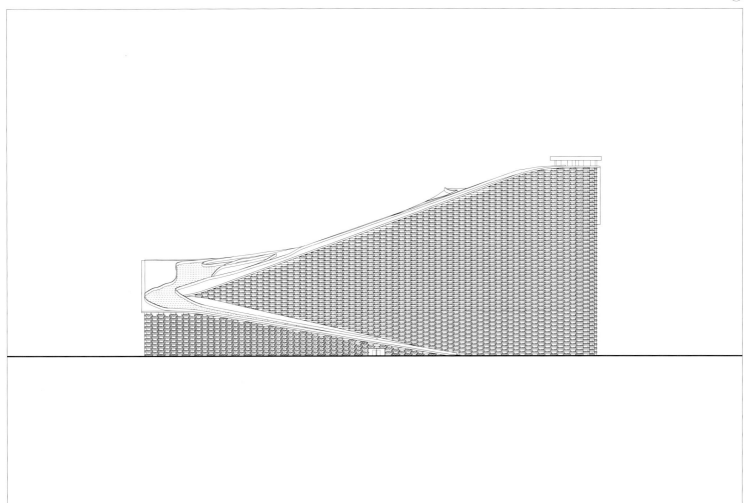

Elevation.

Land[11] to form an open space that offers leisure sport activities throughout the year. On the building, plants are used less as decoration than as camouflage, a way to neutralize what would otherwise appear as a massive, conspicuous reality of human existence.

Energy Efficiency and Environmental Benefits

Denmark is a country considered to be at the forefront of environmental awareness, for example with a large proportion of its population choosing to cycle rather than to drive. With Copenhagen being determined to become carbon-neutral by 2025 through the CPH Climate Plan 2025,[12] the Amager Bakke plant fits right into the larger ambitions of the city. Rather than using the traditional method of burning coal to produce energy, biomass will become the primary source for heat production. Other additions to Copenhagen's power grid will be based on wind and solar energy.

Amager Bakke is part of the city's Climate Plan, with goals to meet the energy needs of 97% of Copenhagen's homes with district heating and provide 4,000 homes with electricity.[13] Framed by residential buildings on one side and industrial estates on the other, Amager Bakke is located in one of two smart "back yards"[14] of Copenhagen. Unlike many other cities where landfills are still a solution to waste management, the Amager Bakke is special in two aspects: rather than disposing of waste, it burns it to create energy for the city, creating a feedback loop of energy production. Because of the plant's proximity to the city, this feedback loop of waste and energy production becomes highly efficient, with an estimated 100% energy content of the waste being utilized.

In total, the Amager Bakke will burn waste collected from 500,000 to 700,000 inhabitants and 46,000 companies in and around Copenhagen.[15] The plant will have at least 25% more energy output[16] than the Amagerforbraending, one of Europe's first waste-to-energy plants. With steam generated at 440°C and a pressure of 70 bars, the electrical efficiency is double that of the replaced Amagerforbraending.[17] More importantly, the new plant will reduce nitrous oxide (N2O) emissions by 85% and bring down the sulfur content of smoke by 99.5% as compared to the existing plant. The new plant is expected to offset emissions of 107,000 t of carbon dioxide (CO_2) per year compared to a traditional coal burning plant.

Critique

Not only does Amager Bakke redefine the typical program of a power plant, the plant itself becomes a project of public engagement for visitors as well as residents of the surrounding neighborhoods. The vertical plane of green becomes crucial in the experience of the project's artificial ski slope as well as the view of the energy plant from afar and for creating the image of a green mountain with a white top.

1. Bjarke Ingels, Founder and Partner, BIG.
2. *Ibid.*
3. Source: http://www.orestad.dk/byliv-oplevelser/orestad_natur/naturpark_amager.aspx
4. Source: http://www.dac.dk/en/dac-life/copenhagen-x-gallery/cases/amager-slope/
5. Source: http://www.visitcopenhagen.com/copenhagen/copenhagen-cable-park-gdk639724
6. David Zahle, Partner & Project Leader, BIG.
7. Source: http://www.big.dk
8. Source: http://www.waste-management-world.com/articles/2013/03/big-waste-to-energy-ski-slope-under-construction-in-copenhagen.html
9. Source: http://www.theguardian.com/environment/2011/jul/03/bjarke-ingels-incinerator-ski-slope
10. Source: http://www.dezeen.com/2011/01/27/waste-to-energy-plant-by-big/
11. Source: http://www.bustler.net/index.php/article/big_puts_a_ski_slope_on_copenhagens_new_waste-to-energy_plant
12. Source: http://subsite.kk.dk/sitecore/content/Subsites/CityOfCopenhagen/SubsiteFrontpage/Business/Growth_and_partnerships/~/media/F5A7EC91E7AC4B0891F37331642555C4.ashx
13. Source: http://www.urbanista.org/issues/issue-1/news/bigs-amager-bakke-mixed-use-waste-to-energy-plant-in-copenhagen-breaks-ground
14. *Ibid.*
15. Source: http://www.power-technology.com/projects/amager-bakke-waste-energy-plant/
16. Source: http://news.nationalgeographic.com/news/energy/2013/08/130801-amager-bakke-europe-waste-to-energy/
17. Source: http://www.power-technology.com/projects/amager-bakke-waste-energy-plant/

Columbia Boulevard Wastewater Treatment Plant Support Facility

Skylab Architecture

Building Type: Infrastructure
Climate Zone: Marine West Coast
Location: 5001 North Columbia
Boulevard, Portland, OR 97203, USA
Coordinates: 45°35'45"N 122°43'6"W
Date: 2013

Height: 7 m / 1 floor
Gross Floor Area: 1067 m²
Gross Green Area in Building: 1,314 m²
Gross Green Area to Built-Up Area: 123%

Oregon's oldest wastewater treatment plant, the Columbia Boulevard Wastewater Treatment Plant (CBWTP) in Portland, was constructed in 1952 amidst public outcry over the unsanitary conditions in the Columbia Slough and Willamette River, two key waterways of the local urban ecology.[1] Skylab Architecture's recent addition, the Support Facility, strives to better integrate the wastewater treatment plant with the ecology while also providing an educational interface between the treatment plant and the public. Through a variety of distinct architectural features, the design injects a relatively ordinary building program with an elaborate perspective on the relationship between infrastructure, the city, and the environment. It has become an exemplary project for the issues that many communities face in terms of waste and stormwater management as well as regarding the effects of development on naturally occuring water management systems.

Today, the CBWTP serves a population of 600,000 people and treats an average of 73 million gallons of wastewater per day, with a peak capacity of 280 million gallons per day.[2] Situated within the North Portland neighborhood of Portsmouth, which borders the site on the southern side, the plant is located next to Columbia Slough in the north, a slow-moving marshy waterway that historically connected the Columbia and Willamette Rivers. At the time when the plant was constructed, the surrounding land was largely used for industrial and agricultural purposes. Today, some remnants of these past uses remain, while the city's relentless residential expansion has pushed to abut the wastewater treatment plant along Columbia Boulevard. The entire area has historically served as a critical part of Portland's natural watershed, helping to reduce flooding in other parts of the city. During heavy rains, the absorptive soils found in the small tributaries, ponds, and wetlands of the low-lying floodplain would soak up much of the excess water, resulting in little visible change of the water levels in the area's major waterways. However, in the decades following the plant's construction, building development in the catchment area greatly reduced the effect of these naturally occuring systems.[3] In 1999, it was estimated that impervious surfaces covered 54% of the watershed. Stormwater runoff that had previously taken days to reach the Columbia Slough, only took hours. The resulting, often sudden demand on CBWTP, which treats both wastewater and stormwater, can easily exceed the plant's capacity, causing untreated sewage and industrial wastewater to overflow directly into the Willamette River and Columbia Slough.[4] While the treatment plant has undergone a series of expansions in recent years to rectify these issues,

the Support Facility offers an additional solution—extensive integration of green roofs and other porous surfaces that help to undo years of overdevelopment and overpaving in this sensitive ecosystem.

Skylab Architecture was initially brought in to design a support facility to mainly serve as office and training space for 38 engineers, whose offices had previously been housed in temporary buildings on CBWTP's sprawling campus. However, early on in the design process, additional issues facing the campus became clear, most importantly the need for the building to serve as a public interface. Skylab's design proposal sought to integrate these functions with solutions for a host of site issues of access, security, and parking. In the end, an 1,067 sqm building was constructed that seamlessly integrates office, training, and educational spaces with an overall approach to site planning and serves as a showcase for best practices of stormwater management.[5]

The building is organized in seven cast-in-place concrete segments, which support an undulating green roof that folds into the surrounding landscape in the south. This strategy maximizes the green roof's southern exposure, benefiting the year-long growth of the indigenous plants used on the roof. Furthermore, the building's massing gently curves to frame a stand of old-growth trees on the north side of the site, opening up to draw in ample amounts of northern daylight while also opening views to the trees and campus beyond.[6]

The pattern of the fin-shaped building sections defines the interior spaces by ordering the relationships between public educational and more private office spaces. The building is entered from the south, through an opening in the undulating roof landscape. The lobby, which doubles as an educational space informing visitors about Portland's wastewater management system, provides direct access to a theater to the right and office spaces to the left. The small theater is used for informational and educational presentations as well as a host of other public functions. The office spaces are arranged under the sawtooth roof to maximize the natural daylighting reaching the individual workstations, while minimizing glare. A series of conference rooms are nestled into the trembankment to the south side of the building, while the open-plan work areas are pushed toward the sawtooth glass facade on the north. In all, the building's functions are carefully defined by a fundamental interest in incorporating the integrated stormwater management and green roof system in the project.

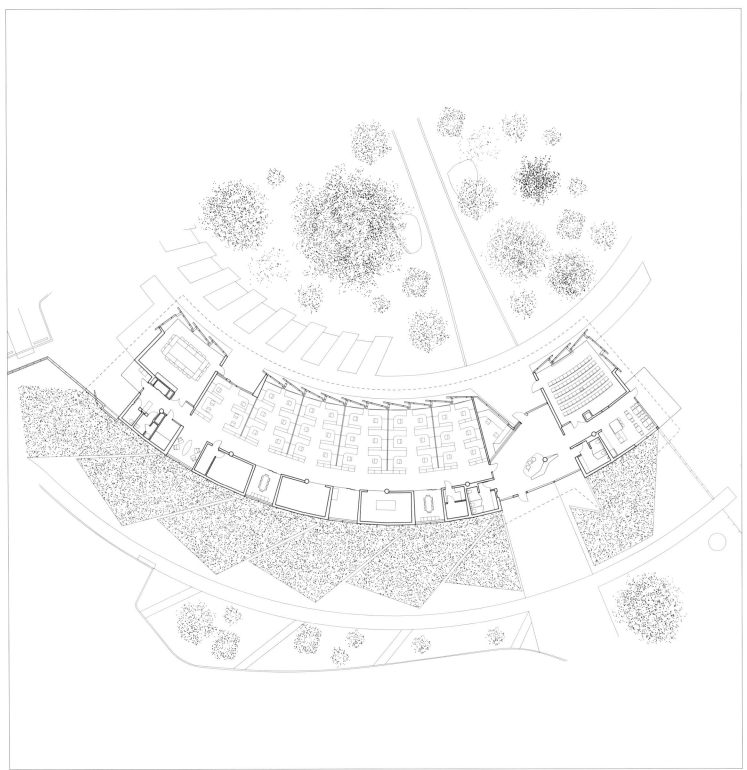

Site and ground floor plan.

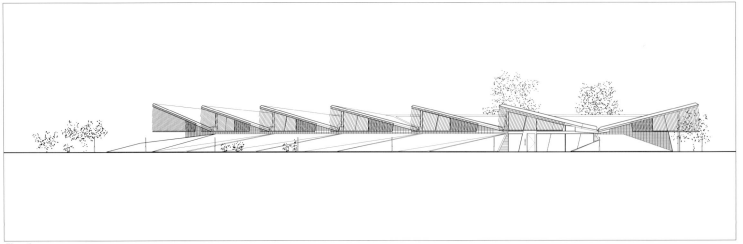

Elevation.

The massing of the roof as well as the building's integration with the landscape provide a number of environmental benefits. The offset arrangement of the fin-shaped building sections allows for generous clerestory windows; steel louvers provide an even distribution of natural daylight into the work spaces below. With the combination of large clerestory windows and the glass curtain wall on the north facade, the building can be naturally lit for much of the workday. The integration with the bermed landscape to the south not only creates the opportunity of a clear and dramatic entrance but also provides a substantial thermal mass to help minimize the heating and cooling costs. The resulting effect is increased by the use of a fully integrated hydronic heating and cooling system, which draws its preconditioned water from the treatment plant's water supply.

The entire facility provides space for and fosters talks and other public events related to continued improvement of Portland's watershed and its overall integration with the environment. The building's green roof is included as a real-world extension of these ideas: it should not be viewed as an add-on but as an integral part of the project that ostensibly drives the design of the structure's form and function. The green roof incorporates best practices of stormwater management with the intention to let these become the norm over time.[7] Beyond its insulating benefits, the roof utilizes highly absorbant soils typical of the adjacent watershed. The roof soils are specifically designed to absorb the region's heavy winter rains and release the water slowly over time. The green roof of CBWTP proposes a future in which the development and growth of our cities could incorporate a number of biological aspects in a distributed infrastructural network rather than creating massive facilities purposefully isolated from the city.

Critique

The project offers an integrated approach to the construction of the built environment in which infrastructure can be seamlessly incorporated with the requirements for functional space. This design approach leads to a strategic resolution of a number of site issues and requirements, such as access, security, and watershed management. Against criticism due to cost overruns,[8] the project's defenders maintain that the building's integrated approach will not only save money in the long run, but will inspire similar educated and forward-thinking decisions about the built environment.

1. The City of Portland. "Columbia Boulevard Treatment Plant Overview" (source: http://www.portlandoregon.gov/bes/article/40645).
2. Griffiths-Sattenspiel, Bevan. "Wastewater Treatment Plant Generates Clean Energy, Has Room for Improvement." River Network blog (source: http://www.rivernetwork.org/blog/7/2010/07/14/wastewater-treatment-plant-generates-clean-energy-has-room-improvement).
3. The City of Portland. "Wastewater Treatment History" (source: http://www.portlandoregon.gov/bes/article/41962).
4. Portland Bureau of Environmental Services. Columbia Slough Watershed Characterization, "Chapter 5: Stream Flow and Hydrology." p. 9 (source: https://www.portlandoregon.gov/bes/article/63585).
5. Furato, Alison. "Columbia Boulevard Wastewater Treatment Support Facility / Skylab Architecture." ArchDaily, 25 July 2012 (source: http://www.archdaily.com/256588/columbia-boulevard-wastewater-treatment-support-facility-skylab-architecture/).
6. "Water treatment facility by Skylab Architecture features a roof of grass-covered fins." dezeen, 15 April 2014 (source: http://www.dezeen.com/2014/04/15/wastewater-treatment-plant-skylab-architecture-portland-oregon/).
7. Madsen, Deane. "Star Turn" in Architect Student Edition, February 2014 (source: http://mydigimag.rrd.com/article/Star_Turn/1629393/195816/article.html).
8. Mesh, Aaron. "Space of Waste" in Willamette Week, 30 April 2014 (source: http://www.wweek.com/portland/article-22479-space_of_waste.html).

Transbay Transit Center

Pelli Clarke Pelli Architects

Building Type: Infrastructure
Climate Zone: Marine West Coast
Location: 425 Mission Street,
San Francisco, CA 94105, USA
Coordinates: 37°47'23"N 122°23'46"W
Date: Under construction

Height: 23 m² / 4 floors with 2 basements
Gross Floor Area: 112,000 m²
Gross Green Area in Building: 22,000 m²
Gross Green area to Built-Up Area: 20%

Transbay Transit Center in downtown San Francisco proposes a return to the railway station holding the role of a placemaker within urban environments. The project draws from the economic, symbolic, and civic status afforded by many of the world's most iconic stations such as Grand Central Station in New York City, Paddington Station in London, and Gare de Lyon in Paris. Each of these stations is synonymous with the cities they serve. While the new transit center will bring together a multitude of transportation options under one roof, the key component of the project—the lasting image for visitors—is a 5.4 acre rooftop park, which will serve as a waiting area, a connection to neighboring residences, and a living room and recreation space for the city. By integrating landscape, architecture, and infrastructure in the center of the city, the design holds the potential to redefine the role of infrastructure as it relates to social, recreational, environmental, and economic well-being in the city.

In 2006, the Transbay Joint Powers Authority (TJPA) announced a competition for design and development teams to submit proposals for a redesigned Transbay Transit Center and an adjacent tower on the publicly owned site of the outdated and underused San Francisco Transbay Terminal. Maria Ayerdi, then Executive Director of the TJPA, noted that the Transbay Transit Center would "be the first major urban intermodal station to be built in the USA in nearly 70 years." The train service in the station built in 1939 had ended in 1959, when the station became a bus-only facility. Since then, the large elevated ramps that provided direct access to and from the adjacent Bay Bridge formed imposing structures that cut off San Francisco's bustling city center from the industrial buildings of the once busy waterfront. Despite its rather bleak appearance, the Rincon Hill neighborhood surrounding the terminal was seen as ripe for redevelopment at the time of the competition. In fact, the TJPA cited the economic potential of development around a world-class transit hub as a prime reason for the development of the Transbay Transit Center.

The new transit center is bordered on the north and south by Minna and Natoma Streets respectively, and will stretch five blocks from Beale Street to the east to 2nd Street to the west. In order to minimize its effect on traffic and pedestrian flow, the building will bridge over Fremont Street and 1st Street, allowing traffic to pass smoothly through the site. The tower is located directly to the north of the transit center between Fremont and 1st Street. The new center is intended to provide nine types of transportation including bus, train, and high-speed rail services for 100,000 passengers per day, with a target of 29 million passengers per year by 2020. More importantly, the building's site positions the project at the center of the redevelopment of San Francisco's aging port and waterfront district further to the east and south.

Contrasting typical railway stations organized as horizontal behemoths, the Transbay Transit Center is distributed vertically throughout the section of the building. The regional and high-speed rail is logically pushed to the lowest levels, while bus transportation remains at the uppermost one. Sandwiched in between are a range of ground transportation, administrative, and retail spaces purposefully located in close proximity to the ground level. A series of skylights and funiculars distributed along the length of the project draw light through the diverse functions of the project to the lowest levels of the structure. These vertical voids also attract views and people up to the lush 5.4 acre City Park, which caps the development and projects the image of a lush garden park to visitors, defining a new type of gateway into the city.

The massing of the building takes on a particular character within the city. No longer is the transit center a single iconic facade, opening to a large public square at street level. Instead, as the Transbay Transit Center spans the streets, it confronts the city in innovative and unique ways. At street level, it is never viewed as a whole, but rather as small glimpses of a glowing, shimmering facade capped with a verdant greenscape that is carefully framed by ordinary streetscapes and pedestrian alleys. The clean, light, and open image of the facade is achieved through the design of a structural exoskeleton formed into "basket" or "petal" shapes. This approach creates a rhythmic and dynamic quality along the street. The baskets are clad in a patterned metal mesh, which shimmers in the sunlight and allows the building to "glow" at night.

City Park

The incorporation of a public park on the roof transforms the transit center into a living and breathing part of the urban environment, which attracts its residents to engage with those who are arriving at and departing from San Francisco. The design of City Park foreshadows the future density and requisite high-rise construction of the surrounding neighborhood. Its landscape design merges a range of features, including a 100 seat amphitheater, cafe, playground, and an arts education center, which blur the landscape with the architectural features of

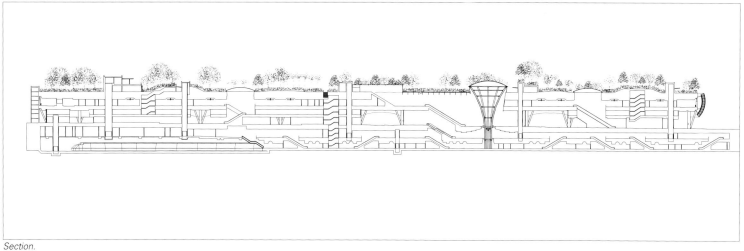

Section.

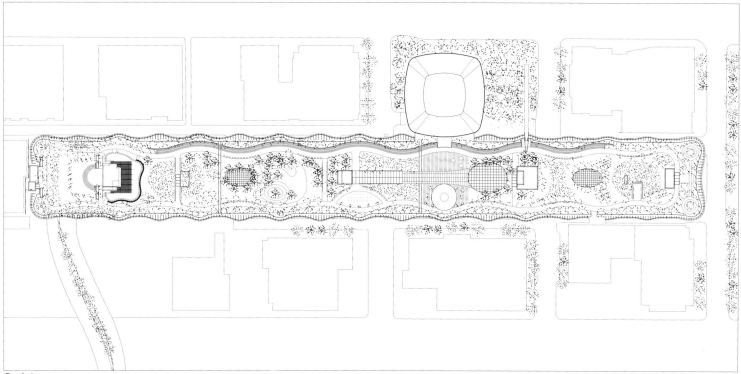

Roof plan.

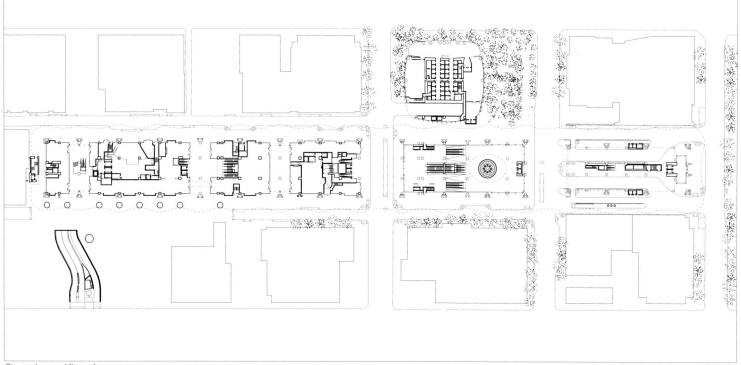

Site and ground floor plan.

City Park. On the roof, a mounded landscape mediates between quiet areas of reflection and busy areas of communal socializing, while also integrating access points and the domed skylights and funiculars that draw light deep into the station below. To better connect with the transit programs, artist Ned Kahn designed a 365-m-long bus jet fountain, in which buses moving through the interior of the terminal just one level below will trigger jets of water on the roof park.

The park serves also as an environmental buffer, filtering both air and water, which is intended to offset the environmental impact of the station below. Water features that define the long edges organize the park—one is a stream, the other a wetland—and play vital roles in the building's stormwater retention and cleansing system. Located in between these water features is a gently undulating landscape that promotes biodiversity and incorporates local ecologies including grassland, riparian, chaparral, marsh, and oaks. The plants and soil of the landscape absorb and process the carbon dioxide and other pollutants from the buses, trains, and the central power plant on the levels directly below.

Such recreational green space does not exist anywhere in the area. Creating such an amenity for the neighborhood is to spurn real estate development and the increase of land values. This kind of concern for public space has recently manifested itself in the form of many Privately Owned Public Open Spaces (POPOS), which are the result of a 1985 zoning law that required developers to construct 1 sqft (0.1 sqm) of public space for every 50 sqft (4.65 sqm) of commercial space. This law has created an informal network of POPOS throughout the downtown core of San Francisco. While there are obvious issues with public spaces that are constructed and managed by private entities, many of these are largely responsible for engendering the downtown area with a lively urban environment. The City Park at Transbay Transit Center is not itself a POPOS but serves to extend the city's understanding about the value of public space. Furthermore, in hopes of putting the POPOS regulations to further good use, the city is working to require new developments abutting City Park to dedicate their POPOS requirement for access to the park.

Critique

San Francisco's Transbay Transit Center encourages us to demand more from our public spaces. Infrastructure here is no longer pushed to the edge of the city, or lowers real estate values. Instead, infrastructure and public buildings serve as an amenity by providing attractive spaces and services for the benefit of the city at large. This type of integrated development does require additional support and resources. For example, in the case of City Park at Transbay Transit Center, there are ongoing funding and budgetary issues. However, given the amount of development that is predicated on the construction and implementation of City Park, it seems improbable that the constituents will not be able to come to an agreement on how to fund such a critical public project. Provided that this can happen, the Transbay Transit Center in San Francisco provides a new model for the development of infrastructure within the city that integrates recreational and social spaces, a new type of public infrastructure that supports continued growth and well-being of the city.

1. TJPA and Pelli Clark Pelli. "SF Transbay Transit Center and Tower" in *Architecture Plus*, 17 (December 2007). pp. 109-113.
2. Borgen, Scott. "The Grand Central Terminal of the West" in *Rail Magazine*, 21. pp. 18-24.
3. Ibid.
4. Clarke, Fred W. *City Connect*, 2012.
5. Transbay Joint Powers Authority. Transbay Transit Center: Key Investment in San Francisco's Future as a World Class City. November 2013.
6. TJPA and Pelli Clark Pelli. "SF Transbay Transit …"
7. Clarke, Fred W. *City Connect* …
8. Vinnitskaya, Irina. "Transbay Transit Center in San Francisco/Pelli Clarke Pelli Architects" in ArchDaily, 13 April 2013 (source: http://www.archdaily.com/356982/transbay-transit-center-in-san-francisco-pelli-clarke-pelli/).
9. PWP Landscape Architecture
10. Clarke, Fred W. *City Connect* …
11. King, John. "S.F. guide to private sites for public use" in SF Chronicle, 4 December 2012 (source: http://www.sfgate.com/bayarea/place/article/S-F-guide-to-private-sites-for-public-use-4090503.php#ixzz2EwY8zA3d).
12. Anderson, Lamar. In Architizer (source: http://architizer.com/blog/popos-san-francisco/).
13. Dineen, J.K. "Transbay Transit Center will open without signature park." SFGate, 26 June 2014 (source: http://www.sfgate.com/bayarea/article/Transbay-Transit-Center-will-open-without-5580008.php).

Changi Airport Terminal 3

CPG Consultants/SOM

Building Type: Infrastructure
Climate Zone: Tropical Wet
Location: 65 Airport Boulevard,
Singapore 819663
Coordinates: 1°21'22"N 103°59'14"E
Date: 2008

Height: 30 m/4 floors, 3 basements
Gross Floor Area: 380,000 m²
Gross Green Area in Building: 7,000 m²
Gross Green area to Built-Up Area: 1.8%

The third terminal of Singapore's Changi Airport opened its gates on January 9th, 2008[1] after eight years of construction. Terminal 3 added a capacity of 22 million passengers per year to Changi by providing 28 additional aerobridges, eight of which are suitable for the Airbus 380. At the same time, Terminal 3 has increased the overall retail and F&B (food and beverage) spaces by 70%, from 28,000 to 48,000 sqm.[2] It covers an area of 250 m by 300 m,[3] and is 27 m high.[4] The project's main architect was the Singapore firm CPG Consultants. Two of the building's major architectonic features were designed by specialist consultants: the spectacular, daylighting roof by the US firm Skidmore, Owings and Merrill (SOM), and the massive Green Wall that divides the terminal into two parts, by the Singapore landscape architecture firm Tierra Design.

Changi Airport's master plan, with Terminal 1 completed in 1981 and Terminal 2 in 1990, "was driven by practical considerations rather than a search for aesthetic uniqueness."[5] In a similar spirit, Terminal 3's design was approached from a rational perspective. As a starting point, the Civil Aviation Authority of Singapore (CAAS) defined four guiding criteria: clarity, natural lighting, external views, and maintainability.[6] In CPG's design of the terminal, these criteria are clearly legible. The building is conceived as a clear and uncluttered glass box, without large subdividing elements and with an emphasis on long vistas. The departure hall, for example, is laid out as a single street along the terminal's transversal exit. The single exception to the rule of reducing subdivisions is the large wall that divides the terminal into two halves. It is five stories high and spans the whole volume of the terminal. On the landside, where the wall demarcates the check-in hall and the baggage claim area, it is greened with a Vertical Garden interspersed with water features.

Besides the Green Wall, the second unique part of Terminal 3's architecture is the roof designed by SOM. It features a large number of skylights covered by actuated so-called "Butterfly Panels", which are operable and can rotate to achieve various degrees of openness to the sky.[7] The panels can adjust the amount of natural light reaching the building's interior to both current climatic conditions and programmatic needs. They are complemented by a secondary system of reflector panels mounted below the terminal's ceiling, which serve to direct natural light toward specific locations such as circulation areas and plant features. Terminal 3's daylighting system is thus strongly interrelated with its interior use of greenery.

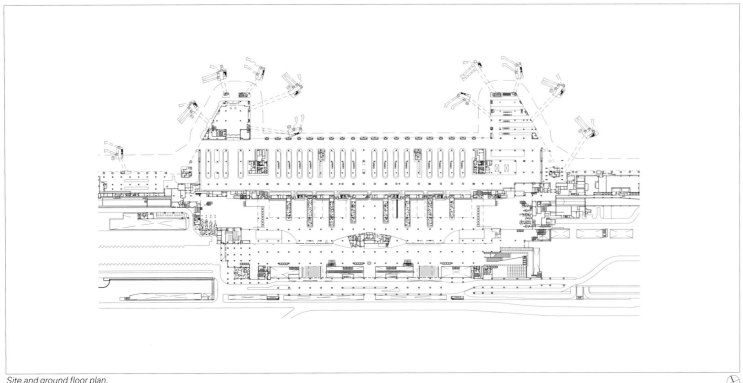

Site and ground floor plan.

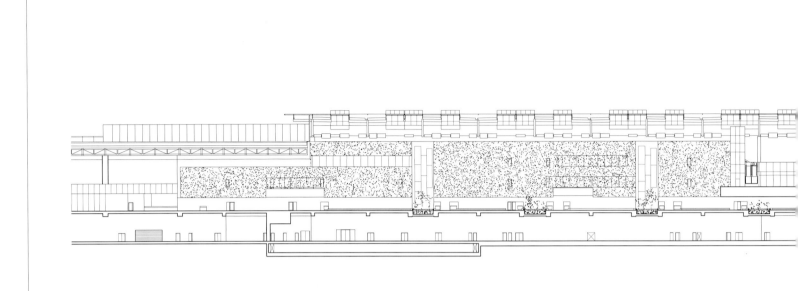

Section.

The Daylighting Roof System

Structurally, the intricate roof system consists of a gridded frame of steel trusses, with varying depths between 4.1 m and 4.5 m. It is supported by a grid of 12-m-high concrete columns.[8] In their main direction, the trusses are cantilevered on both the landside and airside. The roof structure is perforated with 919 skylights, with two Butterfly Panels located centrally above each skylight. These are louvers whose position can be mechanically adjusted to control the amount of natural light entering through each individual opening. Their positions are determined by an array of brightness sensors located on the roof that feed data into a central controller.[9] This allows for adjustment to Singapore's tropical environment in an optimal way: on cloudy days, for example, the panels open to allow in a maximum of daylight, while on cloudless days, the Butterfly Panels close to prevent glare and overheating. In the closed state, the perforation of the compound aluminum louvers still achieves a daylight coefficient of 5%. Over the course of a day, the louver orientation adapts to the sun's position in the sky. Overall, the intelligence of the system allows the terminal to be naturally lit for at least eight hours per day, regardless of the actual cloud cover.[10] This extensive use of daylight leads to significant energy savings due to a reduced need not only for artificial lighting but also for cooling, since there is less excess heat from lamps. Terminal 3's overall energy consumption is estimated to be about 20 kWh/sqm, which is 17% less than the energy consumption of the older neighboring terminals, with about the same shape and volume.[11]

A second set of louvers is located below the terminal ceiling. Installed at various fixed angles, but manually adjustable via a rope system, the inner louvers serve to diffuse and reflect light.

They are perforated like the outer louvers, which helps to generate a good interior acoustic ambiance.[12] Some are positioned to reflect light back onto the ceiling to achieve indirect lighting effects; others concentrate light onto the planters and Green Wall. Circulation areas are also enlivened by larger amounts of light. At night, the sun's role is taken over by 1000 W spotlights installed on the roof's exterior,[13] so that the terminal is indirectly illuminated via the skylights and reflector panels. With this, consistent lighting levels can be achieved at all times.

Beyond elegantly addressing functional needs, the design of the inner louvers was also driven by an aesthetic agenda: "Although the components of the roof system have been arrayed to fulfil specific technical requirements in various zones of the building, their overall appearance is intended to be homogenous. The large number of angled metal surfaces blurs the legibility of the structural trusses, skylight openings and ceiling plane to soften their otherwise technical quality."[14] Together with the Green Wall, the sculptural, mobile-like effect of the inner louvers helps to transcend the engineered rationality that is characteristic for most aspects of the terminal's design.

The Green Wall

This Green Wall is the most explicit manifestation of a general design strategy that aims to soften the clean efficiency of the terminal's shell. Complementing the cool and technological materials on the terminal's exterior such as steel and glass, the terminal's interior finishes include timber, limestone, and granite, thus employing warmer tones and a more natural and haptic materiality. Plant features such as palm trees are

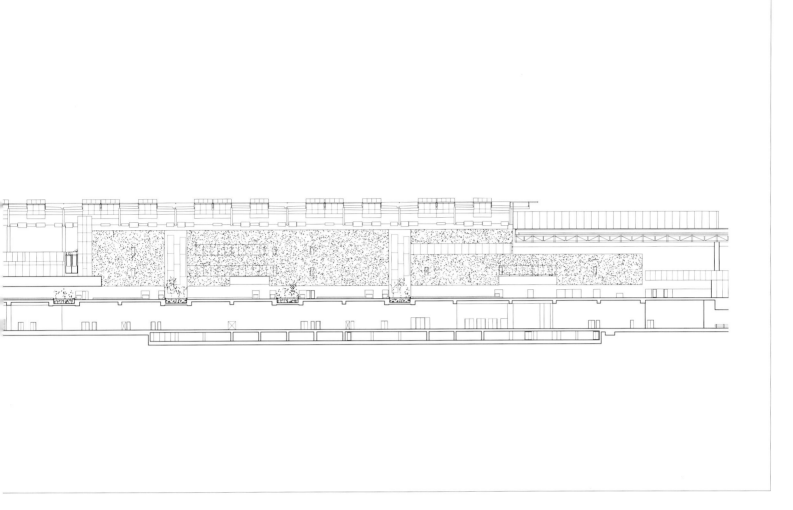

spread throughout the terminal to create a "tropical" atmosphere. Extending the design concept of long vistas, the terminal's interior landscaping aims to establish a connection with the airport gardens, which are located outside of the terminal.[15] Of all these landscape features, the Green Wall is the most prominent one.

The Green Wall's scale makes it a landscape in the building rather than a mere decorative element. Spanning its width and reaching the ceiling, the wall is an impressive element that divides the neutral glass container into two distinct zones on the landside and the airside. In the wall's center, a single opening on the second floor contains the emigration area, where passengers proceed from check-in to the departure hall. On the wall's far left and right, stairs allow arriving travellers to proceed down onto the ground floor, where immigration and the baggage claim areas are located.

The baggage claim area is structured by wide planters oriented perpendicularly to the Green Wall, seemingly growing out of it. The planters contain ground covers and approximately 10-m-high palm trees. The floor slab of the second floor check-in area is recessed from the Green Wall, thereby creating a vertical connection with the baggage claim area below. This relationship is strengthened by the verticality of the Green Wall and the palm trees. In this sense, the Green Wall is Terminal 3's most prominent architectural element: simultaneously connecting and separating the building's most important functions and delineating Singapore's border with a metaphorical gesture: the "City in a Garden" is secured by a Green Wall.

The Green Wall or Vertical Garden is a massive wall veiled by a thin screen, or tapestry, of climbers. Stainless steel beams cantilever from the granite-clad element to support horizontal strata of fiberglass planters. Maintenance walkways are located between the planters and the wall. Screens of vertical stainless steel cables are placed both in front and behind the planters and provide a substructure for the climbing plants. As a result, the wall's visual impact is not so much one of a forest-like, dense three-dimensionality, but rather a semi-transparent layering of different planes. Also contributing to this appearance is the indirect lighting scheme, with backlighting reinforcing the impression of a thin, two-dimensional screen of plants.

On four occasions, this semi-transparent screen is divided by a so-called Waterfall: vertical water features that are enclosed by glass, with water flowing down a geometric relief constructed of stainless steel plates coated with shredded glass, imbuing the Waterfall with a "sparkling" appearance. A sandstone relief covers the wall on the ground floor and provides passengers with a tactile experience in addition to the visual one.

The Green Wall is composed of more than 10,000 plants, including seven species of climbers and a dozen epiphytes or "airplants" (a type of plant that does not have to be rooted in soil). During a four-year period of testing in Changi Airport's Terminal 1, these plant species were carefully selected according to their suitability for the new terminal's indoor climate. The plants are watered and fertilized via a drip irrigation system. They do not need any artificial light sources, since the natural daylighting system provides them with enough sunlight. Weak plants are replaced from a stock of pre-grown plants to ensure the consistent appearance of the Green Wall.

Critique

The natural lighting system with its sculptural appearance and the Green Wall as a central element provide both a visual and physical sense of relief from what would otherwise be an efficient, but bland and neutral interior, scores of which can be found in airports around the world. In the Green Wall's combination of plants with an engineered substructure, the natural is constructed with a precision similar to other technological aspects of the terminal. In recognizing its own artificiality, the Green Wall convincingly acknowledges the paradox that is involved in introducing a large amount of vegetation into an air-conditioned and enclosed space. At face value, the needs of tropical plants in terms of humidity and light are rather different from levels of human comfort. At the same time, plants introduce a sense of soft serenity that is conducive to human well-being. As a solution to this difference, Terminal 3's Green Wall is interpreted as a tapestry with strands of plants growing out of regularly spaced horizontal elements.

A complex effort of design, engineering, and manufacturing was necessary to achieve what seems to be simplicity itself: a naturally lit interior. Terminal 3's sophistication lies in the way in which both complex and blatantly artificial means were employed to achieve deceptively simple and natural effects. Terminal 3 makes a compelling case for this design strategy, embracing the artificiality of architectural environments even in the inclusions of seemingly natural elements.

1. "Changi Airport's Development." Changi Airport Group
(Source: http://ne.edu.sg/files/ljs/Backgrounder%20-%20The%20Development%20
of%20Changi%20Airport%20for%20LJ.pdf).
2. "Changi Airport Terminal 3" in *The Singapore Engineer*, March 2008. p. 16–22.
3. "Airspace: Singapore—Changi International Airport Terminal 3." Dialogue, Skidmore, Owings & Merill, July 2008
(source: https://www.som.com/resources/SOM.com_Dialogue_July2008.pdf).
4. "Green Airports" in *FuturArc*, vol. 10 (July 2008). p. 78.
5. "Changi Airport's Development ..."
6. Fact Sheet on Singapore Changi Airport Terminal 3. Civil Aviation Authority of Singapore, July 2008.
7. Airspace: Singapore …
8. "Changi Airport Terminal 3 …"
9. "Terminal 3 at Changi Airport in Singapore inaugurated with a daylight system built by durlum GmbH from Schopfheim, Germany." Durlum GmbH, 3 June 2008 (Source: http://www.durlum.de/P/07_aktuell/pdf/Pressemeldung%20durlum_Changi-Airport.pdf).
10. "Airspace: Singapore ..."
11. "Green Airports ..."
12. "Terminal 3 at Changi …"
13. *Ibid.*
14. *Ibid.*
15. American Society of Landscape Architects. 2009 Professional Awards: Honor Award (Source: http://www.asla.org/2009awards/043.html).

Urban Mountain

schmidt hammer lassen architects/LOOP architects

Building Type: Mixed Use
Climate Zone: Marine West Coast
Location: Postgirobygget, Oslo, Norway
Coordinates: 59°54'42"N 10°45'16"E
Date: 2019 (estimated)

Height: 138 m/31 floors, 2 basements
Gross Floor Area: 79,000 m²
Gross Green Area in Building: 21,700 m²
Gross Green Area to Built-Up Area: 27%

Urban Mountain is a project conceived for the Nordic Built Challenge, an initiative that promotes building sustainability and biodiversity for its region.[1] The project was successful as the Norwegian national winner of the Challenge.[2] The underlying Nordic Built Charter promotes ten principles for architecture, among them that projects should "push the limits of sustainable performance, as a result of an innovative mindset and a high level of knowledge"[3] as well as that buildings should further "merge urban living with the qualities of nature, as well as achieve zero emissions over its lifecycle."[4] The project brief called for "transforming an already existing 50,000 sqm office tower in central Oslo into a 79,000 sqm icon of sustainability that would ultimately be Norway's tallest building."[5]

Urban Mountain is a 31-story mixed-use office building with two basement levels housing technical uses, the first three stories above ground housing retail, the fourth story featuring a restaurant, the fifth conference rooms, and the sixth story and above offices. The project site is located in Oslo City and is flanked by major roads (Biskop Gunneruds Gate to the north, Bispegata to the south, Nyandsveien to the east, and Jernbanetorgetl to the west), with the train and the central bus station located directly next to it. With a new gallery and a new train station currently underway, pedestrians will not only have access to Urban Mountain from Levels 1 and 2 but also from across the adjacent streets. The building's new main entrance is located on the new north side, easily accessible from Biskop Gunneruds Gate, to connect to the future development of the neighboring Crystal Clear landmark towers. Urban Mountain provides an automated bicycle parking system. The project aims to achieve an almost full score under the BREEAM-NOR rating system.[6]

Green Lungs and Other Sustainable Features

The Urban Mountain proposal differs significantly from conventional mixed-use office typologies. The building is stacked in stories of four that are configured around green walls and pockets. Interior living walls or Green Lungs run through the building, from the facades all the way to the internal atria that are carved into the overall volume. The atria occupy the building core and expand, creating a series of smaller green atria that are four stories tall and located next to the office spaces. This expansion of green space within the innermost core of the building helps to increase the number of naturally lit spaces next to elevator cores, which are typically artificially lit in conventional office buildings. Green Pockets, four-story-high atria on the periphery of the building mass, add depth to the facades.

The Green Lungs also work as natural air intakes, cleaning, humidifying, and reducing the concentration of carbon dioxide in the interior.[7] They extend deep into the building, forming a void filled with living elements. With solar chimneys cutting through the entire height of the building, the exhaust is naturally driven through a thermal stack effect generated by solar heat gains.[8] The Green Lungs are further part of a solar chimney system. The facade openings are controlled automatically to allow for an optimum indoor climate through the use of natural ventilation.

Following ecological principles in their design, the architects seek to actively support biodiversity. Diverse plants are used throughout the building to clean the air, produce oxygen, and reduce dust and carbon dioxide,[9] as well as keep the temperature and humidity at comfortable levels.[10] The project uses plants from various parts of the region for different parts of the building. For the roofs, plants were sourced from the Oslomarka Forest, including conifers, heather, and moss. On the building's north facades and in the atria, the plants originate from the Alna River Valley and include herbs, grasses, deciduous trees, and moss. On the south facades and also in the atria, they include herbs, deciduous trees, and shrubs mostly from the Oslo Fjord Islands. Some local plants stem from Oslo City's urban environment and are used mostly on the east and west facades and at the street level, including herbs, deciduous trees, and moss.

Among the many environmental components of the building is an innovative ice storage system to store energy during the winter for the summer months. Ice is used in the summer months as a natural cooling device. In the colder months, it serves as a heat source by using an adapted heat pump system. Conceptualized as an energy saver as well as an educational tool, the ice storage is made visible through a large window on Level -1 of the project.[11]

Of all environmental components employed in Urban Mountain, the Green Lungs are among the most innovative ones. On a social level, these large air-purifying volumes double up as recreational spaces that allow for semi-public interactions to take place. On an environmental-performative level, the Green Lungs purify the air in the building and provide buffer spaces to prevent drastic changes in temperature moving from the inside to the outside of the building and vice versa. By allowing these spaces to be open or closed to the outside via the facade opening system, temperatures can be controlled, keeping summer temperatures in the atria relatively constant and winter temperatures at a minimum of 5°C.

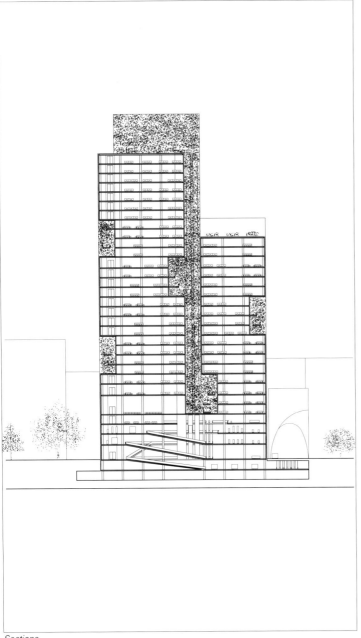

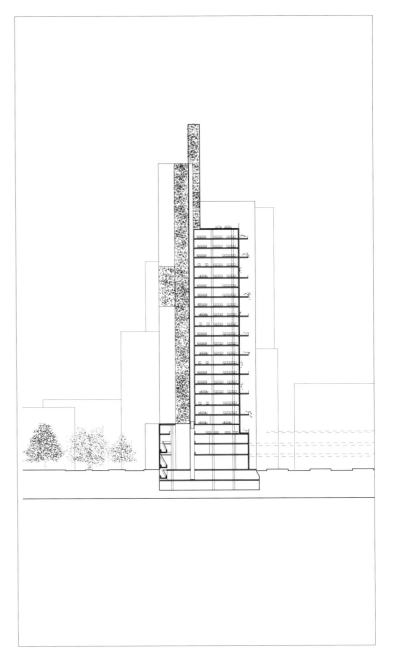

Sections.

Critique

In adopting the ten principles set out by the Nordic Built Charter, Urban Mountain integrates architecture and landscape elements through the use of Green Lungs throughout the project. The innovative design and integration of these not only significantly improves the interior climate of the building, it also encourages social interaction of its inhabitants. With its innovative use of green spaces that feature many local plant species, the project defines a distinctively Nordic "green" high-density building typology.

1. Source: http://www.nordicinnovation.org/Documents/Nordic%20Built%20documents/ Challenge%20Projects/Norway/017_URBAN%20MOUNTAIN_A3booklet.pdf
2. Source: http://www.nordicinnovation.org/nordicbuilt/the-challenge/
3. Source: http://www.nordicinnovation.org/Documents/Nordic%20Built%20documents/ Challenge%20Projects/Norway/017_URBAN%20MOUNTAIN_A3booklet.pdf
4. Ibid.
5. Source: http://persquare.com.au/2013/11/10/nords-building-sustainable-urban-mountains/
6. www.breeam.org
7. Source: http://www.archdaily.com/428959/urban-mountain-team-wins-nordic-built-challenge-in-norway/
8. Source: http://www.nordicinnovation.org/Documents/Nordic%20Built%20documents/ Challenge%20Projects/Norway/017_URBAN%20MOUNTAIN_A3booklet.pdf
9. Source: http://sourceable.net/super-sustainable-skyscraper-wins-nordic-built-challenge/
10. Source: http://www.nordicinnovation.org/Documents/Nordic%20Built%20 documents/Challenge%20Projects/Norway/017_URBAN%20MOUNTAIN_A3booklet.pdf
11. Ibid.

Maquinnext

MVRDV

Building Type: Mixed Use
Climate Zone: Mediterranean
Location: Carrer Ferran Junoy, 42, 08030
Barcelona, Spain
Coordinates: 41°26'26"N 2°11'48"E
Date: Under development

Height: 24 m/2 floors, 3 basements
Gross Floor Area: 45,000 m² shopping
center, 57,000 m² residential
Gross Green Area in Building: 31,000 m²
Gross Green Area to Built-Up Area: 69%,
30% including future residential

MVRDV's Maquinnext shopping center follows the firm's longstanding interest in exploring the integration of architecture, landscape, and the city. This interest started with their seminal Netherlands Pavilion for Expo 2000 in Hanover, Germany, and has since then found further expression through a number of projects. The opportunity to continue their explorations with a project for an often banal building type – a mixed-use retail and residential development on the periphery of the city – resulted in a powerful statement about the lifestyle such a project could encourage. Long conceived as hermetically sealed for the sole purpose of expanding the commercial realm into our daily lives, the shopping center as a typically generic and often cheaply constructed building type is pushed here to become an important part of the urban context. Maquinnext integrates a dense forested park with a shopping center to redefine the shopping, retail, and lifestyle experience for the public.

Maquinnext is located in a peripheral neighborhood in the north of Barcelona, Spain, on the site of the parking lot for an existing, approximately ten-year-old shopping center, La Maquinista, directly to its east. As the new building is replacing the existing lot, two levels below grade are reserved for parking, while the retail spaces occupy the 2.5 levels above grade. On its western side, Maquinnext is bounded by Carrer Ferran Junoy, a main boulevard and one of the main train corridors providing access to the city center. The northern and southern sides of the site are bound by Carrer de Potosí and Carrer Sao Paulo respectively. The project is located on the threshold of the residential enclave of Sant Andreu across the rail tracks to the west, and an industrial and commercial district to the east. Further to the east, the Besòs River, lined on both sides with a linear park, cuts through the city, creating another dividing line within this rather heterogeneous part of the city.

In 2008, as Spain's economy experienced a major crisis, one of Europe's largest developers of retail property, Unibail-Rodamco, purchased the 74,400 sqm La Maquinista. It was viewed as one of the country's most resilient developments, due to its well-connected location and low rental cost. The purchase included the adjacent parking lot, which the developer saw as an opportunity for further development.[1] MVRDV was brought in on the basis of their interest in redefining shopping typologies through the integration of retail and residential spaces with a rooftop forest. However, due to the poorly performing Spanish economy, the brief called for a phased construction in which the 45,000 sqm retail and underground components would be built first, followed by 57,000 sqm of residential space four to

five years later. To further complicate matters, Unibail required that the retail component be undisturbed during the future construction of the residential component.[2]

Green Building Strategy

In developing the organizational strategy for the project, MVRDV adapted their ideas about optimizing the relationship between the city and its inhabitants. The site was widened to the east by demolishing some structures of the existing shopping center in order to better integrate the new development with the central plazas of the original La Maquinista. This allowed for an open-air shopping experience. The residential buildings are pushed toward the residential district to the west of the site so that they will help to frame and enclose the public space of the park. By virtue of the railroad tracks being situated directly opposite the busy street to the west, long-range views across the city and toward the Catalan foothills were made possible, creating a connection to the project's natural surroundings.

MVRDV's proposal is characterized by an undulating forested roof structure that provides generous access to the gardens from the street as well as the retail spaces. The design idea is not to camouflage an otherwise unsightly shopping mall with greenery. On the contrary, the roof structure provides ample and inviting entrances into the open-air retail spaces below. Although the planting is kept to the roof surface, the intention is to put consumers in constant contact with nature.[3] A series of cuts through the building define the circulation spaces and draw light, trees, views, and even animals to the interiors. Three rectangular volumes are positioned on top of the green roof and serve as shop connectors. These volumes allow for the public to fully access the roof, combining the shopping experience with that of being in a forest. This combination produces a tension between two unlikely neighbors – retail and nature, based on the understanding that natural elements within the city attract people and in turn investment.[4]

Drawing cues from earlier projects, the design strives to integrate shopping with urban recreation, promoting a range of planted spaces that merge the natural with the artificial. MVRDV co-opts many of the approaches and methods explored in the project for Les Halles in Paris, France, where they conceived a below-grade shopping area topped with a garden and recreation space. Also, the project for Les Halles featured a new axis that is not reserved for circulation, but cascades to all levels, opening the entire depth of the building to the sky. Maquinnext puts a forest at the place of

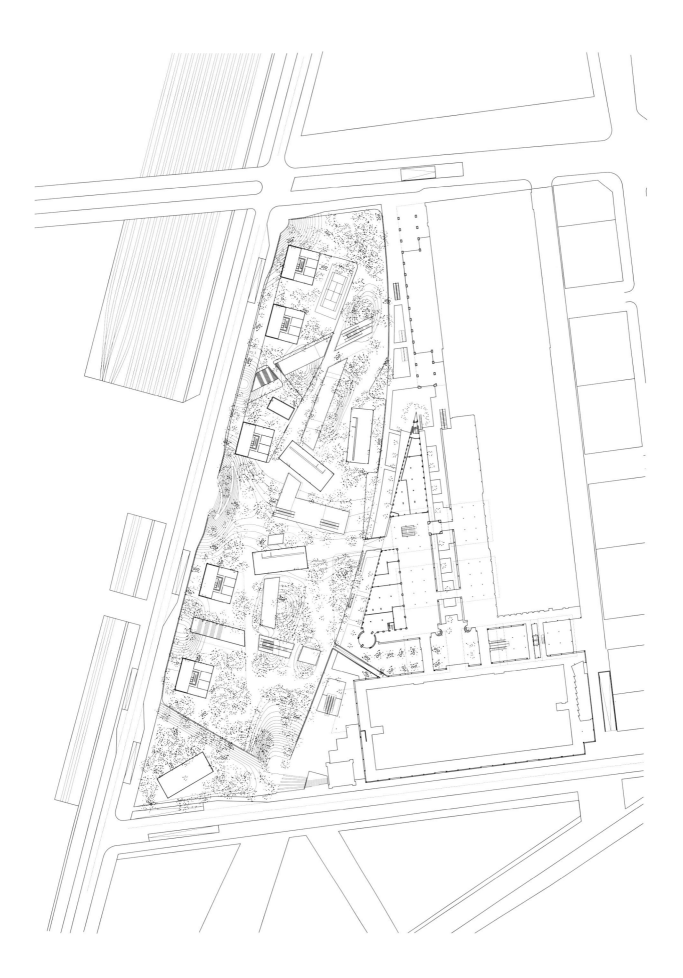

Site and ground floor plan.

the urban park and stretches the green space in section, creating a thickened ground that undulates in order to combine the city with nature. Another project of MVRDV's portfolio – BiodiverCity, The Why Factory – also proposes combinations of landscape and architecture that benefit from each other.

Critique

MVRDV's work is not based on conventional ideas of sustainability. Rather, it can be understood as responding to a more fundamental need – that the experience of living in dense urban environments can be enriched with the provision of nature. For example, the forest of Maquinnext can serve as a park for children to play while their parents run errands in the shopping center below. Or customers can go for a run or bike ride through the forest before buying their groceries at the market. While architecture is often about separating city and nature, MVRDV truly embraces a contrasting notion, that the 21st Century will be focused on living in the city in harmony with it.

1. Unibail-Rodamco. *UK Annual Report*. 2008.
2. Architect's Statement. MVRDV
(source: http://www.mvrdv.nl/en/projects/GREEN_SHOPPING/#).
3. *Ibid*.
4. Chiesura, Anna. "The Role of Urban Parks for the Sustainable City", in *Landscape and Urban Planning*, 68 (2004). pp. 129–138 (source: http://carmelacanzonieri.com/library/6123/ChiesuraRoleUrbanParksSustainableCity.pdf).

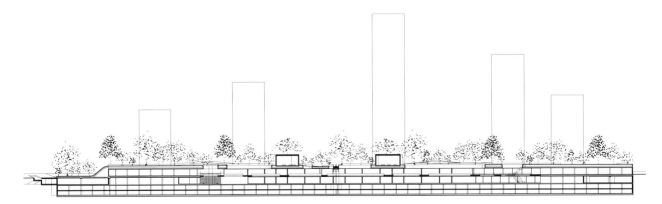

Section.

One Central Park

Ateliers Jean Nouvel/PTW Architects

Building Type: Mixed Use
Climate Zone: Humid Subtropical
Location: One Central Park, 26-60 Broadway, Chippendale, NSW 2008, Australia
Coordinates: 33°53'7"S 151°12'1"E
Date: 2014

Height: 116 m/34 floors, 4 basements
Gross Floor Area: 67,626 m²
Number of units: 623
Gross Green Area in Building: 4,000 m²
Gross Green Area to Built-Up Area: 6%

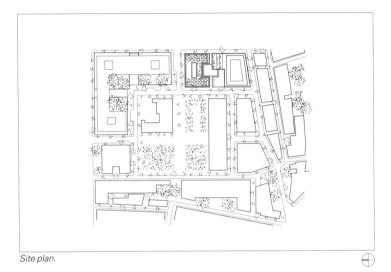

Site plan.

One Central Park integrates a range of green systems with its architecture. Most notably, the project features the world's tallest green wall. A heightened understanding of the microclimates created by the building informs the deployment of integrated green systems that temper the internal or external environment. Green facades climb from the park towards the sky, while a massive cantilever allows for natural light to reach deep into the building's interior and the park beyond.

One Central Park is part of a larger master plan developed by Foster + Partners for the redevelopment of the former Kent Street Brewery, a 5.8 ha site bought by Frasers Properties Australia in 2007.[1] Central Park is the city's second-largest urban renewal project[2] within the Sydney 2030 framework, a set of forward-thinking principles to improve environmental, social, and economic sustainability.[3] The master plan deploys best practices at the scale of the precinct in terms of energy production and consumption, water management, and renewable energy sources in the development of 2,000 residential units, student housing, a hotel, a retail center, and a commercial campus, covering more than 250,000 sqm of development.[4] Central Park provides 6,400 sqm of park space.[5] It carefully integrates the rich history of the surrounding area through the preservation of 33 heritage sites and an important public art program. Situated at the confluence of Haymarket, Ultimo, Central Station, and the University of Technology, Sydney, Central Park will serve these neighborhoods as a "village" center,[6] in particular the trendy arts district of Chippendale and the University across the street. The development is well positioned to make use of Sydney's vast public transportation networks, with Sydney's Central Station, the largest railway station in Australia, directly to the northeast of the site. The project includes allowances for bike paths connecting to the existing cycling and walking path network as well.[7]

The master plan takes an integrated and localized approach to sustainability. Rather than plugging into Sydney's existing water and power infrastructure, Central Park incorporates the latest in power production and water treatment facilities on site.[8] The localized strategy of water and power production is able to adapt more quickly to fluctuating demands. A state-of-the-art plant provides power, hot water, heating, and air-conditioning from a single system.[9] The recycled water network contains the largest membrane bioreactor recycled water facility in the world.[10] The system harnesses water from roofs, planter boxes, and other impermeable surfaces, groundwater, sewage, green wall irrigation, as well as drinking water from the public water main. The water is filtered to different levels of purity and redistributed

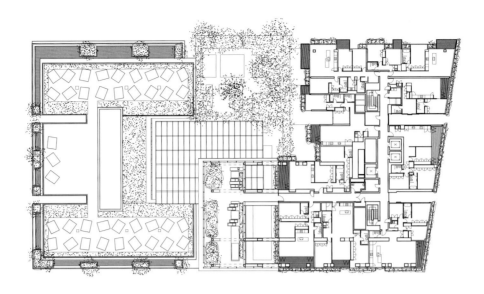

Typical floor plan.

Section.

according to need, bringing the technology in tune with the lives of the residents.

One Central Park is located at the northwest corner of the former brewery site, closest to Sydney's Central Business District. Chippendale Way sits to the west, while Carlton Street and the old Kent Street Brewery Gatehouse are located directly to the east. To the south is an open green space that serves as the centerpiece of the master plan. The building fills its entire site and maintains the clear urban street edge of Broadway directly to the north. Two residential towers comprising a total of 624 apartments[11] rise above a six-story retail podium. The taller East Tower, with 33 stories, is 116 m high, while the lower West Tower, with 16 stories, has a height of 64.5 m. The floor plan layout of the towers is standard. Double-loaded corridors provide access to a range of unit types, from one-bedroom to three- and four-bedroom units on the penthouse floors. The dramatic views and generous rooftop spaces provided by the cantilevered levels are occupied by a private sky garden as well as penthouses spanning the top four levels.

At Level 29 of the East Tower, a massive 42 m cantilever extends outwards toward the West Tower. This cantilever is understood as a response to the siting at the northwest corner of the central green space.[12] Given Sydney's setting within the southern hemisphere, the towers cast considerable shadows south across the entire brewery site and the retail atrium situated between them. An elaborate heliostat system mounted to the underside of the cantilever captures and redirects natural light into the retail atrium and the park space, as well as onto the residential terraces below.

Planting Strategies

One Central Park employs a mixture of vertical gardens, creeper walls, and slab-edge planter boxes to cover about 50% of the building's facades with plants, thereby becoming the tallest green facades in the world to date.[13] Relating to its context, the project deploys two facade types. The outer ones (the east and north facades of the East Tower, and the west and north facades of the West Tower), which receive maximum solar exposure, integrate Patrick Blanc's green wall system with creepers and planter boxes. There are only few balconies, giving residents limited access to the plantings. By contrast, the inner facades (the south and east facades of the West Tower, and the south and west facades of the East Tower) which face the community-oriented spaces of the development, feature deep facades with a large number of randomly staggered balconies and planter boxes within and around them, bringing residents in close proximity to greenery.

One Central Park's 1,200 sqm of green facades[14] feature a total of 370 plant species, 200 of which are from Southeast Australia, especially the Wentworth Falls area, introducing a high level of biodiversity to the project.[15] In total, nearly 30,000 shrubs and 70,000 plants spread across 21 panels of green wall. The ensuing biodiversity reduces the need for maintenance by decreasing insect or disease damage. The green walls' growing medium is produced from recycled polyamide clothes. This material is not biodegradable, which minimizes the need for maintenance.

An important consideration for the design team in creating the green walls that run nearly 150 m across the full building height was a detailed understanding of the microclimates that exist on

the various facades. The specification of the plants is based on a mapping of the environmental conditions on the facades. For example, in many zones at the top of the building, the plants are exposed to strong winds, which tend to dry out the leaves. These zones require hardy, small-leaved plants, while the lower facade areas require more shade-loving species with larger leaves. The designers used color-coded elevations to indicate different zones of wind and sun exposures to help with the plant selection process.

There are considerable environmental benefits to the use of green facades in the project. According to Blanc, "the vertical garden is very efficient and aids in lowering energy consumption both in winter by protecting the building from the cold, and in summer by providing a natural cooling system."[16] The gardens reduce the urban heat island effects and also act as a natural air purification system, absorbing polluting particles from the air to slowly decompose and mineralize them, transforming them to plant fertilizer, effectively reducing the maintenance required to three times a year. Irrigation water is collected from the roofs and open areas. Grey and black water is recycled as part of the master plan's overall water system.

The Heliostat

One Central Park takes a sophisticated approach to the conditioning of the microclimates of its surrounding environments. The heliostat is a sophisticated system consisting of 40 sun-tracking reflective surfaces, positioned on the roof of the project's West Tower. It reflects sunlight to 320 fixed, mirrored reflector panels mounted to a 110 ton steel frame on the underside of the cantilever at the 29th floor of the East Tower. The mirrored underside distributes the reflected sunlight to the retail atrium and residential balconies directly below, as well as to the public park further to the south. For activation of the public space at night, artist Yann Kersalé integrated LEDs into the panels, creating a massive light installation that dynamically illuminates the space between the two towers.[17] In much the same way that the green walls purify air for the city as a whole, the heliostat system reframes architecture as a device that tempers its internal as well as its external environments.

Critique

Vertical gardens introduce new ways of integrating plant life into the city. They take advantage of the many large vertical surfaces that can be found within our urban environments. The vertical gardens of One Central Park consider how nature and our rapidly densifying urban environment can be reconciled. As Blanc puts it, "vertical gardens are not a criticism of the city and concrete is not pushing nature further away."[18] Through its design, One Central Park situates itself typologically as residential infrastructure, with the plants providing considerable environmental benefits. However, given the amount of planted areas and the lush appearance of the building as a whole, the impact on the lives of its residents can be questioned. As the most invasive and permanent plantings cannot be experienced by the residents from within their apartments, the interior remains largely disconnected from the project's green features and its support systems (save for a few leaves obstructing the panoramic views from the upper level apartments). The integration of the planting creates an image of green sustainability, without drastically altering the residential experience inside. In this sense, the project misses an opportunity in radically, or incrementally,

transforming the residential and retail experience of a high-density mixed-use development.

However, from an urban point of view, the plants are an important feature in defining the building. The project concerns itself greatly with the tempering of the environment. In this way, One Central Park raises the bar for a new type of urban development in which environmental systems, such as on-site water and power generation, are merged with cultural amenities, landscaped public spaces, and planting strategies. The project's environmental systems – the power generation, the public space, the green facades, and the water recycling network – embedded within the Central Park master plan, do much to set an example for the way in which we redevelop former industrial sites. For example, the ongoing redevelopment attempts at the Domino Sugar Factory in New York City, and Carlsberg Brewery in Copenhagen, would be well served to implement the urban infrastructure approach of One Central Park, wherein environmental systems become embedded within the framework of the design efforts. In doing so, One Central Park purposefully and unabashedly conceives of architecture as infrastructure for the city around it.

1. "Central Park Sydney." Frasers Property (source: http://www.centralparksydney.com/).
2. Salhani, Peter. "Towering Ambition" in *ArchitectureAU*, 8 February 2013 (source: http://architectureau.com/articles/towering/).
3. "Sydney 2030." Sydney 2030 (source: http://www.sydney2030.com.au/).
4. Salhani, Peter. "Towering Ambition …"
5. "Central Park Sydney – Architecture and Design." Frasers Property, Australia & Sekisui House
(source: http://www.centralparksydney.com/live/one-central-park/architecture-and-design).
6. "Village Hubs – Sydney 2030" Sydney 2030 (source: http://www.sydney2030.com.au/live-in-2030/out-and-about/village-hubs).
7. "Central Park Sydney – Getting Here." Frasers Property, Australia & Sekisui House
(source: http://www.centralparksydney.com/explore/getting-here).
8. Taylor, Donna. "Cantilevered residential heliostat takes shape in Sydney." Gizmag, 11 February 2013 (source: http://www.gizmag.com/residential-heliostat-sydney/26197/).
9. *Ibid.*
10. "Central Park Sydney – A Sustainable Habitat." Frasers Property, Australia & Sekisui House (http://www.centralparksydney.com/explore/a-sustainable-habitat).
11. "Jean Nouvel – One Central Park." Designboom, 30 July 2010 (source: http://www.designboom.com/architecture/jean-nouvel-one-central-park/).
12. Bunting, Eva. "Jean Nouvel's Gian Mirrors and Vertical Gardens." The Generalist (source: http://www.thegeneralist.com/places/jean-nouvels-giant-mirrors-and-vertical-gardens/).
13. "Patrick Blanc Creates World's Tallest Vertical Garden for Jean Nouvel's Sydney Tower." dezeen, 9 September 2013 (source: http://www.dezeen.com/2013/09/09/patrick-blanc-creates-worlds-tallest-vertical-garden-for-jean-nouvels-sydney-tower).
14. *Ibid.*
15. Tello, Veronica. "One Central Park Vertical Gardens." Curating Cities: A Database of Eco Public Art (source: http://eco-publicart.org/one-central-park-vertical-gardens/).
16. *Ibid.*
17. "Jean Nouvel – One Central Park …"
18. Tello, Veronica. "Curating Cities …"

Oasia Downtown

WOHA

Building Type: Mixed Use
Climate Zone: Tropical Wet
Location: 100 Peck Seah Street,
Singapore S079333
Coordinates: 1°16'33"N 103°50'41"E
Date: 2016 (estimated)

Height: 198 m AMSL/27 floors
Gross Floor Area: 19,416 m^2
Number of units: 314 hotel rooms,
100 office units
Gross Green Area in Building: 5,923 m^2 +
28,000 m^2 (Green Facade Mesh)
Gross Green Area to Built-Up Area: 250%

Oasia Downtown, a 198-m-tall mixed-use tower,[1] is characterized by large voids, the Sky Terraces, and wrapped with a continuous green facade that only leaves the windows uncovered. The generous Sky Terraces transform this tower into an innovative contribution to a building typology that is well-suited for the tropical climate and outdoor living.

Oasia Downtown is located in Tanjong Pagar, an area close by Singapore's Central Business District (CBD) and characterized by a mix of conserved historic buildings and more recent large-scale developments. The project is situated at the intersection of contrasting urban fabrics: Singapore's container terminals are about 500 m to the south, public housing blocks to the west, historic low-rise shophouses to the north, and a strip with commercial high-rises directly to the south of the site (the 163- and 122-m-high Icon Loft residential towers completed in 2007). The 190-m-high International Plaza directly to the east was, at the time of its construction in 1976, one of the three tallest buildings in Singapore. SOM's Tanjong Pagar Centre, a neighbor to the northeast under construction in 2014, is projected to become Singapore's tallest building: up to a height of 180 m, the glass tower mainly houses offices; on top, a block with 181 private residences rises to 290 m.[2] The area to the site's north is a park, while the area to the west is not occupied but zoned for commercial developments.[3]

While all of these projects are more or less geared at maximally profitable volumes, Oasia Downtown differs significantly from its late-modernist neighbors in terms of its treatment of both volume and surfaces, reflecting the design goal "to create an alternative imagery for commercial high-rise developments."[4] Large portions of the tower's volume are void spaces. While the architects describe the building as a programmatic "sandwich,"[5] or horizontal layering of different programs, in structural terms the tower is better understood as an empty bookshelf. Its four main columns, about 12 m wide and located in the filleted corners of the tower, are connected by four horizontal, 6-m-high floors that transfer horizontal loads between the columns. The transfer floors on Level 6, 14, 25, and 29 are inaccessible and only serve structural purposes.[6] They divide the tower into five parts: the base, the SOHO offices, the hotel, the hotel club, and the roof space inside the building's crown.

Oasia Downtown's footprint is a filleted square with a side length of 48 m that covers the site almost completely. The 29-story-tall tower is a vertical extrusion of the footprint all the way up to the roof terrace and crown located 159 m above ground. The five-story-high base, occupied largely by a car park, is the only

accessible part that is completely solid. The SOHO offices, hotel, and hotel club each can be understood as an L-shaped smaller building placed between the transfer floors. Their relatively thin volumes leave large areas on top of the transfer floors unoccupied, thereby providing the space for the Sky Terraces outdoor areas.

The Sky Terraces

The eight-story volume of the SOHO offices sits on a Sky Terrace at a height of 33 m. The 100 individual office spaces, each with an area of 40 to 50 sqm and complete with a kitchenette and bathroom, have a floor-to-floor height of 5 m.[7] Resting on a Sky Terrace at 84 m height, the hotel occupies 11 floors with 224 rooms. Located on top of the hotel volume at 132 m, the hotel club is a more exclusive part of the Oasia hotel with five floors and 90 larger rooms.[8] On top of the highest transfer floor, at 159 m, the hotel's dining facilities are located in the spectacular space formed by the tower's crown.

While the L-shaped programs share the same orientation, the hotel volume located between them is positioned on the opposite sides of the tower, so that no two building masses are on top of each other. This arrangement of the programmatic volumes is the structural reason for the design's massive transfer floors. The tower exhibits an interesting play of solids and voids and appears like an almost empty structure from some perspectives—a striking contrast to typical commercial high-rise developments.

The maximum permissible plot ratio for the site of 8.4 (i.e. a maximum floor area of 8.4 times the site area)[9] would typically have generated a much smaller building of perhaps 17 stories, as opposed to the Oasia Downtown's 27 stories. The architects explain that the height difference results from the tower's massing, as the Sky Terraces are considered outdoor spaces in terms of the relevant regulations and are therefore not included in the plot ratio calculation.[10] Additionally, the floor plates of the L-shaped building volumes are much smaller than the footprint of the tower. The openness of the massing allows the Sky Terraces to be cross-ventilated and ensures that all rooms have sufficient access to daylight.

The architects characterize the Sky Terraces as multiplied ground floors.[11] Their large floor-to-ceiling heights of 43 m, 40 m, and 20 m respectively make them feel like outdoor spaces more than partially enclosed loggias. They feature a variety of plants, including grass, bushes, and trees. The soil compositions

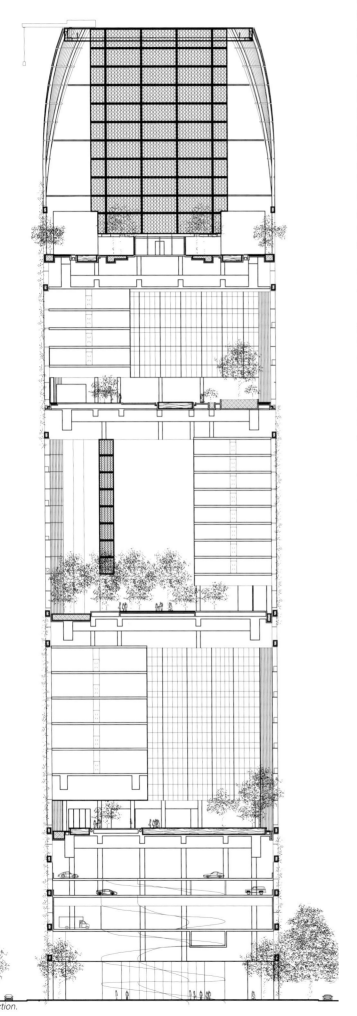

Section.

and thicknesses of up to 1.5 m vary depending on the types of vegetation. On higher elevations with increased wind speeds, the trees' roots are tied down with steel rings.[12] Since the terraces are open only on two sides and some of the neighboring buildings are quite tall, the daylight conditions were studied carefully.

The Sky Terraces are not only intended to function as gardens but also serve other programs. Many functions that, in a typical hotel, would be enclosed are located on the cross-ventilated, greened terraces. The architects imagine a desk-less reception area as well as lounge and meeting areas in the outdoor setting. A roofed dining area is placed onto the topmost Sky Terrace. Consistent with this approach, the hotel has no enclosed lounges, conference spaces, or similar standard features.[13] As the architects put it, "the public areas become functional, comfortable tropical spaces with greenery, natural light and fresh air instead of enclosed, internalized air-conditioned spaces."[14]

This enclosure-minimizing approach is reminiscent of Singapore's famous, colonial-era Raffles Hotel which first opened in 1887.[15] There, the rooms are arranged around a series of open, greened courtyards, featuring a lounge, cafe, and restaurant. Oasia Downtown reinterprets the colonial typology of the greened courtyard, with the important improvement that by stacking several half-enclosed green spaces, the site can be used more intensively, as is commercially appropriate for the project's central location. Just as importantly, the vertical stacking improves natural ventilation with increased wind speeds. While the original design envisioned the terraces' ventilation to be supported by large, high-volume low-speed fans, climate simulations proved that such fans are unnecessary.[16]

Planted Facade

At first glance, Oasia Downtown's planted facade is its most spectacular feature. With a height of about 180 m, it will be one of the highest continuous green facades to date, comparable to the 166-m-tall green wall at One Central Park (see p. 226–233).[17] It also covers the rounded corners of the tower, the edges of the transfer floors as well as partially the shields of the crown. The edges between the glassed facade areas of the offices and hotel and the greened areas, which make up about 75% of the surfaces, are blurred with an apparently random pattern, contributing to the tower's overgrown, soft appearance, allusive of an algae-covered shipwreck or moss-blanketed tree trunk. However, the tower's straightforward yet distinctive form never loses its architectural shape, balancing an architectural with a natural expression.

From a technological point of view, the green facade is relatively straightforward. Continuous, horizontal planter boxes divide the surfaces into 3-m-high segments. The 75-cm-wide and 1-m-high planter boxes rest on cantilevered beams and are accessible via maintenance walkways between the planters and the outermost layer of the facade, which is composed of perforated metal panels about 1 m wide and 3 m high. These panels, colored in various shades of pink, hide the planter boxes. They hold various types of creepers and flowering plants, with different perforation sizes according to the species. In order to achieve the soft edges and intended random appearance of overgrowth, some panels are not planted, contrasting their pink color with the green of the surrounding plants. This strategy also helps to preserve the coherent appearance of the facade, as plants will need maintenance or replacement. The tower's crown will be greened from below, with creepers growing out of planter boxes located at the height of the roof terrace.[18]

The implementation of this green facade is anything but simple. Initially, the architects were planning to include only three different plant species. However, the environmental conditions along the facades are so varied that a wider plant selection is necessary. Higher elevations necessitate hardier plants that can cling to their substrates at faster wind speeds. Sunlight conditions also vary based on orientation and shading by the neighboring buildings according to their differing heights. The landscape contractor was brought early into the construction process and experimented with a selection of a dozen plant species, including creepers and flowering plants.[19]

Critique

Combining the Sky Terraces and the facades, the Oasia Downtown achieves a green plot ratio of 750%,[20] which is significantly more than the empty grass field on which the tower was built. However, this claim does not capture the building's main quality. The intent of the project's green facade is largely aesthetic. According to the architects, "the building form is softened by a living green façade…, creating an alternative image distinct from the surrounding glassy towers …"[21] The sheer magnitude of the green facade, an impressive piece of building engineering and botanical know-how, transforms the building into a visual hybrid between the built and the natural.

Probably the tower's most innovative aspect is its massing strategy.[22] The scale of the Sky Terraces in relation to the built volume imbues them with a genuine outdoor quality that transcends the "enlarged balconies" more commonly found in greened high-rises. Even more important is the strong integration with the building's programs. By proposing that functions like the hotel reception, lounge, and meeting spaces are accommodated by the Sky Terraces, the building relies less on air-conditioned spaces. In this respect, Oasia Downtown may be considered WOHA's most successful attempt to date in developing typological innovation specifically adapted to tropical, high-density environments. Projects like Newton Suites (see p. 178–183) and the School of the Arts (see p. 120–125) also provide greened outdoor spaces, yet are less radical in their rethinking of program in light of the tropical climate. Oasia Downtown, beyond projecting a green image, promotes a way of high-density living that is closer to nature.

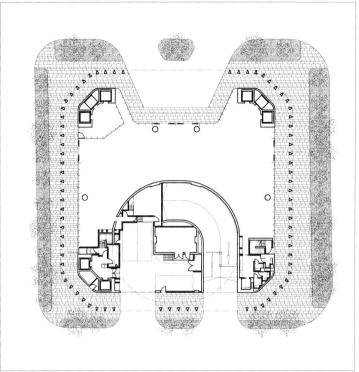

Site and ground floor plan.

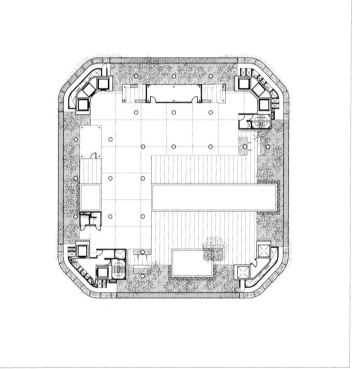

Sky garden floor plan.

1. WOHA, Oasia Downtown, 2013.
2. Source: http://www.tanjongpagarcentre.net
3. Source: http://www.ura.gov.sg/uol/master-plan/View-Master-Plan/master-plan-2008/Growth-Area/City-Centre/Tanjong-Pagar.aspx
4. WOHA, Architect's Statement, 2013.
5. *Ibid.*
6. Ang, C.H. (Architect Designer with WOHA). Oasia Downtown, Interview with T. Wortmann, 9 December 2013.
7. "Far East" in *Homenews* Supplement "Business SoHo@Oasia Downtown", August 2012.
8. WOHA, Oasia Downtown …
9. URA. *Island-wide Master Plan 2008 [Map]*. 1:50,000. 2008 (source: http://www.ura.gov.sg/uramaps/?config=config_preopen.xml&preopen=Sales%20Of%20Plans&saleIndex=1).
10. Ang, C.H. Oasia Downtown …
11. WOHA, Architect's Statement …
12. Ang, C.H. Oasia Downtown …
13. *Ibid.*
14. WOHA, Architect's Statement …
15. Source: http://www.raffles.com/singapore/about-hotel/
16. Ang, C.H. Oasia Downtown …
17. Source: http://inhabitat.com/patrick-blanc-is-growing-the-worlds-tallest-vertical-garden-in-sydney/
18. Ang, C.H. Oasia Downtown …
19. *Ibid.*
20. WOHA. Architect's Statement …
21. *Ibid.*
22. Source: http://www.fosterandpartners.com/projects/commerzbank-headquarters/

South Beach Road

Foster + Partners/AEDAS

Building Type: Mixed Use
Climate Zone: Tropical Wet
Location: 38 Beach Road,
Singapore S189673
Coordinates: 1°17'39"N 103°51'18"E
Date: Under construction

Height: 182 m/45 floors & 42 floors
Gross Floor Area: 146,800 m²
Number of units: 192 residential units,
654 hotel rooms, 50,000 m² offices
Gross Green Area in Building: 5,800 m²
Gross Green Area to Built-Up Area: 4%

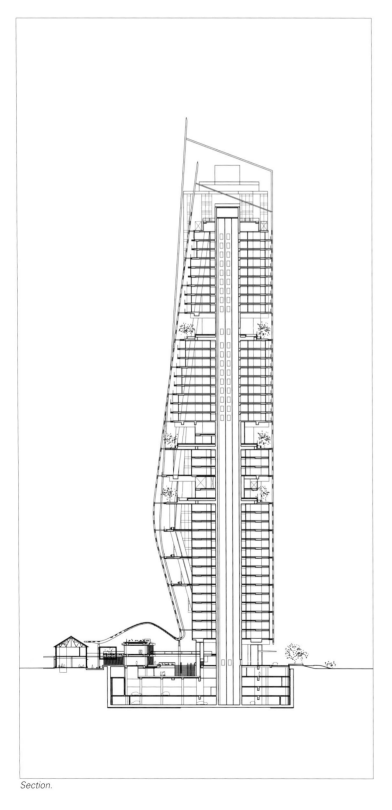

Section.

South Beach Road is located directly east of Singapore's Central Business District and in close proximity to important civic institutions and monuments. The project occupies an entire city block, which was formerly used as a military site. The development's two high-rises, four new buildings, and four conserved buildings feature a programmatic mix of office, residential, and commercial programs to revitalize the location while also preserving parts of its heritage. The project is the result of a competition that paired developers with architects. Each of the seven bids for the government-owned land was submitted in combination with an architectural design proposal. Important selection criteria were the provision of an attractive public space, the contribution to the city's skyline, as well as a high level of architectural quality.[1]

The overall design for South Beach combines ideas of a "Circle of Green" and a pedestrian network into the concept of a "Green Spine."[2] Complementing the "horizontal green" of the pedestrian level, the architects made a considerable effort to include "vertical green" into the two high-rises. Richly planted sky terraces and sky gardens provide recreational spaces for office workers, hotel guests, and residents, and give a lush and vegetated appearance to the towers.

The rectangular site of approximately 285 m by 125 m comprises four conserved buildings with preservation status from the early 20th Century. Together with a number of mature trees that date back to the same time, the site has a historical character that is distinct from many of the surrounding developments.[3] It is surrounded by major traffic arteries on all four sides, with Raffles Boulevard to the southwest and Nicolls Highway to the southeast, and most importantly by adjacent areas with individually distinct characters, which provided important references for the design by Foster + Partners.

Suntec City on the southeast side is a late 20th-Century shopping and business complex that presents itself with largely closed facades. A green corridor is situated on the southwest side, formed by the directly adjacent park of the Memorial to the Civilian Victims of the Japanese Occupation and, further on, the large open green public space of the Padang. The site's long side to the northwest is characterized by a dense fabric dominated by traditional shophouses, a common building typology across Southeast Asia that has a narrow street facade and is typically two to three stories in height. The iconic Raffles Hotel is located toward the south. Eventually, the northeast points toward the city's Ophir-Rochor corridor, an area currently under

Site and ground floor plan.

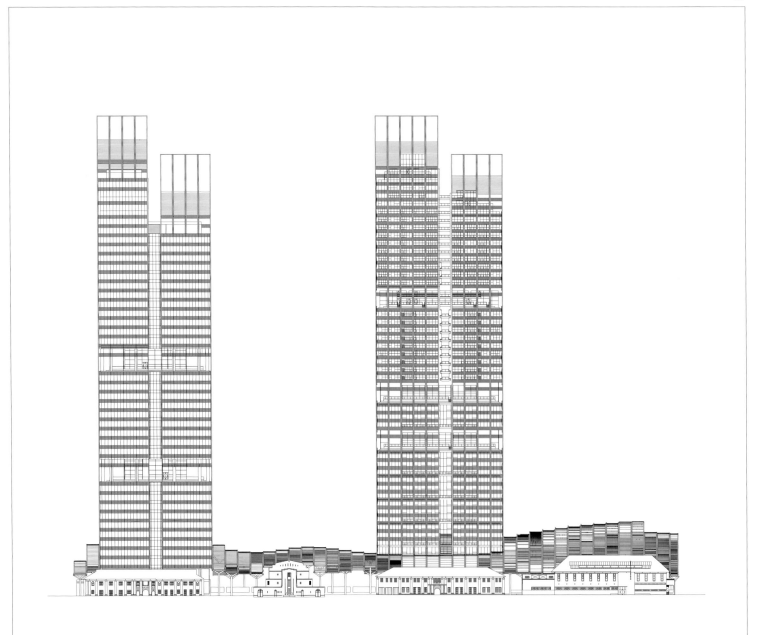
Elevation.

development and envisioned as a cluster of office buildings set in a park-like environment.[4]

Foster + Partners developed two main design concepts to respond to the boundary conditions. On a large urban scale, the site is understood as a link in a "circle of green" formed by the Padang, the Ophir-Rochor corridor, and other surrounding green spaces. Secondly, a structuring network of pedestrian connections is imposed onto the site, with the main route, the Spine, as the main structuring element. The Spine runs diagonally toward the visual focus of the Civilian War Memorial, incorporating important pedestrian transport nodes. Three smaller routes run perpendicularly to the main axis, connecting to the existing urban fabric in the northwest as well as to a pedestrian bridge in the southeast. The site is kept largely car-free.

The development's gross floor area of 146,800 sqm is divided into ten smaller areas on the ground floor that are connected by a pedestrian network. The two 182-m-tall mixed-use high-rise buildings are located to the left and right of the main pedestrian axis. Retail as well as food and beverage outlets, a private membership club, a meeting space for a veterans' association, and a nightclub and bar assure 24-hour activity in the area. The site's conserved buildings fit neatly into this design concept: together with the new low-rise buildings and high-rises, they structure the spaces along the main axis into a series of courtyards and plazas; passengers exiting the subway arrive in sunken courtyards. In this way, the main spine and courtyards provide diverse spatial experiences defined by new and conserved buildings that are enriched by different water features and plants. Naturally, the conserved mature trees have also been integrated into the design concept.

Horizontal Green and the Canopy

South Beach Road aims to provide an environment that is naturally ventilated, rich in plants and water features, and yet shielded from the extreme heat and torrential rains that characterize the Singapore climate. This is achieved with an environmental Canopy, a large, undulating roof that covers much of the site. The Canopy conforms to the ridge heights of the conserved buildings and, in other places, opens up to invite the public into the project, as well as cooling winds. In analogy to the foliage of trees, the Canopy filters both sun and rain, its permeability modulated by different types of louver configurations.[5] The design combines the urban qualities of the adjacent planted courtyards and traditional open streets in the northwest with the comfortable climatic conditions found within the air-conditioned enclosure of Suntec City; at the same time, it creates an artificial landscape that connects the area to the green spaces to the southwest and northeast.

The horizontal green in South Beach Road is mainly composed of conserved and newly planted trees, as well as of hanging planters, and, in some instances, green walls.[6] These elements are integrated into an artificial landscape of paved courtyards and plazas, marked by level differences and diverse water features. This rich and inviting landscape is almost completely covered by the Canopy, which filters sunlight, rain, and wind. The large, undulating roof of the Canopy is composed of steel ribbons, with powder-coated aluminum louvers spanning in between. The steel ribbons are supported by Y-shaped steel

columns, which enhance the "floating" appearance of the Canopy. The louvers are coated with a range of warm brown colors that evoke a natural material such as wood. In some areas, e.g. toward the edge of the site, they perform in a way similar to conventional shutters when they are open, providing a degree of shading and rain protection but allowing air to circulate freely. In other areas, the openings between the louvers are filled with glass, so that they allow for the penetration of natural light but not rain. In the areas that have the strongest requirements for sun and rain protection, the louvers resemble the closed state of shutters: they are rotated to provide a solid skin that is completely closed.

The louvers are equipped with various technological elements relating to the development's energy and water use. Some louvers have been fitted with components for solar heating to provide hot water to the hotel. On louvers located in areas of particularly high solar gain, PV cells generate the energy that is needed to light the pedestrian spaces at night. The Canopy also performs rainwater harvesting to irrigate the plants beneath and in the tower's sky gardens, which receive little or no direct rain.

The Canopy has been shaped in a way to control the wind flow; it is high in the southeast, which is the direction of the prevailing winds, and thus allows cold air to stream under it, where the air follows the Canopy's shape to fall down unto the ground level. Here, the air takes up some of the heat energy stored in the surrounding surfaces and environments, and then rises up to exit from the Canopy via open louvers on the site's northwestern side. In this way, the Canopy's shape and the configuration of its louvers work together to create a sufficient airflow.[7]

Different louver types are employed to calibrate the microclimates facilitated by the Canopy. Variables such as access to natural light, solar heat, air velocity, ambient temperature, surface temperature, thermal sensation, and rain protection are carefully considered and optimized. The central pedestrian axis is the area that is most protected from the elements. Here, the Canopy is fully closed to provide optimal rain protection and shading, with daylight penetrating through the glassed louvers to the sides of the main axis. Around the edges of the site, where most of the conserved trees are located, the Canopy becomes more permeable, with open louvers that allow a measure of sunlight and rain to penetrate the Canopy.

Vertical Green

Turning the Canopy into the vertical, shields of louvers also provide shading for the two high-rises. South Beach Road encompasses several types of vertical green. The most prosaic of them is the green roof, which is found on top of the four new low-rise buildings, as well as on the two high-rises. Of more interest are the sky gardens and sky terraces of the towers. The sky terraces are planted balconies located on approximately every third floor. They are accessible to hotel guests, residents, and office workers, and, when seen from the inside, provide visual relief. To a certain extent, the plants also provide shade to the facade behind them.

South Beach Road's most spectacular elements of vertical green are the three sky gardens that each tower houses. These open spaces extend through a full floor plate and are three stories high. Extensively planted and crucial to the towers' lush

vegetated appearance, they are accessible to the residents as recreational spaces with spectacular views over Singapore's CBD and the newly developed Marina Bay. From a programmatic perspective, the sky gardens provide an elegant separation of the hotel and the apartments of the South Tower. Those related to the apartments are connected with a vertical shaft for air circulation. In this way, natural cross-ventilation is facilitated for all apartments in a manner that is similar to the "wind towers" found in traditional Persian and Middle-Eastern building typologies.

Like the Canopy, the towers are shielded by louvers on their northwest and southeast facades. The facades are composed of slightly folded vertical ribbons, which alternate darker, more reflective glass with clear glass, in a way that the clear glass is shielded by the darker glass during the midday hours but maintaining a clear view.

Critique

South Beach Road can be understood as a synthesis between the natural and the artificial. Clearly, the environment of the sky terraces and sky gardens is largely artificial; they are not open to the sky and are shielded by louvers on two sides. The Canopy creates an environment that is comfortable for humans without resorting to mechanical means, which, in tropical Singapore, is a significant achievement. However, to some degree, the Canopy also shields the plant cover from the sun and rain it needs. In this way, South Beach demonstrates that the dialectic between the natural and the artificial cannot be overcome by merely introducing decorative greenery. Rather, both need to be carefully adapted to each other in order to create a new and compelling synthesis.

1. Rashiwala, K. "Size of winning bid colours green project: CityDev consortium clinches deal while a bigger bid fails to make the cut." Business Times, 11 September 2007.
2. "South Beach by Foster and Partners." Interview by T. Wortmann with D. Glaessl, Architect with Foster + Partners, and R. Schnizer, Foster + Partners Resident Partner in Singapore, 14 August 2013.
3. Dorai, F. "South Beach: From Sea to Sky: The evolution of Beach Road." South Beach Consortium, Singapore, 2012.
4. Masterplan 2014: Beach Road/Ophir-Rochor Corridor. Singapore: Urban Redevelopment Authority, 2014.
5. "South Beach at Beach Road." The Singapore Engineer, May 2013.
6. Rashiwala, K. "Size of winning bid …"
7. "South Beach at Beach Road …"

DENSE+GREEN

PRACTICE REPORTS

Foster + Partners Practice Report
Environmental Performance Optimization on the Urban and Building Scale

Our cities are getting bigger and denser: increasing numbers of people in the developing world are moving into cities in search of prosperity and a better life, and they are doing so at an unprecedented speed. In the developed world, cities are also experiencing a renaissance: London is growing again after a significant loss of population in the second half of the 20th Century, and there is evidence that in North America people are starting to turn their backs on the suburbs and are re-discovering the benefits of city living.

Cities offer greater diversity in employment and lifestyle opportunities, and afford a wider range of cultural and entertainment choices. They also pose challenges, as people are more packed together more closely. Is there enough space for everybody to live and work? How do we move around? Where are the breathing and relaxation spaces? Looking at places that score well in quality of life surveys, it becomes apparent that a variety of strategies have arisen in response to these and other questions. What all these places have in common, however, is providing a good public realm and, more specifically, access to nature. They provide places that let us enjoy the company of others or a quiet moment surrounded by trees with a view of the sky. Understanding the importance of these spaces and developing the policy tools to protect and grow them goes hand in hand with a greater sensitivity to other natural elements, such as access to sunlight and air quality, not just between the buildings, but inside them as well.

A growing body of research is showing how the natural environment has a positive effect on human well-being. These effects have been particularly well examined in the context of the hospital environment: studies have shown how merely the sight of vegetation can have a measurable effect on recovery times, and can even reduce the need for pain medication. In the workplace, access to nature can be related to lower levels of perceived job stress and increased job satisfaction. But there is also a lot of evidence to demonstrate how green spaces and physical activity can lead to a better lifestyle: one study highlighted an increase in body weight for teenagers living without access to green areas, compared to their peers who do have access to nature.

Advances in building technologies have allowed us to set the conditions inside a building, independently of the outside environment. It is evident that the mechanical control of temperatures in extreme climates can be beneficial and, similarly, that artificial light is needed in the winter months. But does the internal building temperature need to be the same throughout the seasons? Studies have demonstrated that this approach is not only energy-intensive, but also does not make us feel comfortable.

We have to consider nature, not as an adjunct to architecture, but as an integral component in the design process. Starting with the urban environment, we intend to illustrate how we can enhance the microclimate through seasonally responsive design strategies, and explore the role that natural elements can play in an urban regeneration scheme. Turning then to the building scale, this essay describes how green elements can help buildings integrate more successfully with the environment and provide better environments through that integration. Finally, we focus on the application of both of these scales in a tropical context.

Urban Landscapes and Ecology

Since the early days of the practice, we have been driven by performance optimization. Better architecture should be comfortable to use, more efficient to construct and operate and, taken as a whole, should seek to minimize the finite natural resources it consumes. Design strategies that build upon natural systems and minimize reliance on mechanical systems are critical in this regard. In a hot climate, for example, shade can create a better public realm and can reduce the cooling loads on buildings. Similarly, the study of the sun path and the orientation of buildings can minimize a building's demand for heating and cooling. It is a design philosophy that is as much concerned with the aesthetic aspects of buildings and their environment as it is with the invisible elements—breezes, air, the motion of the sun, and the movement of people—that make a building an integrated part of the wider urban landscape.

As early as 1975, the practice undertook a strategic planning study for sustainable tourist development on the island of La Gomera, for which there was no real precedent. It pioneered a holistic approach to issues of energy, water, waste, and transport. Behind this design lay detailed analysis of the terrain and climate patterns, and the landscape became an active component of the strategic plan for the island, rather than its passive surroundings. Almost 40 years later, this understanding of the interconnectivity and unifying qualities of energy systems and the environment has been applied at the scale of an entire city, with the design of the master plan for Masdar City in Abu Dhabi.

Masdar was conceived as the world's first low-carbon modern desert community. Given the arid desert climate, we developed

Foster + Partners, Gomera master plan, Spain, 1975.
The study proposed energy self-sufficient houses, as described here. The drawing shows
how a house could be supported by natural resources; wind power generates electricity for
lighting; sea-water deliveries allow drinking water to be distilled in solar stills; and anaerobic
generators digest household waste to create methane gas for cooking.

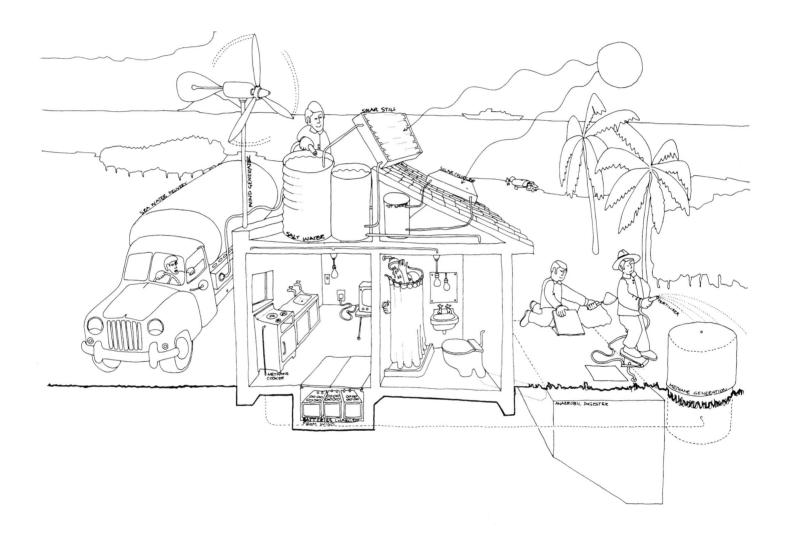

a number of strategies to ameliorate the heat, to introduce comfortable microclimates, and to effectively extend the season in which outdoor life is possible. These spaces are designed to a human scale and invite people to walk as their main mode of transport. Our design features narrow streets—a departure from the wide, heat-soaking roads that create an urban heat island surrounding our project site—allowing the buildings to overshadow the ground plane. These pedestrian routes connect a sequence of landscaped public spaces, which incorporate native, drought-resistant planting and help to create a more comfortable microclimate, as well as engender a sense of community. These landscaped spaces connect like stepping stones, as a network of cool pockets throughout the city, protecting pedestrians from the intense heat. A reinterpretation of the vernacular wind tower is employed to help naturally cool the public realm. In a post-occupancy exercise, the office tested the effectiveness of these strategies around Masdar's first buildings. Compared to central Abu Dhabi, the perceived temperature in Masdar was lower by up to 20° C—in effect, prolonging the moderate season. As the spaces between buildings are made more comfortable, the need for them to be closed off from their environment decreases; and by increasing comfort in the public realm, pedestrian life is encouraged, creating a more convivial atmosphere and conveying a unique sense of place.

The Relationship between Nature and the Creation of Successful Social Spaces

In addition to utilizing nature as part of the functional aspects of a master plan, many of the practice's designs have sought to engage with nature in different and sometimes surprising ways. Several of our projects have involved inserting buildings within sensitive natural landscapes. Where possible, the design has used the topography of the site to minimize a structure's visual impact, physically embedding the building within nature. Examples include the family hideaway Cockpit in the Cornish landscape, the National Botanic Garden of Wales, the Elephant House at Copenhagen Zoo, and the Bodegas Portia winery for the Faustino Group, whose earth-toned Corten steel shingles harmonize with the soil of the Ribera del Duero wine region in northern Spain.

The practice's research has explored the spatial and design implications of alliesthesia, the human need for sensory stimulation and variety, with the awareness that at a psychological level, the stasis of a climate-conditioned building can be negative. The constant subtle changes that we associate with nature, such as a fresh cooling breeze or the shifting tones of light or seasonal colors, can create a sense of delight through connection with the outside world. It seems obvious today that natural daylight creates a better atmosphere in a building. But when the practice was invited to design Stansted Airport in the early 1980s, the situation was a very different one: airports were predominately hermetically sealed boxes, optimized for the flow of luggage rather than people. Our design turned the building upside down, banishing the heavy environmental service installations usually found at roof level to an undercroft that runs beneath the entire concourse floor. This allowed for the building to be entirely daylit on all but the most overcast of days and provide views out to the natural landscape surrounding the terminal. The constantly changing play of light gives the concourse a poetic dimension and also has significant energy and economic advantages, leading to running costs that were half those of any other British terminal at the time.

The Great Court at the British Museum followed a similar strategy, turning an unused courtyard space into the active heart of the museum by means of a glazed roof. The sensation of being "open to the sky" and a part of the outside world is intrinsic to the space's attraction, since it is precisely this openness that conveys the sense that it is true public space. Changes in the sky and weather outside animate the space, which remains a flexible, protected enclosure for visitors.

This relationship between nature and the creation of successful social spaces has been particularly explored for its utility in many of the practice's designs for workplaces. The modern office is increasingly designed to encourage the informal face-to-face connections that can promote collaboration and spark ideas. Natural environments have therefore been incorporated to provide calming, humanizing social spaces, and when placed within sight of the workplaces themselves can contribute to a more relaxed working environment. The courtyard gardens of HM Treasury in London, for example, provide a natural gathering space, as does the rooftop garden of Willis Faber and Dumas in Ipswich, a building that was radical for its reinvention of the workplace. The rooftop garden was not only a social focus point, but also provided insulation for the floors below and helped to retain rainfall.

As buildings grow bigger and taller, providing a high-quality work environment becomes more difficult. A significant challenge for naturally ventilating tall towers is the imbalance of wind pressures and higher speeds at altitude, leading to a closing-off and dislocation from their natural surroundings. Furthermore, office towers were also socially disconnected, as the vertically

Foster + Partners, Commerzbank Headquarters, Frankfurt/Main, Germany, 1997.
Although each of the sky gardens is unique, they share a similar layout and are planted
on the principle of "themes and variations." Four-story sky gardens spiral up through the
height of the building. The gardens are planted with trees and shrubs drawn from one of
three different regions, depending on their orientation.

stacked spaces within them reduce opportunities for staff to engage with each other. In the design of the Commerzbank Headquarters in Frankfurt, we had the opportunity to question some of those preconceptions.

In the design of the Commerzbank every office is daylit and has openable windows, which—external conditions permitting—allows occupants to control their own environment. A series of sky gardens provides valuable social space while contributing to an efficient natural ventilation strategy. The gardens work in synergy with the social and environmental aims of the design. "In a sense the whole building is a garden… the gardens are always naturally ventilated," explains Lord Foster: "They can be thought of not as interior spaces, but as sheltered exterior spaces; together they read not as a multi-story hothouse, but as a sequence of vertically linked courtyards." In each section, a garden faces windward to admit fresh air, and a garden faces leeward to exhaust it, allowing efficient through-ventilation. The sky gardens are inserted in each of the three sides of the building and distributed evenly along its entire height, affording all offices a view of the gardens and the world beyond. In addition, the sky gardens' social function as cafe spaces conceptually breaks down the scale of the tower and helps to foster interaction and a greater sense of community. Through articulating the gardens with different plantings, we have been able to offer a feeling of privacy in social areas with a high level of concentration of users. In this way, the natural world can create a sense of ease and conviviality in even the busiest, most densely occupied places.

The Commerzbank's gardens remain one of the most successful examples of sustaining mature trees in a high-rise building. The planting was carefully considered, in parallel with the architecture. Each of the sky gardens has a slightly different microclimate, and changes in the planting reflect these variations. The south-facing gardens enjoy the hottest climate and the greatest exposure to sunlight, so Mediterranean species—olive trees and citrus plants—are key elements. In the west-facing gardens, North American and Northern European plants, such as maples, are used. The east-facing gardens have an Asian theme and incorporate a bamboo garden. "The planting was the subject of an extraordinary amount of research: buying mature olive trees from Italy, maples, bamboo, rhododendrons, importing them, moving them, working to give the fullest possible variety of foliage, and gain a mix that worked with the scale of the building," explains Spencer de Grey, Co-Head of Design at Foster + Partners. Just as the different plants give each garden a subtle individual character, these themes are carried through in the

Foster + Partners, Stansted Airport, London, UK, 1991.
Interior of the main concourse with travellers waiting to board and check in.
Entirely daylit on all but the most overcast of days, the constantly changing play of light
gives the concourse a poetic dimension and also has significant energy and economic
advantages, leading to running costs half those of any other British terminal.

choice of materials for benches and planter-tops: terracotta in the Mediterranean gardens, timber in the North American and European gardens, and slate in the Asian gardens.

Although each of the Commerzbank's vertical gardens is unique, they share similar layouts. Typically there is a deep planter for trees in the middle of the garden and a shallow planter for foreground planting and shrubs on the atrium side. Between these areas are a small bar and vending machines. The planting medium is a mixture of soil and volcanic aggregate, which is dense enough to support the mature trees, but light enough to minimize live loads on the floors. Irrigation hoses are embedded in the soil, while the bottoms of the planters are lined with thick felt over a layer of gravel to ensure good drainage. The moisture content is monitored and can be adjusted automatically.

Localism in a Tropical Context

A fundamental concern is the design of buildings and public spaces that reflect the unique culture and climate of each place where we work. Southeast Asia is a region particularly pertinent in many ways when discussing the relationship between natural elements and density. The population in the region has doubled in the last 40 years and much of that growth has been in the urban centers—the city of Kuala Lumpur has grown almost fourfold during that time span.

In the context of this rapid urban growth, the Malaysian government promoted further development nodes away from the capital. The Petronas University of Technology, Seri Iskandar, for example, is set on a former mining site. The climatic conditions demanded a highly specific design response, which could provide shade from the intense heat of the midday sun and shelter from the afternoon monsoon rains. The buildings are oriented for views out to their lush green setting and are connected by wide walkways, set beneath crescent-shaped canopies. Unlike typically enclosed institutional corridors, these circulation routes are open to the tropical landscape and ventilated by cooling winds. These two simple steps, providing shade and inviting airflow, helped to create an attractive social environment, bringing a sense of cohesion to the whole campus.

Some 450 km southwest, in a much more urban setting, we have built on those simple passive design strategies to create a new high-density, mixed-use urban quarter in the heart of Singapore. Combining new construction with the restoration of existing buildings, the scheme brings together places to live and work with shops, cafés, restaurants, a hotel, and new public spaces. A wide landscaped pedestrian avenue—a green spine—weaves through the site and is protected by a large canopy, which shelters the light-filled spaces beneath from the extremes of the tropical climate.

Having worked on a number of projects in Singapore, we were often struck by the parallel considerations of building sympathetically with the environment and engaging with regional styles. David Nelson, Co-Head of Design at Foster + Partners, explains how the client for Singapore's Supreme Court was keen to develop "an adaptive architecture" that was respectful of the city's colonial era buildings. Singapore's architecture during the 1960s and 1970s was international in its style, and Liu Thai Ker, the local architect for the project, "felt that it was time to search for an interpretation of an architecture which belonged in a tropical climate." To achieve this, the design team's research was wide-ranging: investigating the climate, cultural influences, and elements of existing architecture, such as natural shading devices, the use of deep recesses and formal colonnades— all aspects of the Singaporean vernacular. In parallel, they looked at the use of landscaping in traditional buildings and sought a way to allow natural light to penetrate deep into the Supreme Court, while minimizing solar heat gain. A dense urban pattern of blocks, streets, and lanes was established within the boundaries of the site, creating something more like a sheltered pedestrian precinct than a conventional building, and opening up the possibility of a connected internal urban landscape.

This strategy was similarly applied in the main "street" through the South Beach project. While the landscape along the public route at ground level provides respite from the dense urban setting, the canopy above is designed to regulate the microclimate, harvest rainwater, and channel natural breezes. Creating ideal thermal comfort relies on the integration of the canopy and landscape below. The roof structure is made of a series of laminated aluminum slats staggered in a shingle pattern. These are fixed within steel ribbons, which form the undulating structure of the canopy. At the low points, this canopy is supported on a series of light hollow columns. The canopy's solid panels are angled strategically to provide appropriate levels of shading and indirect sunlight. We were interested in the effectiveness of providing shading from the intense midday heat—our research showed that this is three times more effective than providing maximum practical air movement. Overall, 85% shading is sufficient to minimize solar radiation to an acceptable level.

The distribution of shading density is laid out according to the use of space within the canopy, with a higher density along the major pedestrian pathways and increased porosity around the outdoor gardens and courtyards. The overlapping canopy allows diffuse daylight to be introduced through a series of reflections with minimum heat gain. A common misconception is that large amounts of skylights are required to illuminate the interior of the building. In fact, in Singapore only 2% of the daylight on a typical overcast day is required to illuminate an office (500 lux), while even less (300 lux) is sufficient for a comfortable visual environment in retail and circulation spaces. Introducing excessive daylight presents a high risk of glare and a strong contrast between light and dark areas.

The roof's geometry has been optimized to funnel breezes through the site's main pedestrian thoroughfare, increasing wind speed by up to 60%. The canopy is profiled to capture the prevailing winds during the monsoon periods. Air movement can effectively counter the effect of high humidity in Singapore and can significantly improve thermal comfort within the canopy during specific times of the year. The porosity of the canopy and angling of the shingles has been optimized such that users will remain dry under the main pedestrian areas, even in driving rain, but warm air is able to escape through spaces between shingles, helping to reduce the interior air temperature. Where the canopy dips, rainwater is channelled into the hollow columns that hold up the canopy. These valleys are angled to prevent the accumulation of stagnant water, thus avoiding the possibility of creating breeding grounds for mosquitoes. In this way, the design embodies a climatically and culturally responsive urban model in a tropical context.

South Beach demonstrates that performance, in environmental and social terms, relates very strongly to local resources and climate. It also implies global viability coupled with local appeal, which means that while the underlying goals might be the same for cities across the world, the forms and the spaces will relate very specifically to each place.

MVRDV Practice Report
New Nature

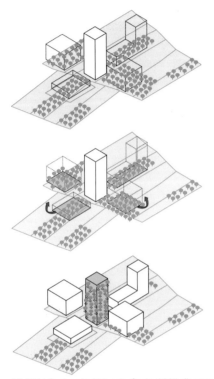

MVRDV, Sociopolis, Valencia, Spain, 2007, diagram.
The project "transplants and transports" the agricultural plots, which will be swallowed by real-estate development, to the future building, thereby creating a vertical orchard. All the apartments have a balcony/orange orchard.

The 21st Century is being marked by sustainability. It is a powerful term that has gained universal attention. Unfortunately, it is commonly associated with drama rather than optimism and happiness. Framed by a situation perceived as confusing or even apocalyptic, sustainability is, or at least appears to be, a source of fear and conformism instead of intelligence and newness. The wider public should become aware that sustainability is enjoyable and not a sacrifice, that it is possible to combine lower resource consumption with more ambition, more comfort, higher density and higher quality of life. Can we imagine new ways of ecology that reflect an exciting and intense interaction between urbanity, nature, and humans?

New Nature

In the era of sustainability, the world is facing a challenging reality: the increasing density and degree of interaction between city and the non-urban, urbanity and landscape, nature and artificiality. While nature is being invaded by man-made elements, many cities, especially in developed countries, are incorporating nature into the urban fabric for its obvious social and environmental benefits, but also to improve their competitiveness. At the same time, urban agriculture is evolving in different forms, providing fresh organic food that often citizens help to grow in their free time. Some cities offers indoor ski resorts or beaches where high-tech systems allow featuring mountain slopes or surfing waves.

This relatively new pattern of artificialized nature or naturalized urbanity offers new fields of experimentation. It pursues a sustainable balance of man-made spaces, nature, and technology, blurring the boundary between architecture, landscape, and urbanism, creating a realm where people can benefit from nature while supporting the expansion of nature into the city. One can imagine a new kind of world emerging from this process, a (new)nature that would constitute a hyper-dense landscape in place of the current formal arrangement of gardens and parks. Echoing the desire of the inhabitants for healthy and enjoyable cities, this development challenges nature to become urban and the urban to build with nature. With it, our cities would take a step back from their current artificiality, establishing a positive coexistence between the natural world and the networks of cities: you walk into a forest stepping out of the shopping mall, or enjoy your own farmland as an extension of your living room, or walk through a mosaic of 3D pocket gardens in your neighborhood.

MVRDV, Maquinnext, Barcelona, Spain, 2012, rendering.
The symbiosis between nature and architecture creates intriguing combinations
of landscape and building functions.

MVRDV, Natural History Museum, Zhejiang, China, 2014, rendering.
The design reflects and extends the surrounding nature,
celebrating the natural wonders of the region.

MVRDV, Folie Richter, Montpellier, France, 2014, rendering.
The architectural composition of this project brings together a collection of neighborhoods and a variety of intense green spaces. The resulting mix is more open, more diverse, and more natural.

In order to create a greener city, we need to look at pure nature and find effective ways to bind them together. Families often prefer houses over apartments. Sociopolis is a tower of social housing located in an area where the population is very attached to local agriculture. Instead of stacking apartments on a green plot, the building offers an individual balcony-orchard to each and every apartment. You could grow your own fruit, or have holidays on your balcony!

MVRDV's proposal for a new mixed-used complex in Barcelona represents an intense encounter between nature and the city. While the brief called for the development of a shopping center and residential towers, a forest became an additional and crucial element of the program during the design process, creating a new (eco)system in the neighborhood with the help of advanced technology. The intense nature stimulates the shopping experience, pumps life into the district, cleans the air of the city, and contributes to cool the environment in the Mediterranean climate of Barcelona.

Creating an enhanced interaction between the urban and nature sometimes leads to building in a natural environment. We need to regain a sense of humility when facing the beauty of landscape. The celebration of nature by means of a building can be highly attractive and may bring the opportunity to preserve and even improve the ecological value of the site. The design of the Zhejiang Museum of Natural History in China has the aim to raise the awareness for the role of nature in general and more specifically of the regional natural wonders. With its compact volume and "lift nature" on the roof, the design is an exemplary solution for respectfully letting nature take over architecture by allowing trees, plants, and little animals to enter the building and create their habitats inside and on top of it.

Dense Mix of Nature and Urbanity

Imagine you could live in a tower characterized by the variety and richness of a mixture of intense nature, sports, and leisure, combining a wide range of living and working spaces so that everybody could find their own style. It would be a tower with relaxation areas, pocket gardens, plazas, and even pieces of jungle where residents would experience nature in the normal course of work, play, shopping, and living.

Our cities often stand in stark contrast with this, presenting high-density structures that are not more than piled-up spaces, highly concentrated vertical buildings with no soul.

MVRDV, Peruri 88, Jakarta, Indonesia, 2012, rendering.
The project proposes a network of buildings and collective spaces, interwoven with the lush vegetation.

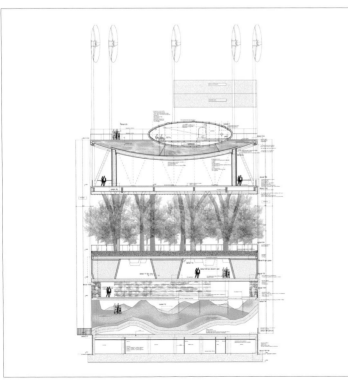

These high-density structures are in many cases called "mixed-use," which stands for the stacking of functions on top of each other. This terrible simplification fails to respond to the need to create liveable and rich environments. It does not lead to urban renewal or innovation, nor does it reflect a sustainable scheme for the growth of cities. Such structures tend to become shoddy eyesores, as the typologies they offer often have very little sense of community and hardly any connection with the streetscape.

We want to incorporate wildlife in our cities, collective spaces at a variety of levels, all kinds of functional programs. The challenge and the ambition are to make such a mix more open, more natural, and more productive. One can imagine, in a collection of neighborhoods, patio homes, collective houses, penthouses, studios, and elderly houses combined with warehouses, work spaces, and shops linked by means of terraces, gardens, squares, forests, and eco-farms. It is a celebration of the Small and the Big, a Village within a City. The neighborhoods offer quality and attractive environments, both unique and suitable for all type of users, young and old, families and singles.

MVRDV's design for a housing development in Montpellier, France reflects the concept of accumulation of neighborhoods and identities, merging different residential typologies, shops, and leisure with plazas, terraces, and collective pieces of nature in a vibrant ecosystem.

3D Density and 3D Nature

Density is and remains a hot issue for the coming generations. The claim of density, however, is often made too simplistically, without taking into consideration a more social and cultural environment. High density is not only about going up and down again. The new, advanced concept of density should enhance social factors, which will lead to more complexity and more interaction between buildings and hence between people. Integrating public spaces within the buildings creates opportunities for people to make contact. Blending different functions with infrastructure and public spaces stimulates the experience of the inhabitants and creates places where people like to live and work.

The exploration of options for public life between buildings and involving nature, not only at street level but especially at higher levels, brings new spatial articulations and with these the possibility to open up the dense cities and make them more liveable, more enjoyable, healthier, and more comfortable. In this spirit, imagine that you walk from one tower to another through a hanging garden, that you sit on a public plaza overlooking the city and from here you reach a forest growing in the building and cooling down the environment. The current 2D zoning of our former urbanism will shift toward a 3D zoning: urbanism will become vertical. Beyond the green facade and parks at street level, we can create a 3D mosaic of green spaces in the city. Peruri 88, a large and ambitious mixed-used development in Jakarta, Indonesia, reflects the richness of this approach in architecture and landscape. It combines Jakarta's need for green space with the city's need for higher densities while respecting the typologies of the existing urban fabric. By interweaving buildings and connectors, ample spaces and opportunities for social interactions are created in an urban-natural environment.

Since the beginning of its practice, in response to the observation of vast areas being filled up with low-density elements, turning our environment into a "sea of mediocrity," MVRDV has examined the possibilities of density. The following projects walk the fine line between reality and experiments, conceiving this term as a broad concept that includes density of information, density of lifestyle, density of buildings, density of countryside, and density of farming, weaving nature and urbanity.

Expo 2000 Pavilion: Nature Helper

The Netherlands Pavilion for the World Expo 2000, designed by MVRDV, shows a new and efficient way of adding nature to our urban environments by expanding vertically. The 9,000 sqm building with a height of 40 m consists of six stacked Dutch landscapes. Together they form an independent ecosystem: a survival kit, combining an increase of diversity with an increase of cohesion. The stacked landscapes, integrated in the water and energy cycles, become the building's service system: plants produce biomass as alternative fuel, produce food, and clean the water. Warm air generated in the auditorium is used for the floor heating. Natural ventilation helps control temperature, odor, and humidity.

Mixing technology and nature, the striking pavilion provides multi-level public spaces as an extension to existing public spaces, in the shape of a monumentalized multi-level park. This act of stacking and connecting saves space, energy, time, water, and infrastructure. At the same time, the ensuing density and diversity of functions build new connections and new

relationships. The structure presents the paradoxical notion that as diversity increases, so too might cohesion.

Floriade 2022: Symbiotic City

The Floriade World Horticultural Expo takes place once a decade in the Netherlands. MVRDV's plan for the 2022 Floriade in Almere is not for a temporary expo site, but for a lasting green *cité idéale*—a green extension of the existing city center of Almere.

The Floriade takes as its premise the simple pleasure of plants and trees integrated into our everyday lives and the city around us. This idea will translate into an urban landscape that integrates the qualities of different species into the built environment, thereby creating a rich variety of architectural and urban experiences that embrace, rather than eschew, the natural world. Can such a symbiosis between city and landscape be a solution to the rapidly growing resource consumption that results from a rapidly urbanizing planet? The challenge of this project is to enrich our everyday lives with plants, while creating a world-class, energy- and food-generating city center.

Almere Floriade will be a grid of gardens on a 45 ha square-shaped peninsula. Each garden block will be devoted to different plants and a wide variety of programs, from pavilions to homes, offices, and even a university, which will be organized as a stacked botanical garden, a vertical ecosystem in which each classroom will have a specific climate to grow different plants. Visitors will be able to stay at a Jasmine hotel, swim in a lily pond, or dine in a rose garden. The city will offer homes in orchards, offices with planted interiors, and bamboo parks.

Bastide Niel: Democratization of the Sunlight

Bastide Niel is to become a lively extension of the city center of Bordeaux as well as a striking eco-quarter by the transformation of 35 ha of former barracks and rail yards. The question was how to create a vibrant neighborhood in the tradition of, as well as an update to, the European city center: architecturally diverse yet dense; open and well-lit but intimate, and sustainable as well as literally green.

The project proposes the creation of a dense neighborhood by maintaining and extending vertically all historical structures, railways, and platforms. The new envelopes of the buildings, developed from strictly applied daylighting concepts, offer

MVRDV, Floriade 2022, Almere, The Netherlands, under development, rendering.
"Floriade will be a symbiotic world of people, plants, and animals" (Winy Maas),
creating an energy- and food-generating city center.

MVRDV, Bastide Niel, Bordeaux, France, 2010, under development.
The project combines maximal densification of the historical structures with sunlight access to all levels of every building. The result is a master plan that is architecturally diverse yet dense; open and well-lit but intimate, and sustainable as well as literally green. The neighborhood offers a network of pocket gardens that captivate nature at a small scale, using different plants and materials, serving various functions, and representing a variety of themes: the Mirror Garden, the Bird Cage, the Sports Garden, the Winery Garden, the Wisteria Garden, the Buxus Sculpture Garden, the Geranium Garden, and the Tropical Garden.

sunlight for everybody, even at ground level, while at the same time creating a contemporary European city roofscape.

In addition to aiming at becoming a zero-energy quarter, all residents will live within 150 m of a pocket park. The project creates a high-density network of small green collective spaces with a big variety of uses: playgrounds, sports, events, and eco-farmland that the children themselves will help to grow. The pocket parks and all the north rooftops will be planted with native species and provide a local biodiverse habitat. To foster an intimate quarter, the street width will be limited to 6–10 m, leading to a safe traffic system with equal rights for cars, public transport, bikes, and pedestrians. This network will result in an intimate and capillary city.

China Hills: Hyper-Dense Autarkic City

The concept of China Hills, developed for the "Future China" exhibition at the Beijing Center for the Arts in 2009, envisions a new typology of the future urbanization to cope with the high rate of economic and urban growth in a sustainable and self-sufficient way. Winy Maas explained the basic assumptions of this project: "As the Asian context is still developing and hence flexible, its design culture has a bigger tolerance for new typologies and the ideas that help shape it. The Asian context is characterized by a collectivism which is organized from the bottom up."

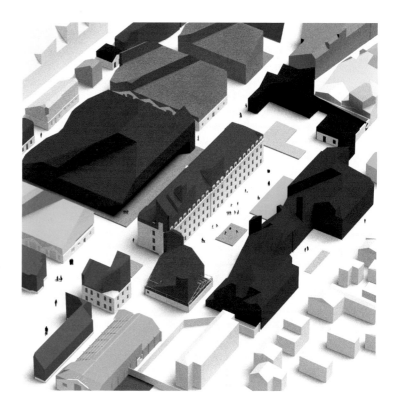

A series of green hills houses apartments and work spaces in their shells and giant voids in the interiors. Spacious terraces contribute to attractive and liveable spaces for housing and offices. The generous dimension of the voids accommodates leisure—cinemas, museums, and concert halls—as well as technology for storing and cleaning water, cooling capacities, and industry. The development also creates new opportunities for agriculture and energy production. As a new type of urbanization, this concept reacts to the current land shortage in both agricultural and urban areas in China, as well as to a lack of quality in the current types of towers. It explores how to intensify the forested and agricultural areas, as well as how to densify future cities with mixed programs in a sustainable and self-sufficient way.

The new urbanization would undertake the task of rebalancing the need for space, agriculture, energy parks, and water storage. Following this direction, China could be considered autarkic in ecological terms 20 years from now … Wouldn't that be desirable?

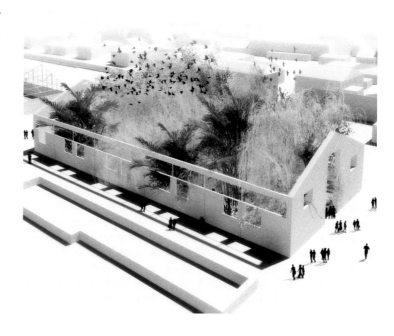

MVRDV, The Why Factory with JUT Foundation for Arts and Architecture, The Vertical Village, 2011. Installation of the Vertical Village exhibited in the Museum of Tomorrow, Taipei.

Vertical Village: Individual, Informal, and Intense

Vertical Village is a new model of urbanization envisioned by MVRDV and The Why Factory for the development of cities as an alternative to the prevalent monotonous sea of blocks.

For centuries, the fabric of East Asian cities has been shaped by urban villages consisting of small-scale, informal, often lightweight architecture. Urban villages form intense, socially connected communities where strong individual identities and differences are maintained. Today, driven by demographic and economic forces, Asian cities are rapidly changing. Massive towers, slabs, and blocks with repetitive housing units, floor plans, and facades are invading the cities, scraping away the urban villages. These alien buildings provide a Western standard of living, while destroying indigenous communities and rich social networks in the process. They obstruct urban innovation and discourage diversity, flexibility, and individually tailored ideas and solutions.

Is there a better way to develop these areas? Can they be densified without sacrificing the informality of the urban village? Could we apply the principles of informality to generate new neighborhoods? This approach may provide housing types with terraces and roof gardens that accommodate leisure activities; homes could be combined with small-scale offices and workspaces. In contrast to the block, this new village type might enable an architecture based on individual expression and identity. To develop the Vertical Village, a self-organized and self-initiated manner of city building is required, following a model that combines individuality, diversity, and the collective with the need for densification.[1]

Sustainability is a tool to increase the quality of life and to create a positive enjoyable living environment, even though it has often been associated with the downgrading of our lifestyles and the ensuing need to save the planet and ourselves. In a similar discourse, fragments of our daily life reflect that we prefer the artificial to the natural, while recently we have seen movements toward a lifestyle more connected with nature and other forms of life. How can architects practice under this contrasting reality? What is the direction to follow?

There are signs to be optimistic. There is still a certain flexibility and wiggle room to operate. High levels of technology and creative forms of engineering will allow nature to coexist with city networks in a way that does not show any tension or subordination, a way that would work for both sides. It is possible to create advanced density by combining functional spaces with forests, agriculture, and gardens where outdoor and indoor spaces combine their functions and allow interaction between them.

Imagine a city where individuality blends with collective responsibility, architecture melts with urbanism and becomes landscape. Imagine that this city can contribute to equalize the distribution of world resources. It would be a green global city, a place where everybody would want to go and be part of its environment!

---

1. MVRDV and The Why Factory with JUT Foundation for Arts and Architecture. *The Vertical Village: Individual, Informal, Intense.* Rotterdam: NAi Publishers, 2012.

MVRDV, China Hills, "Future China" exhibition at the Beijing Centre for the Arts, Beijing, China, 2009. A truly mixed city would emerge from the blend of programmatic functions with forest, agriculture, and energy production, taking the shape of supersized hills.

WOHA Practice Report
High Density, High Liveability

Asia's rapidly growing metropolises demand an alternative strategy for city planning and architecture that addresses the need to live appropriately and sustainably with urban densities. This pursuit of high density and high liveability produces a pressure on land-scarce cities that calls for a paradigm shift in our design approach at both masterplanning and building scale in order to create progressive, sustainable, and humane environments that propagate a high quality of dense urban living in the tropics.

Club Sandwich Typology

In all our recent projects, WOHA seizes the opportunity to find radical ways of organizing functional programs of diverse natures into distinct, self-sustaining strata each with their own unique quality and character, and then synergizing these varied strata into innovative high-density, high-amenity building typologies designed for the tropics. We refer to this concept of stratum synergy, where the integrated whole achieves more than the sum of its component parts, as a Club Sandwich approach. The Club Sandwich buildings not only result in richness and diversity of cross-programming, but also achieve the triple objectives of minimizing the building's footprint, opening up the ground level for activity generators/landscaping, and maximising areas for facilities by considering the ground plane as an essential, duplicable layer of the city that can be replicated at strategic horizons within and between buildings in the sky.

This concept was first clearly demonstrated in the School of the Arts (SOTA) in Singapore, which combines a high-density inner city school with a professional performing arts venue. WOHA's primary design strategy involved separating the school into its two constituent parts. The lower stratum, named the "Backdrop," comprises three publicly accessible lower levels that accommodate a concert hall, drama theatre, studio theatre and several smaller, more informal performance spaces within an exciting, multi-level urban plaza. This is overlaid by the upper stratum, named the "Blank Canvas," which is a six-story private, secure zone with a singular point of controlled access wherein all the academic spaces are located. For lack of actual physical ground space, a new ground level was created as an elevated level, conceived as a large sky park at the rooftop instead of at grade. This is the school's play field, complete with a 400 m running track.

Three years after SOTA was completed, WOHA had the opportunity to expand this vision by demonstrating how an integrated approach to building use is critical for promoting liveability, sustainability, and community on an urban scale through the commission of BRAC University in Dhaka, Bangladesh, one of the fastest-growing and densest cities in the world with the least amount of open space *per capita*. BRAC is located on a *tabula rasa* urban lake site and WOHA drew inspiration from the region's Sundarbans, the mangrove forests, which have separate ecosystems above and below tidal level. Instead of entirely displacing the water body, our strategy was to create two distinct programmatic strata: by floating the "Academia" as a canopy of learning above the lake and revealing a "Campus Park" below, the design reflects the synergistic coexistence between mankind and mangrove. Raising the "Academia" also increases airflow throughout the site by allowing wind to travel below the building, thereby reducing any wind-shadow effects caused by the multiple blocks. Coupled with the presence of the lake and its lush surroundings, air-cooling is naturally enhanced as gentle breezes pass over the water surface. The landscaped lake serves as a bio-retention pond where storm water pollutants are removed through a number of processes including adsorption, filtration, volatilization, ion exchange, and decomposition before the water recharges the ground. Part of this water is also recycled for irrigation and other non-potable uses.

This idea of synergizing both architecture and landscape into an "archiscape" was further explored in WOHA's unbuilt competition entry for Plot B of the Singapore University of Technology and Design (SUTD), where layers of student accommodation blocks were envisaged as an organic network of interconnected branches spread over an enfolding, undulating, sports and recreational "Activity Terrain." By contrast, an inverse scheme was tested in WOHA's unbuilt competition entry for an Integrated Town Hub, a one-stop community service center in Singapore's largest residential area, by lifting the sports stadium as a new ground level to the top of the building and placing the commercial and civic facilities below. In doing so, the Club Sandwich approach effectively reduced the site coverage by half, allowing the ground level space to be an uninterrupted pedestrianized plane that is fully open, visually porous, and physically connected to the existing neighboring linear park. This seamless merger of park, plaza, and people was proposed to root a new Community Town Green at the heart of the flourishing public housing estate. These ideas were eventually realized in the current Kampung Admiralty, which is a flagship public housing project in Singapore's Woodlands District that brings together a whole fleet of programs under one roof. Here, a vibrant People's

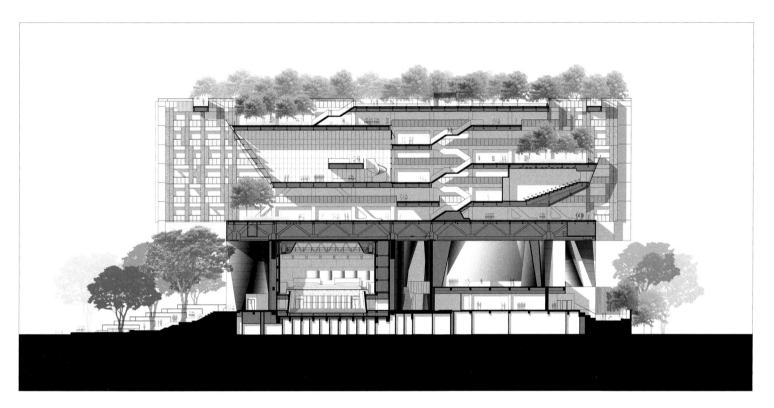

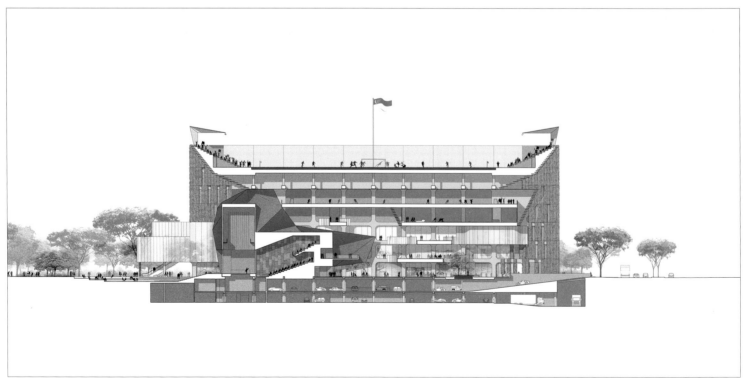

Plaza with sheltered tropical community spaces, retail, and a hawker food center anchors the ground tier, while a Specialist Medical Centre spreads out across two floors in the mid-tier, and a tranquil, more intimate and semi-private Community Park with an Integrated Day Facility (IDF), childcare center, sky deck and two towers of studio apartments for seniors are elevated to the upper ground tier.

WOHA has extended the Club Sandwich typology beyond housing and institutions and applied it to commercial projects as well. In programmatic response to the client's brief of having distinct areas for SOHO ROOMS, a hotel, and a club in the Oasia Downtown, WOHA created a series of five different strata, each with its own sky garden that is treated as an urban scale "Breezeway Atrium." The base strata comprise the real ground level, which contains common shared facilities such as the main entrance, taxi stand, retail shops, and services, as well as three levels of above-ground car parking and services. The SOHO is stacked above the base stratum, with its own exclusive sky terrace. The hotel is located at the mid-segment of the building, with a dedicated sky terrace comprising a veranda with lawn and function rooms. Above this tier are the club guest rooms, with a members-only sky terrace comprising a swimming pool, lounge, outdoor bar, and cabanas. A roof trellis garden with a swimming pool, and proposed restaurant/bar crowns the building, forming the topmost stratum. These distinct layers of sky terraces serve as multiple elevated ground levels, which allow the precious but limited ground floor space to be multiplied, creating generous public areas throughout the commercial high-rise.

In WOHA's recent competition entry for a Jakarta New Town master plan, we have gone a step further and extrapolated these integrated land use ideas from a building to a town scale; from 20th-Century 2D masterplanning to 21st-Century 3D masterplanning, which considers not just the horizontal parcels of a town but also the vertical layers of a city. By adopting the metaphor of a rainforest with its multiple layers of stratification, each with its own environment and ecosystem, this New Town is conceived to have four distinct strata, namely the "Forest Floor Ground Layer," which is the services and vehicular zone of the town; the "Forest Understory Layer," which features an uninterrupted, pedestrianized "Community Terrain" (new ground level) raised 6 m above grade; the "Canopy Dwelling Layer," which elevates the level of habitation to better views and fresher air; and the "Tropical Umbrella Emergent Layer" that stretches out as renewable energy farms above all the housing blocks for the harvesting of solar energy, rainwater, and "Skyfield" urban

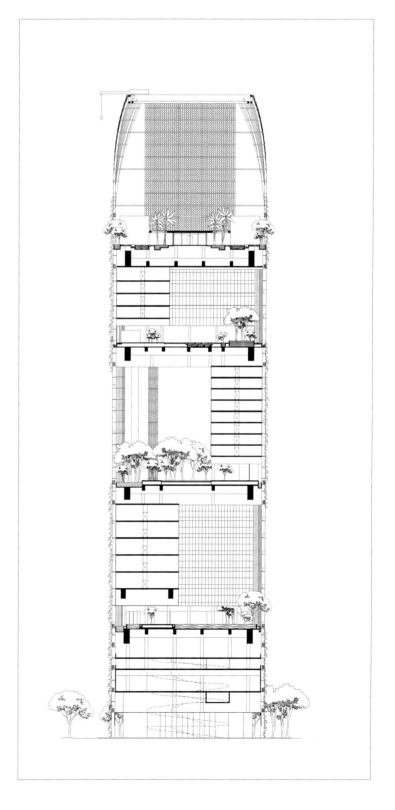

WOHA, New Town master plan, Jakarta, Indonesia, 2014, section.
WOHA, BRAC University, Dhaka, Bangladesh, under development, section.

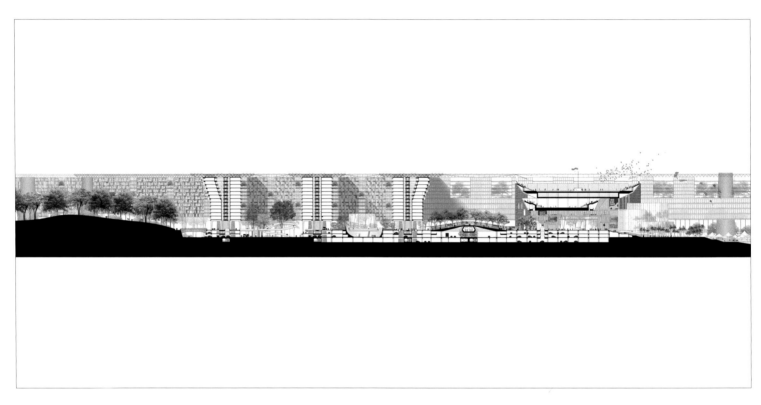

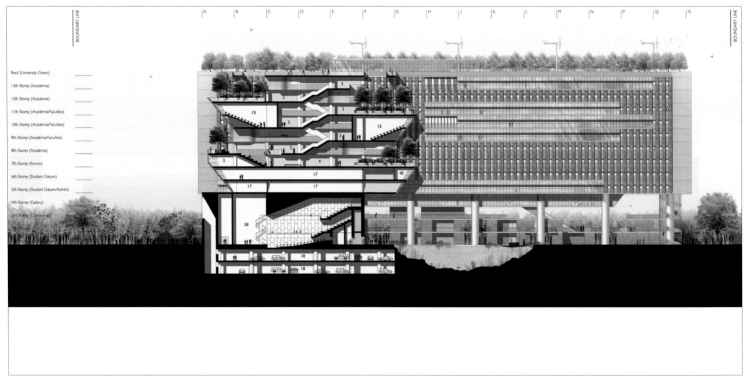

268

farming crops to power, shade, irrigate, and feed the entire town. This multi-layer Club Sandwich approach effectively frees up the real ground level for the preservation of up to 50% of the site's existing forest and offers a strategic way of segregating pedestrians from vehicles at the new ground level. This not only increases commuting safety, but also renders the scale of activity on the "Community Terrain" completely humanized.

Urban Umbrella Tropicality

Built into the Club Sandwich typology approach is the devising of passive sustainable design strategies that factor shade and porosity into the building's inherent form and composition. The multi-layered arrangement gives rise to intermediate and roof levels that comprise social, public, and/or civic functions. These form Urban Umbrellas that shelter and shade the outdoor gathering areas situated below from the sun and rain alike, making them usable in and adapted for the tropics. This combination of urban canopy and strategically sculpted and positioned breezeways make up the comfortable, delightful tropical urban community spaces that are designed to weave nature, in the form of cross-ventilated breezes, natural daylighting, and landscaping, into the building, thereby minimizing energy consumption while maximizing environmental comfort and human delight.

Such is the case for SOTA and BRAC (see the description above, as for all projects mentioned here), where the largest floor plates of the upper stratum's main student assembly and rooftop playfield (new ground levels) shelter and shade the public and academic spaces below. Visual links connect the various levels, with breezeways inserted between the linear blocks where intermediate decks of sky gardens are strategically positioned. Both campuses are designed as "wind machines," with their key facilities, such as the lecture theatres and resource libraries, prominently suspended between the academic blocks and shaped to catch and channel wind to the gathering spaces beneath, even in low wind speed conditions. In SUTD, the network of student hostels collectively form the Urban Umbrella over the "Activity Terrain." To minimize solar heat gain and maximize natural ventilation, the blocks ends were specially orientated, staggered, and shaped to act as natural breezeways to catch and direct the prevailing winds through the site and under the elevated buildings. This active combination of wind and shade offered by the building massing above formed the "Breezeway Canopies," under which a delightful and comfortable tropical environment was created,

one that would be perfectly conducive for student life to sprout and flourish.

These ideas were brought together in the Integrated Town Hub, where the large footprint of the sports stadium was lifted to the upper strata to form the cover over the entire development, thus ensuring continuity of programs below. With their linear arrangement, the facility blocks were specially designed to act as wind funnels, channeling airflow movement between the buildings. Aerodynamically shaped western block ends and rows of forest trees extending from the existing park further enhance the wind-directing design, making up the comfortable tropical "Breezeway Atria" at ground level, which serve as the alternative sheltered tropical town square of the development. Likewise, in Kampung Admiralty, the large footprint of the Specialist Medical Centre is raised to the mid strata, forming the Urban Umbrella over the People's Plaza. The Medical Centre is organized horizontally over two levels for efficient patient circulation/flow, as opposed to a vertically stacked block that would rely heavily on mechanized circulation. All medical areas are arranged around a large central courtyard with scenic views to the Community Park above and to the People's Plaza below.

Expanding this concept to a town scale, WOHA's vision for a Jakarta New Town master plan involved not just a passively protective cover, but also an actively productive one. The presence of a nearby airport meant that aviation flight paths directly impact the town. WOHA adopted a radical approach by turning the blanket building height restriction into a design opportunity. A common denominator of 60 m above sea level (AMSL) was proposed as a town-wide datum, from which the housing blocks were designed top down, with an inverse skyline. This enabled the spread of a large and continuous surface area, eliminating problems of shadowing for the installation of photovoltaic panels on the roofscape that can harvest enough solar energy to make this town Jakarta's first 100% zero energy town.

The PV Parasol additionally offers a good degree of weather protection, shading and sheltering the Community Terrain below. The panels are angled for optimal solar incidence and open up at strategic points to serve as wind scoops that catch and channel breezes into the housing units. Rainwater is also harvested from this town-wide canopy and recycled for irrigation and other non-potable uses. This "touching the ground lightly" by raising the buildings like kampung houses on stilts further permitted the seamless continuation of ground level greenery and the creation

WOHA, Singapore University of Technology and Design, 2010, model.
WOHA, Kampung Admiralty, 2010, under development, rendering.

WOHA, Integrated Town Hub, Singapore, 2011, rendering.
WOHA, New Town master plan, Jakarta, Indonesia, 2014, rendering.

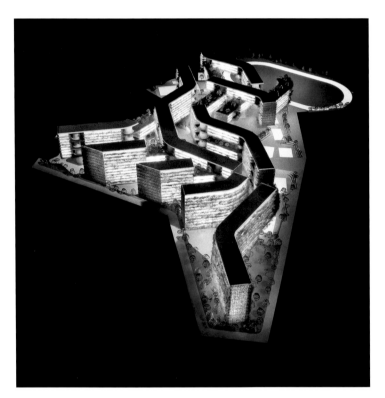

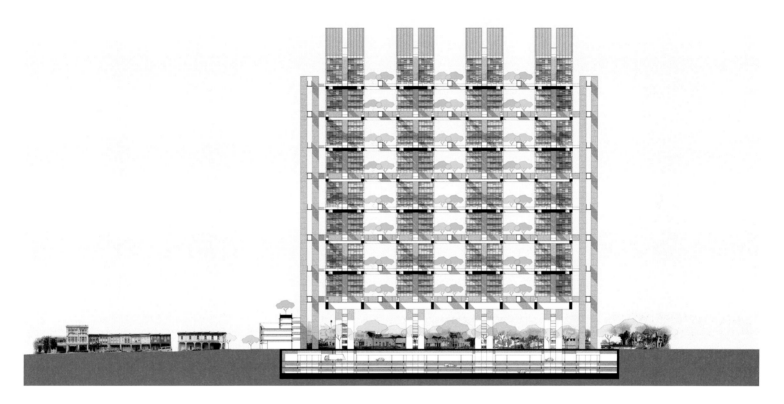

of a town-wide covered community space that is lofty, breezy, and fully pedestrianized.

Community Priority

Beyond achieving thermal comfort, WOHA adopts a humanistic approach to counteract the alienating effect of high-rise buildings. This is achieved by designing for quality of external spaces that encourage neighborliness; crafting physical and visual cues that reduce large or tall building structures to human scale; establishing dynamic visual links between the blocks/buildings; prioritizing thoughtful attention to practical detail; empowering people with choice; engaging the multi-sensorial experience to orientate, navigate, explore, and discover spaces; and providing different scales and characters of place.

WOHA's participation in the Duxton Plain Public Housing competition (unbuilt, the complex known today as The Pinnacle@Duxton in Singapore) led to a thorough exploration of high-density living, in particular of the quality of external spaces and the relationship between the high-rise interior and exterior. The project took the fine historic scale of the neighborhood into the large development. However, when spaces that

work at three stories, such as the typical neighborhood street width, were extruded to 50 stories, the scale turned it into an inhuman vertical slot, rather than a charming well-proportioned street. To avoid this problem, the emerging vertical slots were subdivided with horizontal gardens every five floors, creating more stable proportions that evoke a feeling of comfort rather than dynamism. Additionally, the landscaping features introduced visual cues that are to scale, rather than the abstraction of the curtain wall. Sky streets and sky parks were designed as social spaces, with residents having to take high-speed lifts at each end of the development, walk along their sky street, then take low-speed lifts, or stairs, to their apartment. These pleasant, relaxed social spaces were seen as vital to the development of community.

Eight years after the Duxton Plain competition, WOHA had the opportunity to realize these ideas in Singapore in the SkyVille@ Dawson, where every apartment in this 960 unit public housing development is designed to belong to an 80 unit "Sky Village", which shares a common "Village Green": a landscaped common sky terrace occurring every 11 floors, overlooked by the lift lobby and circulation spaces leading to each apartment. In this way, every inhabitant crosses a common space when entering

or leaving their apartment, and can observe the activities in the study areas, gathering spaces, playgrounds, community gardens, and shed in the "micro white site"—the high-rise version of backyards. Community Living Rooms at ground level provide seating areas overlooking a landscaped park where enormous rain trees are retained and community pavilions are arranged around a 150-m-long bioswale. A "Penthouse for the People" has been created in the form of a rooftop park that incorporates a 400m jogging track and pavilions.

Integrated Greenery

Recognizing the benefits of biophilic design, WOHA treats landscape as a primary design strategy for defining space, cladding a surface, reducing the urban heat island effect, creating a sense of human scale, and injecting delight. Vegetation forms an important part of our material palette for high-rise buildings, both internally and externally, thus improving the environmental quality on both the local and city scale. Every project is an opportunity to maximize the green replacement potential of the given site through integrated greenery, which includes a tapestry of sky parks, roof gardens, landscaped decks, pocket sky gardens, planter terraces, balconies, creeper screens, etc., that utilize simple, low-cost technologies combined with the sensibilities of the planting palette and the practicalities of maintenance access. In all these cases, the landscape acts as an environmental filter, cutting out glare and dust, reducing heat, improving air quality, and dampening traffic noise. It also provides visual relief and psychological comfort, creating a vertical parkscape that not only promotes biodiversity in the city but also forges a refreshingly striking identity, bringing a sense of beauty, wonder, and delight to the ordinary every day.

Part of the design brief of SOTA called for opportunities for students and staff to experience and encounter elements of nature, given the school's urban setting and its location at what was previously a green field. In response to the brief, WOHA developed a green facade system utilizing simple, low-cost technology—deep planters, aluminum expended mesh, and an automatic irrigation system. The green facades act as environmental filters, cutting out glare and dust, keeping the rooms cool, dampening traffic noise, and adding visual interest as these organic facades continue to grow over seasons. The planters are located off walkways, which allows for easy access and maintenance of the plants.

In Newton Suites, a 36 story residential tower also in Singapore, WOHA achieved 130% Green Plot Ratio (counting both horizontal and vertical planted elements) on a dense urban site. Landscaping was incorporated from concept level in every possible location—at the ground level, at the car park podium, at the common lift lobbies, on the vertical walls, and within the private units. The most eye-catching elements are the green walls and the cantilevered gardens. Using a similar green wall system as for SOTA, the design features a continuous wall of *Thunbergia* flowering creepers throughout the entire height of the tower. The success of the device is due not least to the practicality of its implementation: located adjacent to an external staircase, the planters behind the metal mesh can be accessed at every level for maintenance. The cantilevered sky gardens are common spaces that project off the lift lobbies at every four stories. All the lift lobbies are naturally ventilated spaces that overlook these gardens.

The landscaping theme has been taken even further in the PARKROYAL on Pickering hotel, with a Green Plot Ratio of 206%. A total 15,000 sqm of sky gardens, reflection pools, waterfalls, planter terraces, and green walls double the site area (or are equivalent to the footprint of the adjacent Hong Lim Park). A diverse variety of species including shade trees, tall palms, flowering plants, leafy shrubs, and overhanging creepers come together to create a lush tropical setting that is attractive not only to the people but also to insects and birds, encouraging biodiversity in the city. These landscapes are designed to be self-sustaining and rely minimally on precious resources. Rainwater collected from upper floors irrigates planters on the lower floors by gravity, supplemented by non-potable recycled Newater, which is also used for all water features. Photovoltaic cell arrays on the roof power grow lamps and softscape lighting, making these Singapore's first zero energy sky gardens.

WOHA's skyrise greenery has since gotten more radical. Oasia Downtown in the heart of Singapore's Central Business District sets out to create an alternative imagery for commercial high-rise developments. It showcases a perforated, permeable, furry, verdant tower of green, distinct from the surrounding glassy towers. The extensive landscaping is used as an architectural surface treatment and is planned to achieve an overall Green Plot Ratio of 750%.

Vertical Cities Asia

The above concepts were tested at a larger city scale in WOHA's scheme for the Vertical Cities Asia Symposium, where a "Permeable Lattice City of the Future" was proposed. On a

WOHA, *Permeable Lattice City of the Future*, Singapore, 2011, rendering.
WOHA, *PARKROYAL on Pickering*, Singapore, 2013.

1 km² city grid with a population density of 111,111 people, this visionary project proposes a vertical city that uses modules of our 66 story high-rise residential tower The Met in Bangkok arranged as "City Columns" in a staggered alignment to create a high degree of perforation and porosity in the urban fabric, resulting in cross-ventilated breezeways at city scale, ensuring fresh air and natural daylighting to reach every part of the inner city. These "City Columns" free up the real ground level for nature reserves and heavy industries. They are held together structurally by a network of "City Conduits" that serve as elevated ground levels; they are woven socially by layers of "CityCommunity Spaces"; and they are vertically interconnected by multi-cabin lifts and circulation systems that map out a fully pedestrianized city, entirely eliminating the need for cars above the real ground level.

Ultimately, this exercise in urban densities suggests that

by forming layers of stacked live-work-play communities;

by introducing multiple elevated ground levels at strategic horizons that relieve the real ground level;

by creating openness and porosity between the towers that facilitates cross-ventilation of fresh air and natural daylighting;

by crafting out varying scales of tropical community spaces that encourages social interaction;

and by applying vertical greenery and designing sensitively for human scale,

a super-dense vertical city can be both highly sustainable and highly liveable, if such alternative strategies to city planning and architecture are embraced.

T. R. Hamzah & Yeang Practice Report
Systemic Environmental Integration

T. R. Hamzah & Yeang, Horizontal green eco-infrastructure master plan, Macau, China, 2012.

Urbanization, especially over the last several decades worldwide, has led the urban environments in many of our cities and suburbs to becoming totally de-natured. Urban construction displaces the ecology of the land by deleting and simplifying its ecological systems and replacing the natural environment with synthetic, artificial, and inorganic structures. Should this denuding and resurfacing of the land continue unabated, the surfaces of the earth suitable for human habitation will eventually be significantly covered with hardscapes and impervious material. We need to reverse this increasingly artificial synthesizing of our existent natural environment. For those of our densely urbanized areas whose natural systems have been removed, we need to reverse the de-naturing by extensively restoring, rehabilitating, and safeguarding the existent urban environment with new greenery.

Outside the cities, particularly in the developing world, we find large tracts of rural land being callously cleared for urban expansion and for road networks, which are burgeoning and becoming more congested and polluted. These environmental issues must concern not just our design profession but also the building industry as a whole.

Urban greening involves increasing new planting, particularly in the public realms, by the creation of new parks, the greening of the edges of natural features within the city, such as its waterways, and the addition of multi-functional green eco-infrastructures that string together and link new and existent green areas. Where these are interrupted, whether by roads, highways, drains, or rail tracks, the intersections are to be addressed with eco-bridges and eco-undercrofts to create larger interconnected green realms and corridors.

Greening, of course, is not the only criterion in design. Today, where economics has the upper hand, green design still remains a tenuous imperative. However, it is the most important and vital one as the continued sustaining of the health of our planet is in question.

In architectural design, the key factors are function, aesthetics, liveability, and standards. The first criterion that architectural design must address is function. No matter how green the architecture or the city may be, if it does not function well or is simply dysfunctional, then it is useless. The second criterion, aesthetics, although arguably subjective, calls for designing with an artist's eye. In terms of green design, the aesthetic of the green building or green master plan is yet to be universally

T. R. Hamzah & Yeang, Chongqing Tower, Chongqing, China, 2008, vegetated ramp, green roof, and vertical landscaping.

defined. The third criterion that architecture must address is liveability—a green building should not only perform green but also uplift and enhance the physical and emotional well-being of those who use it. This, after all, is the fundamental purpose and power of architecture—engendering a positive impact on people's emotions and behavior. The fourth criterion that architecture must meet are the current standards and in this sense, being authentically green is one of the standards to be met.

What, then, is green design? Simply stated, it is designing to harmoniously bio-integrate our built environment with the landscape, the water, air, and the ecology of the land, that is, the natural environment in totality. Restoring the ecology of our urban environment is much more than just additional planting, more than a physical juxtaposition of the inorganic built systems with planting. The bio-integration must be systemic; it must be seamlessly environmentally benign in the sense that the environment becomes a "living system," functioning as a constructed ecosystem integrated with nature and its functions, processes, and flows—as opposed to an inert cheek-by-jowl relationship of landscape *hinterland* with cities that still emit polluting and contaminating discharges. In order to function as

an integral part of nature, our built environment must no longer form disparate sets of built objects in the landscape, separated from nature, but must function like ecosystems, mimicking the attributes, structures, and processes of natural ecosystems. The built environment must in effect be transformed into constructed ecosystems, working as active constituents of nature. Environmental integration in a systemic way is the key defining function of eco-architecture and the eco-city.

Our current built environment exists in a technosphere in our society, physically disparate from the natural environment. It is a "through-put" system, in that it mostly extracts the inorganic, non-biodegradable, and other materials from the land, materials that are then fabricated, transported, used in construction and afterwards thrown away. However, our planet, being a closed system, has no "away" for us to dispose of our used items. Nature has no "waste," as everything is recycled in an ecosystem where the waste of one organism becomes the food for another. Waste is a human invention. It is this physical dichotomy of the natural with the synthetic, the current non-bio-integration and disruption of the natural processes and flows in the biosphere that causes global environmental devastation. We need to regard all used items from our built environment no

T. R. Hamzah & Yeang, Kowloon master plan, Hong Kong, China, 2009.

longer as objects with no value but rather as having a reusable and recyclable value, to be made useful again within our human technosphere.[1]

Our current built environment is analogous to the abiotic physical constituents in the ecosystem. In order to function as an ecosystem, it should not be entirely inorganic and synthetic but must comprise a structural complement of the natural organic constituents, with both working together in a balanced system. The appropriate design approach could use an indeterminate framework that is defined here as the bio-integration of four strands of "eco-infrastructures" (color-coded here as "green," "blue," "grey," and "red"). The term "eco-infrastructures" refers to the quality that each of them is focused on achieving sustainable objectives that differ from conventional unsustainable infrastructures—which may, for example, be high-energy systems, high-water profligacy, inflexible non-recyclable material usage, etc.

The **green eco-infrastructure** is the key strand, created with the ecology of the locality, which provides an ecological nexus, a continuously linked green infrastructure ranging from the built forms across the landscapes to the natural *hinterland*.

The **blue eco-infrastructure** is essentially the water system intended to close the water-cycle loop with the reuse and recycling of grey water, the natural treatment of black water, rainwater harvesting, and sustainable drainage of surface water run-offs to recharge aquifers.

Together, the blue and green eco-infrastructures form the key organizational framework for eco-masterplanning and greening the city, a framework that relates both to the individual site and its wider context.

The **grey eco-infrastructure** strand comprises the urban eco-engineering systems, including energy systems like Net Zero Energy Built Environment (NZEB), transportation networks, telecommunication and IT systems, street lighting, etc.

The **red eco-infrastructure** strand is our human society, including built forms, enclosures, public realms and recreation spaces, pedestrian networks, as well as administrative and legislative systems, food production, and agricultural systems. Achieving the successful bio-integration of our human society and its activities with the other strands demands significant changes to our society, our lifestyles, and their

T. R. Hamzah & Yeang, DIGI Technology Operation Centre, Shah Alam, Selangor, Malaysia, 2010, vertical eco-infrastructure using green walls.

systems—including our industrial and economic systems that must all become sustainable.

Our eco-architecture and eco-masterplanning designs must interweave and bio-integrate all four eco-infrastructures holistically into a system, connecting our built environment and its inhabitants seamlessly and benignly with nature. This then defines our strategy for designing eco-architecture and the eco-city, and the remaking and greening of the existent ones.

The green eco-infrastructure needs to be a nexus of connected green strands, like greenways or green corridors, with extended fingers within and from the built forms across the landscape to the natural *hinterland*. The ideal eco-master plan is an interconnected ecosystem where wildlife species can traverse the entire landscape and where habitats remain undisturbed by impervious surfaces, roadways, drains, or buildings. Greening our cities means mimicking the biological structure of ecosystems in such a way that the abiotic constituents of our built environment must be adequately balanced by biotic constituents. The addition of biotic content to the built form should not be a simplistic addition of more greenery. Instead, it must be directed following an ecological analysis of the region and locality and

the establishing of habitat areas, with the selection of native and endemic species of faunal life to be brought back to the locality and of flora species that will attract these.

The benefit of the green eco-infrastructures to the city's inhabitants is the enabling of a softer and more biophilic environment that enhances their well-being. Biophilia refers to the connections that humans subconsciously seek with the rest of life, where the natural love for life helps sustain life. Presently, three million people worldwide die prematurely from poor air quality (compared to one million deaths in car accidents); China and India have the highest health costs due to air pollution, taking up 12% and 8% respectively of their GDP/capita. Most of the mega-cities in the developing world are losing 10% of their productivity due to poor air quality.

Eco-infrastructures can create a healthier microclimate. When plants transpire water vapor from their leaves, they pull air down to around their roots. This supplies the root microbes with oxygen. Root microbes convert substances distributed in the air, such as toxic chemicals, into a source of food and energy. They can rapidly adapt to new chemicals by producing resistant colonies and they become more effective at converting

T. R. Hamzah & Yeang, Solaris, One North, Singapore, 2012. The vertical "linear park" connects the basement eco-cell with the upper-floor roof gardens and sky courts.

T. R. Hamzah & Yeang, Ganendra Art House, Petaling Jaya, Selangor, Malaysia, 2010, passive-mode cooling using a downward wind shaft.

toxic chemicals into food the longer they are exposed to these specific chemicals. The efficiency of plants as a filtering device is proportional to the concentration of chemicals in the air, so that, for example, the removal rate of a chemical is much higher at 7 parts per million (ppm) exposure than it is at 2 ppm.

The densification of planting will also reduce the urban heat-island effect. Vegetation improves the urban microclimates and outdoor thermal comfort. Main benefits are the reduction of solar radiation and air temperature, by way of shading and evapo-transpiration, by approx. +/- 2°C. In a scenario where trees cover 30% of the ground plane and 100% of green roofs, the result could approximate the conditions of a natural forest.

Greening also reduces the energy needed for the cooling of buildings. Studies have shown that the Physiologically Equivalent Temperature (PET) decreases with increasing leaf area.

The green eco-infrastructure can repair the ecology of the landscape with increased ecological nexus, especially in the case of landscapes that have been fragmented by human activities and by previously constructed urban infrastructures. The connectivity is crucial for the eco-infrastructure as it enables a greater pool of linked natural resources to be shared by the flora and fauna, as well as greater species interaction and mobility. A system of linkages should also connect isolated green spaces to public parks and other extensive green spaces, encompassing extensions and connections of riversides, roads, streets, parks, as well as vertical planting in the city's built forms.

In the greening of our cities and in enabling them to function as a constructed ecosystem, other functions and attributes of the natural ecosystem also need to be mimicked. These include the reuse and recycling of materials through net waste systems, redirecting energy usage to using renewable sources through the Net Zero Energy Built Environment (NZEB), reducing water through-put by net water systems, reducing carbon emissions through carbon-neutral systems, last but not least reducing construction leftovers, the built environment's operational solid outputs, and its end-of-use materials destined to being directed to landfills.

The above provides briefly the strategy for the greening of our existent densely built environment and cities to become eco-architecture and eco-cities.

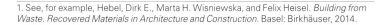

1. See, for example, Hebel, Dirk E., Marta H. Wisniewska, and Felix Heisel. *Building from Waste. Recovered Materials in Architecture and Construction.* Basel: Birkhäuser, 2014.

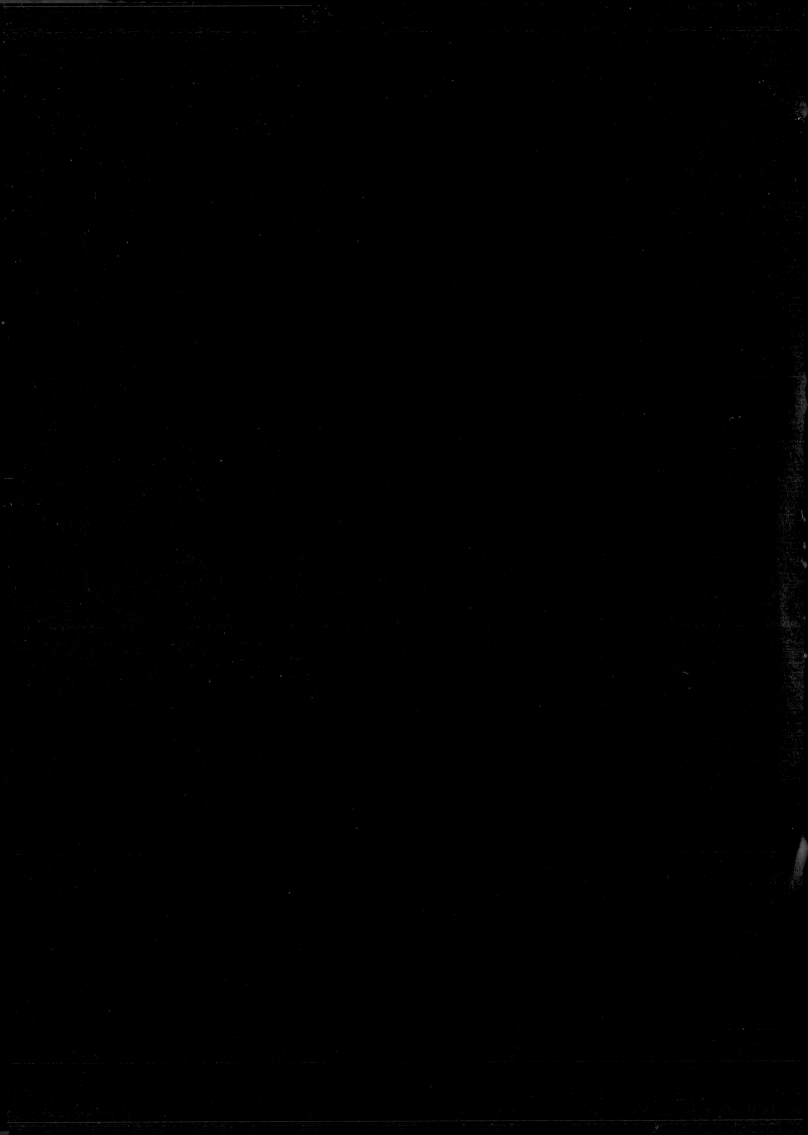

DENSE+GREEN FUTURE

Future Trajectories

Thomas Schröpfer

Conjuring an image of what the cities and buildings of tomorrow will look like is an exercise with a long history.[1] In architecture, these images tend to fall in either of two categories: the utopian and the quantitative. Utopian images are typically conceived around an array of ideals where science and technology are harnessed in ways that enhance life as opposed to making it more challenging, unpleasant, or stressful. The second set, based on empirical data and the observation of trends, charts a future that is anticipative and "probable" and is often used as a base for making decisions. While taking quite different approaches to looking ahead, both of these categories attempt to create a substitute of knowledge in order to effect and channel change, typically change for the better. In the context of the dense and green paradigm, one is probably best served by striking a compromise and combining modes of quantitative, empirical thinking with visionary goals. In striking such a compromise, one may more successfully address the real world problems that the dense and green paradigm must continue to address without divorcing it from the pursuit of a better world, which, although never scientifically quantifiable in its ability to be realized or implemented, has been the conceptual driver behind the most important advancements in architecture and urbanism of our day. The ensuing image, and possible model for a future dense and green paradigm, can be described on three discrete levels: trajectories of the urban, trajectories of architecture, and trajectories of ecology, which are the three main constituent elements developed and demonstrated in this book.

Trajectories of the Urban

Developing compact cities with extensive greenery and highly liveable environments has become an important strategy in addressing the rapid urbanization of the global population.[2] Innovative dense and green building typologies can contribute significantly to the creation of attractive and ecologically balanced urban environments by offering a wide range of architectural, environmental, social, and economic benefits. Dense and green building typologies also have the potential to function as part of larger urban landscape ecosystems.

As many of the case studies in this book demonstrate, the integration of green spaces and "green" technology in buildings can produce new types of high-density urban contexts by designing buildings that include vertical parks, extensive sky terraces, sky bridges, roof gardens, and other public and semi-public spaces. Combinations of all these, often applied to mixes of institutional, residential, infrastructural, commercial,

and mixed-use programs, can help to produce "vertical cities" in which the building section takes on part of the role of the horizontal plane. Density and sustainability in these buildings are not seen as contradictory but rather as mutually dependent and synergistic.

In his concept of a "new pastoralism," Mark Titman explores the potential of such a "green" techno-centric trajectory to overcome the traditional schism between the city dweller and nature.[3] He sees it as the signifying characteristic of a new *Zeitgeist* comprising "gentle, engaging" architecture and urban design that employ biomimetics, hydroponics, cybernetic feedback systems, micro-ecologies and advanced construction methods with natural materials and vertical landscapes. According to Titman, these are used to create "alive spaces that help remind us of our humanity. These soft constructions fulfill a hard-wired human desire to be connected to and delighted by nature. Unlike our ancestors' romantic love of the dramatic power of landscape, these spaces offer a more gentle and artificially tamed nature of 'pastoral' delight."[4] Indeed, this search for a haven or relief has deep roots in the history of architecture, which has time and again looked to natural environments in the attempt to escape and transcend the material constrictions of our removed and "unnatural" day-to-day lives. As Titman explains, "The use of the skies, planting, water, wildlife and the seasons is becoming subtly incorporated into building layouts and onto building surfaces to offer a subtle new interface with our primordial desire to reconnect with nature."[5]

These developments are part of a growing worldwide effort to make our cities more liveable. As urban life becomes denser, the capacity for a city to provide attractive, desirable spaces, including parks and public spaces, seems ever more important. A skeptic could doubt whether we need more public green space if green in buildings is infiltrating the everyday institutional, residential, infrastructural, commercial, and mixed-use spheres. However, parks and public spaces are places that offer more than greenery. They are, in virtually all of their cultural contexts across the globe, the great levelers—places which, if they are made truly accessible and just, provide the proverbial stage on which people of different economic backgrounds, gender, etc. can interact.[6] One may also understand parks and public spaces as a "release valve" for the trend toward densification. Addressing the negative effects of dense living remains one of the most important trajectories for future cities. The provision of innovative dense and green building types in combination with parks and public spaces can provide large urban landscape ecosystems, which are among the most promising strategies for making our cities more liveable.

WOHA, Permeable Lattice City of the Future, Singapore, 2011, rendering.
Office of Ryue Nishizawa, Vertical Garden House, Tokyo, Japan, 2011, perforated floor
plate with plants.

Ateliers Jean Nouvel/PTW Architects, One Central Park, Chippendale, New South Wales, Australia, 2014, green facade.
Atelier Bow-Wow, Miyashita Park, Tokyo, Japan, 2011, aerial view.

Weiss/Manfredi, Seattle Art Museum: Olympic Sculpture Park, Seattle, Washington, USA, aerial view.
UNStudio/DP Architects, Singapore University of Technology and Design, Singapore, 2015, "Learning Spine" with greenery.

Trajectories of Architecture

One of the most important changes in the conception of today's architecture is a move away from concerns premised primarily on questions of form.[7] Form has always been an integral question in the creation of architecture. Its boundaries and shear potential were greatly transformed by the advent of the computer and the fledgling capacities of digital software programs. Since the early 1990s this has led to an array of experimental, wildly ambitious, and novel approaches to architectural form that operate and challenge the limits of materials and construction. As experiments of thought and pedagogy, these express a sense of optimism and boundlessness. This approach has no shortage of heroes and a number of spectacular projects have been realized under its auspices.[8] But it is also not (always) able to keep pace with a number of collateral concerns that are becoming not only too difficult to enumerate but also too difficult to ignore. Pressing issues come from the environmental, social, and political milieus in which architecture exists. Compounded by the fact that experimentations in the digital realm have proven to be in somewhat of a state of overdrive where their ends often prove incommensurate with their means, this has led architecture back to a more open and multidisciplinary state, which rejects or at least seeks to reinterpret the idea of autonomy.[9]

Architecture and the debates around it have once again begun to take up specific, problem-based questions, which make no pretense to tackling a complex large topic all at once. Rather, it has incisively taken up delimited issues and demonstrated a renewed approach as a mechanism for solving given problems that exists outside of architecture, such as global warming or financial depression. Architecture has made a transition away from being the product of tools to being a tool itself. It is not a coincidence that the verb "to tool" has taken on such popularity in today's architectural discourse.[10]

One of the clearest expressions of the "tooling" and problem-solving impulse of today's architecture is the so-called "responsive" architecture, an architectural field that this book has included in the dense and green paradigm and one that is noteworthy for its strong ability to compromise between competing discourses. Steffen Reichert's and Achim Menges' Responsive Surface Structure projects, for example, demonstrate architecture's ability to adapt to conditions and, perhaps even more so at the present moment, to perform.[11] But as many case studies in this book demonstrate, environmentally responsive architecture need not be dynamic in this sense in order to

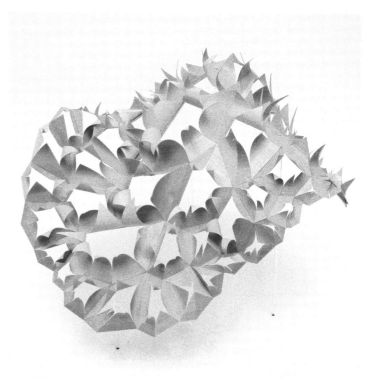

respond to variable conditions and situations and to address larger questions of environmental quality and liveability.

Another specific aspect is the codification and development of our understanding of dense and green buildings themselves. The "high-rise" or "skyscraper" has long been an entity with a quasi-monolithic image where tall rectangular shafts pierce the sky. Their articulation and detail are typically results either of zoning requirements or symbolic paradigms. In recent years, this has shifted as many of the high-density projects featured as case studies in this book demonstrate. Identifying, describing, and developing new ways of speaking about new typologies is a seminal task for updating the parlance and accepted expectations of such buildings.[12]

Trajectories of Ecology

In architecture as well as urban design and planning, it is the ecological turn of recent decades that tends to characterize the complex interrelationship of the built environment with the natural, something George Myerson, who studied *The Language of Environment*, has described as the "eco-pathology of life."[13] As a heuristic comparison, George Myerson has described this in terms of a blocked drain, which can no longer be understood simply as a defective condition but rather as the sign of a problem with deeper roots that have more to do with the water than with the drain itself.[14] Architecture as well as urban design and planning and the wider discourses around them have taken this topic up enthusiastically and without this new embrace, the dense and green paradigm would not have crystallized as thoroughly as it has already.

Organizationally, the ecological turn in architecture has manifested itself through a growing number of institutions, which lobby for novel metrics and mentalities across a range of subtopics and geographical areas. For example, the Lee Kuan Yew Centre for Innovative Cities at the Singapore University of Technology and Design, established in 2012, whose mission to "stimulate thinking and research on the critical issues of cities and urbanization, and to provide breakthrough urban solutions," has positioned itself uniquely as an interface between an important exemplar of the dense and green paradigm—the city of Singapore—and the global need for more and better data—both through research as well as the articulation of the city's policies, successes, and ongoing goals. Other institutions, including the Ford Foundation, The Aga Khan Development Network, the Singapore-ETH Centre Future Cities Laboratory, and the Centre for Liveable Cities, to name just a few, have also rallied around similar objectives and proven to be important forces in making ecological thinking integral to issues of urbanism.

Dense and Green: A New Synthesis

These trajectories and open opportunities of urbanism, architecture, and ecology have the potential to coalesce, support one another, and magnify their relevance through the dense and green paradigm. This will, however, require a broad and committed array of people who make good on the great agency that a single individual can have. This includes not only architects, engineers, and planners. Politicians, business leaders, and policy makers naturally play an important role as well. There is relatively little dispute that the dense and green paradigm is a promising way forward, but it requires a considerable amount of recalibration to the knowledge and decision-making structures that shape society. This points to the need to integrate concerns related to density and ecology as intrinsic, not adjunct, elements of the education of future architects, engineers, and planners but also of political leaders and decision makers.

The cultural values for the future trajectories of the dense and green paradigm are truly innumerable. It would be perhaps utopian but nevertheless productive to imagine a future course where dense and green could become a cultural value in and of itself, a fundamental building block for the way we design and live in cities.

This consideration of the future is, ultimately, intended for the design and planning professions and hence it is important to reiterate here the immense agency the design professions

Ateliers Jean Nouvel, Seguin Island, Paris, France, 2009, garden space, rendering.

hold in steering the dense and green paradigm from its current status to an integrated and tacit element of architecture as well as urban design and planning in the coming decades. Designers and planners must continue to commit their energy to solving the problems posed by the immense and historically unprecedented ecological stress and population pressure with which we are faced today. Design across all institutional, residential, infrastructural, commercial, and mixed-use building types must grapple with and anticipate the challenges that the built environment will have to cope with. We must "retool" the profession to think of these problems as our own task, not of others, to shape a dense and green future for our urban environments.

1. See, for example, the proceedings of the colloquium "Histories of the Future at the Harvard University Graduate School of Design" at http://www.gsd.harvard.edu/#/media/his-04425-00-histories-of-the-future.html

2. These statistics come primarily from studies published by the United Nations. See *World Population Prospects: The 2011* Revision, Volume 1 (United Nations publication, ST/ESA/P/WP224), 4. Accessible online http://esa.un.org/unup/pdf/WUP2011_Highlights.pdf, accessed September 18, 2013.

3. Titman, Mark. "The New Pastoralism: Landscape Intro Architecture," *Architectural Design*, April 2013.

4. *Ibid.*

5. *Ibid.*

6. See a discussion of just urbanism in Fainstein, Susan S. *The Just City.* Ithaca: Cornell University Press, 2011.

7. A notable counterexample is the work and writings of Farshid Moussavi, who contends that formal concerns are not inextricable from larger social and political ones, a contention which has received accord among much of the design profession. See Moussavi, Farshid. *The Function of Form,* Cambridge, MA and Barcelona: Actar and The Harvard University Graduate School of Design, 2009.

8. Architects commonly associated with this include Zaha Hadid, Frank Gehry, and occasionally OMA. The line, needless to say, between what is primarily formal and what is not is incredibly difficult to define and more often than not problematic.

9. See, for example, the rather established discourse of autonomy in architecture, which has been championed by K. Michael Hays and a number of others. Hays, K. Michael. "The Oppositions of Autonomy and History," in Hays, K. Michael (ed.). *Oppositions Reader: Selected Readings from a Journal for Ideas and Criticism in Architecture, 1973- 1984.* Princeton: Princeton Architectural Press, 1998. pp. ix-xiv.

10. See, for example: Aranda, Benjamin and Chris Lasch. *Pamphlet Architecture 27: Tooling.* Princeton: Princeton Architectural Press, 2005.

11. A good example of this is the collaboration between Hoberman Associates and the engineering firm Buro Happold in the Adaptive Building Initiative, founded in 2008, which, according to their mission statement, is "designing a new generation of buildings that optimize their configuration in real time by responding to environmental changes."

12. A 2004 exhibition at The Museum of Modern Art, entitled "Tall Buildings," was an important moment in getting this discussion started. In academia, among some recent attempts is that executed at The Harvard Graduate School of Design, published in the school's annual. See Howeler, Eric (ed.). *GSD Platform IV.* Barcelona: Actar, 2011.

13. For a good summary of the theoretical stakes of sustainability see Crysler, Greig, Stephen Cairns, and Hilde Heynen (eds.). *The Sage Handbook of Architectural Theory.* Thousand Oaks, CA: SAGE, 2012.

14. Myerson, George. *The Language of Environment: A New Rhetoric.* London: Routledge, 1996. p. 51.

APPENDIX

About the Author and the Contributors

Thomas Schröpfer

Thomas Schröpfer is Professor and Associate Head of Pillar of Architecture and Sustainable Design at Singapore University of Technology and Design (SUTD), founded in collaboration with MIT. He directs the University's Advanced Architecture Laboratory (AAL) that investigates the increasingly complex relationship between design and technology in architecture. His design and research projects relate to advances in building structure and form, environmental strategies, performance and energy, computer simulation and modeling, digital fabrication, and building processes. Prior to joining SUTD in 2011, he was Associate Professor of Architecture at the Harvard University Graduate School of Design (GSD). He has published and lectured extensively on his work, which has been exhibited at important international venues, including at the Venice Biennale 2014. He holds a Doctor of Design and Master of Architecture (with Distinction) from Harvard University as well as a Bachelor of Architecture from The Cooper Union. His main publications include *Ecological Urban Architecture* (Birkhäuser, 2012) and *Material Design* (Birkhäuser, 2011).

Naree Phinyawatana

Naree Phinyawatana is Director of the Bangkok and the Singapore offices of Atelier Ten, a leading international building consultancy firm. Her expertise includes environmental design, daylighting and facade optimization, as well as sustainable masterplanning. She has worked on a wide range of projects including LEED Platinum-rated commercial and institutional buildings. Her recent projects comprise several high-performance mixed-use projects in Bangkok, including the Icon Siam, Magnolia Ratchadamri Boulevard, as well as Sindhorn Residences. She has taught at Chulalongkorn University, Harvard University, Singapore University of Technology and Design, University of Pennsylvania, as well as Yale University, and is a LEED AP BD+C, ID+C, Homes, and a TREES Associate from the Thai Green Building Council.

Herbert Dreiseitl

Herbert Dreiseitl is an urban designer, landscape architect, water artist, and interdisciplinary planner. He is a Visiting Professor at the National University of Singapore and an expert in creating Liveable Cities. A hallmark of his work is the inspiring and innovative use of water to solve urban environmental challenges, connecting technology with aesthetics and encouraging people to take care of places. He has realized ground-breaking projects in the fields of urban design, environmental engineering, hydrology, water art, stormwater management, as well as landscape architecture. He lectures worldwide and has authored many publications, including three editions of *Waterscapes, New Waterscapes,* and *Recent Waterscapes. Planning, Building and Designing with Water* (Birkhäuser, 2001, 2005, 2009). As the Director of the Liveable Cities Lab, the think-tank and innovation hub of Rambøll Group, and as founder of Atelier Dreiseitl, a globally integrated design studio with a 35 year history of excellence in urban design, landscape architecture, and ecological waterscapes, Herbert Dreiseitl integrates the organization's strategic design and planning efforts.

Jean W. H. Yong

Jean W. H. Yong finds inspiration in plant diversity and adaptations and uses them for green design. He is an Associate Professor at the Singapore University of Technology and Design, where he runs the Green Solutions Laboratory. He studied botany at the National University of Singapore as well as biochemistry and physiology at the Australian National University. He has written numerous scientific papers and several books in plant science, among them *The Physiology of Tropical Orchids in Relation to the Industry* (World Scientific Publishing, 1997) and *A Selection of Plants for Greening of Waterways and Waterbodies in the Tropics* (Centre for Urban Greenery & Ecology, 2010), providing important information on tropical plants for researchers, institutions, and the plant industry.

Kees Christiaanse

Kees Christiaanse is Professor of Architecture and Urban Design at ETH Zurich and Programme Leader of ETH's Future Cities Laboratory in Singapore. He was educated at TU Delft, then worked for eight years as a partner in OMA before founding his own office KCAP in Rotterdam. Today KCAP looks back at 25 years of practice with branch offices in Rotterdam, Zurich, and Shanghai. Kees Christiaanse has been appointed one of the nine RIBA International Fellows 2016. He specializes in masterplanning in complex urban conditions. Among the projects on which he worked are Olympic Legacy in London, HafenCity in Hamburg, TGV-Quarter in Montpellier, the Regional Plan for Schiphol Airport, and the Wijnhaven Quarter in Rotterdam. Among the buildings he has realized are the Red Apple in Rotterdam, Holzhafen in Hamburg, and GWL housing in Amsterdam. His most important books are *Situation: KCAP Architects & Planners* (Nai Publishers, 2006), *City as Loft: Adaptive Reuse as a Resource for Sustainable Urban Development* (gta publishers, 2013), and *Campus and the City. Urban design for the Knowledge Society* (gta publishers, 2007). His research focuses on Urban Mega Projects, Airports & Cities and Diverse Inner City Neighbourhoods.

Foster + Partners

Foster + Partners is an international studio for architecture, engineering, and design, led by Founder and Chairman Norman Foster and a Partnership Board. Based in London with project offices worldwide, it has an innovative approach to design, whereby architects and engineers work together with other specialist disciplines to develop sustainable, integrated solutions. Over the past five decades the practice has undertaken a wide range of work, from urban master plans, public infrastructure, airports, civic and cultural buildings, offices and workplaces to private houses and product design. The studio has established an international reputation with buildings such as the world's largest airport terminal at Beijing, Swiss Re's London Headquarters, Hearst Headquarters in New York City, the Millau Viaduct in France, the German Parliament in the Reichstag Building in Berlin, The Great Court at London's British Museum, HSBC Headquarters in Hong Kong and London, and Commerzbank Headquarters in Frankfurt. There is also a strong interest in city planning and infrastructure. The practice has received over 685 awards for excellence and won over 140 national and international competitions since its inception in 1967.

Marta Pozo, MVRDV

Marta Pozo is an architect, licensed BREEAM assessor and LEED Green Associate. She has worked with MVRDV since 2007 and has been involved in the conceptualization and execution of projects of various scales, as well as research studies such as the Vertical Village. In MVRDV's Rotterdam headquarters, Marta grew to lead the firm's Sustainability Department, ensuring high standards by forming environmental strategies and energy-efficiency guidelines for each project's design process. Since 2014 Marta Pozo has led MVRDV's asian team, taking on the role of Director of MVRDV Asia to drive engagement across the continent. She regularly lectures and has conducted many workshops on sustainability around the world; she has won several awards for her work.

WOHA

WOHA was founded by Mun Summ Wong and Richard Hassell in 1994. A profound awareness of local context and tradition is intertwined in their work with an exploration of contemporary architectural form-making and ideas, creating a unique fusion of practicality and invention. WOHA has won a great number of architectural awards. A travelling solo exhibition opened at the Deutsches Architekturmuseum in Frankfurt am Main in 2011, accompanied by the catalogue *WOHA: Breathing Architecture* (Prestel and DAM), and three substantial monographs—*WOHA:*

The Architecture of WOHA and *WOHA: Selected Projects, Vol. 1 and 2* (Pesaro Publishing, 2011 and 2013)—have been published.

Mun Summ Wong graduated from the National University of Singapore in 1989. He was a Board Member of the Urban Redevelopment Authority of Singapore and the Singapore Land Authority, and served as member of several Design Advisory Panels for major developments in Singapore. He has mentored students under the National University of Singapore's Embedded Studio in Practice programme and, together with Richard Hassell, served as Studio Master for the University's Master of Science in Integrated Sustainable Design Masterclass since 2011.

Richard Hassell graduated from the University of Western Australia in 1989, and was awarded a Master of Architecture degree from RMIT University, Melbourne, in 2002. He has served as a Board Member of DesignSingapore Council, the Board of Architects, as well as the Building and Construction Authority of Singapore. He has lectured at many universities and served as an Adjunct Professor at the University of Technology, Sydney, and the University of Western Australia.

Alina Yeo joined WOHA upon completion of her Master of Architecture in 2005 from the National University of Singapore and was made an Associate in 2014. Alina's portfolio with WOHA encompasses a variety of projects including institutional and high-rise condominiums, among them the award-winning School of the Arts. Together with WOHA's Founding Directors, Alina has authored numerous published papers and leads in many of WOHA's design competitions, monographic exhibitions, research work, and building contract matters.

T. R. Hamzah & Yeang

Ken Yeang is an architect and ecologist, known for his signature eco-achitecture featuring a distinctive verdant biodiversity-influenced green aesthetic. He trained at the Architectural Association School of Architecture in London, holds a doctorate from Cambridge University and the Plym Distinguished Professorship of the University of Illinois School of Architecture. Ken Yeang is principal of T. R. Hamzah & Yeang in Malaysia, UK, and China, with expertise in distinctive, innovative ecological architecture and master plans beyond conventional accreditation. He has authored more than 12 books on green architecture and received awards including the Aga Khan Award for Architecture, Malaysian Institute of Architects Gold Medal, and the Merdeka Award. *The Guardian* included him among the "50 people who could save the planet."

Illustration Credits

Dense + Green Agendas

The Dense and Green Paradigm
architecturesketch.tumblr.com *19*
Ateliers Jean Nouvel *28*
Iwan Baan *31, 32 top*
Patrick Bingham-Hall *34, 35*
Jakob Boserup *30 top*
Kirsten Bucher *29*
Chuck Choi *24 right*
Dwell *21*
Foster + Partners *22 right, 24 left, 25*
David Friedlander *16 right*
Tim Griffith *32 bottom*
Roland Halbe *36 Right*
Robert Hart *26 bottom*
Dan Hogman *30 bottom*
JDS Architects *36 left*
David Leventi *16 left*
Jonathan Lin *22 left*
MVRDV *27*
North Wind Picture Archives *12 top*
Takashi Ohtaka *17*
Victor Ramos *12 bottom*
relationalthought.wordpress.com *18*
sixty7 Architecture Road *15*
Hans van Reeken *26 top*

Dense and Green Technologies
Naree Phinyawatana *38–46*

Blue-Green Infrastructures for Buildings and Liveable Cities
Herbert Dreiseitl, Rambøll Liveable Cities Laboratory *50–57*

Biological Functionalities of Green
Jean W. H. Yong *61–69*

Green Urbanism
Kees Christiaanse *72–75, 78*
KCAP Architects & Planners *76–77, 81–82*
National Center for Geographic Information and Analysis (NCGIA) *71*

Dense and Green Building Typologies
Iwan Baan *95*
Jan Bitter *90 bottom*
Stefano Boeri Architetti *91 top*
CPG Consultants *93 right top*
Hans Georg Esch *88*
Grits & Guava *85 bottom*
Herzog & de Meuron *85 top, 93 left bottom*
JDS Architects *96 top*
KWK Promes *91 bottom*
Kenta Mabuchi *90 top*
OMA *96 bottom*
Mathieu Proctor *93 right bottom*
Renzo Piano Building Workshop *87 bottom*
Margherita Spiluttini *86*
The Architectural Review *91 middle*
The Office of James Burnett *94*
T. R. Hamzah & Yeang *89*
Western Pennsylvania Conservancy *93 left top*
WolfmanSF, Wikimedia Commons *87 top*

Dense + Green Case Studies

The following drawings of the Case Studies have been prepared by the author's team as mentioned in the Impressum, on the basis of drawings kindly provided by the architects, with the support of the graphic designer, and under the direction of the author: *108, 114, 116, 122, 130–132, 134, 140–141, 144, 148–149, 152, 158, 162, 169–170, 172, 176–177, 181–183, 186–187, 188 bottom, 193, 198, 205, 210, 212–213, 218, 223–224, 226, 228, 236–238, 240*

Regional Chamber of Commerce and Industry of Picardie
Marchand Meffre *101–105*

Brooklyn Botanic Garden Visitor Center
Albert Večerka, Esto *107, 109–113*

Khoo Teck Puat Hospital
CPG Consultants *118 bottom*
Jonathan Ng Ming-En *115, 118 top*

School of the Arts
Patrick Bingham-Hall *121, 123–125*

Nanyang Technological University Learning Hub
Hufton + Crow *127–129*

Ministry for Urban Development and the Environment
Jan Bitter *133, 135*
Frieder Blickle *136*
Sauerbruch Hutton *137*

Phare Tower Project
Jacques Ferrier Architectures *139, 142, 143*

Federal Environment Agency
Jan Bitter *145, 146 bottom*
Sauerbruch Hutton *146 top, 147*

Solaris
Albert Lim *153–155*
Jonathan Ng Ming-En *151*

National University Health System Tower Block
Mauricio Pocholo *157, 159*

Mountain Dwellings
Jakob Boserup *161, 163–164*

Vertical Garden House
Iwan Baan *167–168, 171*

Via Verde
David Sundberg, Esto *173–175*

Newton Suites
Patrick Bingham-Hall *179–180*

The Interlace
Iwan Baan *185, 188 top, 189*

The Amager Bakke
BIG *191–192, 194–195*

Index of Names

of persons, institutions, buildings, and locations

Subject Index